NOW YOU KNOW

NOW YOU KNOW

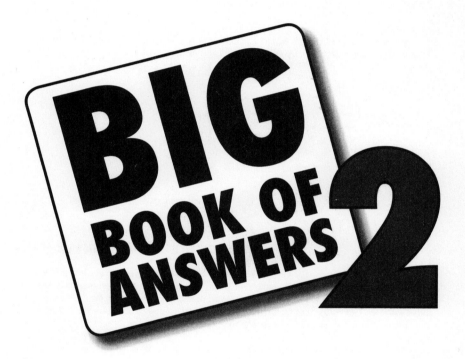

BIG BOOK OF ANSWERS 2

Doug Lennox

DUNDURN PRESS
TORONTO

Editor: Allison Hirst
Design: Courtney Horner
Printer: Webcom

Library and Archives Canada Cataloguing in Publication

Lennox, Doug
    Now you know big book of answers 2 : a collection of classics with 150
new fascinating new facts / by Doug Lennox ; illustrations by Catriona
Wight and Julia Bell.

ISBN 978-1-55002-871-3

    1. Questions and answers. 2. Curiosities and wonders.
I. Title. II. Title: Now you know big book of answers two.

AG195.L453 2008   031.02   C2008-903940-8

1   2   3   4   5   12   11   10   09   08

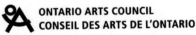

Conseil des Arts
du Canada

Canada Council
for the Arts

ONTARIO ARTS COUNCIL
CONSEIL DES ARTS DE L'ONTARIO

We acknowledge the support of **The Canada Council for the Arts** and the **Ontario Arts Council** for our publishing program. We also acknowledge the financial support of the **Government of Canada** through the **Book Publishing Industry Development Program** and **The Association for the Export of Canadian Books**, and the **Government of Ontario** through the **Ontario Book Publishers Tax Credit** program, and the **Ontario Media Development Corporation**.

Care has been taken to trace the ownership of copyright material used in this book. The author and the publisher welcome any information enabling them to rectify any references or credits in subsequent editions.

J. Kirk Howard, President

Printed and bound in Canada.
Printed on recycled paper.

www.dundurn.com

Illustrations on pages 32, 78, 81, 96, 187, 194, 197, 198, 216, 237, 254, 320, 353, 448, and 465 by Catriona Wight.
Illustrations on pages 85, 214, 323, and 333 by Julia Bell.

Dundurn Press
3 Church Street, Suite 500
Toronto, Ontario, Canada
M5E 1M2

Gazelle Book Services Limited
White Cross Mills
High Town, Lancaster, England
LA1 4XS

Dundurn Press
2250 Military Road
Tonawanda, NY
U.S.A. 14150

This book is dedicated to my Uncle
Gord Lennox, who helped me understand
the heart of a Celtic warrior!

Giants never pass by without leaving footprints.
— DL

contents

acknowledgements

Success requires partners like Tony Hawke,
Beth Bruder, Ali Pennels, Michael Carroll, and Kirk Howard.

preface

It is a wonderful privilege to be able to spend so much of my time exploring the roots of our language and customs and then sharing them with you and your family. I am continually thrilled by what has become a joy of discovery.

Most of what lives between the covers of these books is from the general evolution of the progress and sometimes faltering of the English-speaking peoples. Some are poetic, like the word *window*, which came from the single hole in a thatched roof of the marauding Vikings and began as the "wind's eye." The Germanic tribes from a region called Angle gave the main British island its name — Angle land or England. The British drive on the left-hand side of the road because that's how the Romans drove their chariots. Expressions like "face the music" and the word *fore* in golf both come from the military, while life on the huge sailing ships gave us scuttlebutt for gossip and "son of a gun" for an illegitimate child born at sea. You might not have known that it was the pirates and smugglers who introduced the phrase "the coast is clear." A deck is a roof covering a man-o-war's guns and not a floor or a wooden backyard patio, which is why the title of the Christmas carol "Deck the Halls" means "cover the halls."

Did you know that in Chinese, dim sum means "to touch your heart" and won ton is "swallowing a cloud"? Or that it takes a ton of ore to mine enough gold for one wedding ring?

Each discovery triggers a chain reaction of new thoughts and learning becomes fun — a stimulus for my own imagination and understanding — as I hope it does for you.

Within this modern society's pursuit of self-indulgence, many choose not to learn from history. It was the great Polish pianist and prime minister (1919) Ignacy Jan Paderewski who once said sadly, "men learn from history that men learn nothing from history," while American President John F. Kennedy reminded us that "there is no such thing as the present … only the past rushing into the future." Albert Einstein advised us to "look deep into nature, and then you will understand everything better." He also said that "Imagination is more important than information."

During this time of "Starbucks thinking," our environment, our planet, our very existence demands the courage of free thought and instead of "whistling past the graveyard," I would suggest that we listen for the whispers and build on the wisdom from our ancestors.

Certainly the answers to this world's issues aren't found within this book's cover, but you might find inspiration to look more closely at the isolation and gift of knowledge through your own unique talents. The new direction or salvation of our existence might come from the imagination of that nine-year-old child looking to understand the frightening world that he or she is about to enter and maybe, just maybe, this book might help them realize that learning is exhilarating and comes from an open mind, that the answer to most things is just beyond the obvious, and that a successful society must never forget those in the cemetery.

The expression "whistling past the graveyard" came from "The Grave" (1742) by Robert Blair.

> Oft in the lone church yard at night, I've seen,
> By glimpse of moonshine chequering thro' the trees,
> The schoolboy, with his satchel in his hand,
> Whistling aloud to bear his courage up,
> And lightly tripping o'er the long flat stones …

This book and the others in the series, though thoroughly researched, are intended for fun and, because I'm not a scholar but rather an entertainer, their purpose by nature is to entertain. Anything you learn or rediscover is my pleasure and the workings of your own fine mind. Enjoy!

Doug Lennox
www.douglennox.com

proverbs

What was the original meaning of "variety is the spice of life"?

When William Cowper wrote, "Variety's the very spice of life," in 1785 he was reflecting on the ever-changing fashion of clothes. The idea had been first expressed by ancient writers in different ways, but it was the genius of Cowper that caused "variety is the spice of life" to become an English proverb. Other common Cowper idioms include "The worse for wear" and "God moves in mysterious ways."

Why do we say a hypocrite is "the pot calling the kettle black"?

"The pot calling the kettle black" first entered a dictionary in 1699 with the explanation, "When one accuses another of what he is as deep in himself." When kitchen stoves were fired by wood and coal, both the kettle and the pot would become black through time, so both were equally tarnished. Another explanation is that because both were made of copper, the more prized kettle might have been polished, which would offer the grungy pot a reflection of himself.

What is the real meaning of the proverb "a friend in need is a friend indeed"?

A friend in need could be someone in trouble who needs your help and indeed becomes your friend in order to get it, but it's usually interpreted as meaning a friend who stands with you during a difficult time. But if you accept that "in deed" is two words instead of one, it extends the definition of a good friend from one who stands with you to one who actually helps solve the problem.

music
and musicians

What is the most popular rock and roll song in history?

Because the Kingsmen's 1963 recording of the song "Louie, Louie" was inaudible, people thought the lyrics were dirty, and although they weren't, a United States congressional investigation assured the song's enduring success. Since being sold by its author, Richard Berry, for $750 in 1957, "Louie, Louie" has been recorded by nearly 1,000 different performers and sold an estimated quarter-billion copies.

What is unique about the Beatles song "Yesterday"?

"Yesterday" has had more airtime than any other song in history. The Beatles' Paul McCartney (1942–) said the song came to him in a dream. While writing it he used the working title "Scrambled Eggs." When McCartney recorded the song in 1965, none of the other Beatles were in the studio. He was alone with his guitar and a group of string musicians. Since the release of "Yesterday," more than 3,000 versions of it have been recorded.

Quickies
Did you know...
- that the Beatles is a combination of Beetles and Beat? Heavily influenced by Buddy Holly and The Crickets, the Liverpool boys were known as the Beetles in 1960 then became the Quarrymen and The Silver Beetles before John Lennon suggested a combination of Beetles and Beat.
- that Bob Dylan's real name is Robert Zimmerman? He considered Zimmerman too long so he adopted the stage name from his favourite poet, Dylan Thomas.
- that the Barenaked Ladies is an expression of the innocence a boy child experiences when seeing a nude woman for the first time? The band thought of the name during a Bob Dylan concert.

Which much-married star sang "Stand by Your Man"?

Country and western music icon Tammy Wynette wrote and recorded the 1968 smash hit, "Stand by Your Man." She was married five times. Four of the marriages ended in divorce; the fifth (which lasted 20 years) with her death in 1998. Tammy Wynette also recorded the 1967 hit "D-i-v-o-r-c-e."

Quickies
Did you know...
• that feminists severely criticized Tammy Wynette for "Stand by Your Man"? She replied that the song was an expression of triumph over adversity. She once said, "I spent 15 minutes writing ["Stand by Your Man"] and a lifetime defending it."

Why is Johnny Cash known as the "Man in Black"?

Johnny Cash, the gravelly-voiced singer of country classics like "Folsom Prison Blues," "I Walk the Line," and "A Boy Named Sue" began wearing black on-stage in 1957 when he started playing at the Grand Ole Opry in Nashville, Tennessee. In 1971, he recorded a song called "The Man in Black" that explained why black clothing had become his signature with lines like, "I wear the black for the poor and the beaten down, Livin' in the hopeless, hungry side of town...."

Another reason that Cash may have worn black was that his childhood hero, cowboy actor Al "Lash" LaRue, was known both for his skill with a bullwhip and his black outfits.

Cash got into the music business in 1954 in Memphis, Tennessee, after auditioning for Sam Phillips, the man who discovered Elvis Presley.

Who coined the term *heavy metal*?

Lead, cadmium, gold, and mercury are all classified as heavy metals. The term was also used by the military to describe tanks and heavy artillery. But that was before the May 1971 issue of *Creem* magazine hit the newsstands. It contained a review of an album by hard-rocking band Sir Lord Baltimore, which made reference to the bands MC5 (Motor City 5) and Led Zeppelin. In this review,

Mike Saunders introduced the definition of the term *heavy metal* as we know it today — as a musical genre.

Why is extemporaneous jazz called "vamping"?

Improvised music is called "vamping" because it is music being added onto the original score. In the eighteenth century, *vamp* started out meaning the part of a stocking that covered the foot and ankle. It came from the French word *avant* or "in front" and with the addition of "pie" or "foot" it became *avantpie*. The Anglo version became *vampe*. If an old pair of stockings needed mending or boots needed repairing or patching up, they were "revamped." That's how any adlib added to an established piece (musical or otherwise) came to be known as "vamping."

Who invented sheet music?

Sheet music is another miracle of the printing press, which was invented by Johannes Gutenberg in 1450. Before machine printing became possible, music was written painstakingly by hand on manuscripts, which took a long time to produce. Sheet music made music available to a much larger audience, and amateur musicians soon became commonplace, providing a good source of income for professional composers like Beethoven and Mozart.

By the nineteenth century, sheet music had come to serve the same purpose for music lovers of those days that CDs and MP3 players serve today.

Quickies
Did you know...
- that Ray Charles was born Ray Charles Robinson? He dropped the last name to avoid continual confusion with the great boxer Sugar Ray Robinson.
- that The Grateful Dead first called themselves the Warlocks without realizing that there was another band using that name? A dictionary search found a reference to a series of folk legends wherein the spirit of a dead man mysteriously helps a benefactor. These spirits where known as The Grateful Dead.
- that The Mothers of Invention were originally the Mothers, but because this suggested a crude curse their label convinced them to add "of Invention" to their name?
- that The Doobie Brothers began as The Pud but changed to Doobie, which is slang for a marijuana joint?
- that Dire Straits named themselves after their financial situation at the time they came together?
- that in the beginning, The Who were known as The High Numbers but whenever they took the stage the audience always asked, "The who?" so the band went with it?

What is the difference between an anthem and a hymn?

Technically, an anthem is sung in response to a religious liturgy, but by the end of the sixteenth century this musical form began to be used secularly as a song of praise outside of the church.

By the mid-nineteenth century, the term *anthem* began to be incorrectly applied to "God Save the King," even though it had been named the national hymn of Great Britain. A *hymn* (from the Greek *humnos*) is a song of praise that the Greeks used to honour their gods or national heroes. Over the years, through its use by the Christian church, a hymn gradually became a song of praise to God, a hero, or a country — so a national anthem is, in fact, a national hymn.

Why is earthy-sounding music referred to as "funky"?

"Funky" music is rooted in "the blues" and is a soulful rendition of folk music interpreted with a syncopated and repetitive bass line. It was first used as a musical definition in a 1954 edition of *Time* magazine, though the jazz world had been using *funky* as a slang reference to the earthy, deeply felt music handed down from oppression (slavery) since the early twentieth century.

The word *funky* entered the English language in 1623, meaning "a bad smell." It was derived from the French word *funkiere,* meaning "smoke." It had been used through the centuries as a reference to the smell of strong cheese, bad body odour, and anything else repulsive until that reference in *Time* after which it took on the current meaning of "cool."

A *funk* (1743), meaning a foul mood or a state of panic, comes through the Scots from the Old French word *funicle,* meaning mad or crazy.

Who coined the phrase "a good man is hard to find"?

The phrase "a good man is hard to find" has probably been around as long as the English language but it became an adage from the title of a song written by Eddie Green and offered for sale as a player piano roll at the Christmas bargain price of 90 cents through the *Fort Wayne Journal-Gazette* on December 12, 1918.

> "A good man is hard to find
> You always get the other kind
> Just when you think that he is your pal
> You look for him and find him fooling 'round some other gal
> Then you rave, you even crave
> To see him laying in his grave
> So if your man is nice, take my advice and hug him in the morning, kiss him ev'ry night
> Give him plenty lovin', and treat him right
> For a good man nowadays is hard to find, a good man nowadays is hard to find."
> *Eddie Green — 1918*

**everyday
expressions**

What is correct, "just deserts" or "just desserts"?

If someone gets justice or a consequence they deserve, whether good or bad, they get their "just deserts." The word is pronounced "desserts" (the sweet last course of a meal) but spelled with only one *s*. The reason is unique to this word. It comes from the thirteenth century and is derived from the word *deserved* as in, "he got what he deserved." The confusion arises because of the spelling of *desert*, implying a large arid region — the current common use of the word. The phrase "just deserts" is the only surviving use of the word as a derivative form of *deserves*.

Why do we call a timid person "mealy-mouthed"?

If someone is afraid to speak plainly, they are called "mealy-mouthed." The expression suggests cowardice or fear of saying what someone really thinks. In his writings, Martin Luther mentions "to carry meal in the mouth, that is, not to be direct in speech." Meal was sweet ground flour — a mouthful of which would make it difficult or at least a good excuse not to speak to anyone.

Why do we say that a victim of his own scheming has been "hoisted on his own petard"?

The phrase "hoisted with his own petard" is found in Shakespeare's *Hamlet*. It has come to mean that someone has been or will be hurt by the very device he's created to injure someone else. *Hoist* means to raise something into the air, while *petard* is an antiquated word for "bomb." Therefore, if you were "hoisted on your own petard," it means you were blown up by your own bomb.

Where do we get the saying "think outside the box"?

The phrase is an allusion to a well-known puzzle where one has to connect nine dots, arranged in a square grid, with four straight lines drawn continuously without pen leaving paper. The only solution to this puzzle is one where some of the lines extend beyond the border of the grid (or box). This puzzle was a popular gimmick among management consultants in the 1970s and 1980s as a demonstration of the need to discard unwarranted assumptions (like the assumption that the lines must remain within the grid).

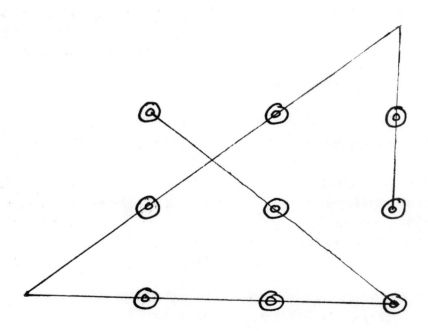

How old is the epithet "son of a bitch"?

Shakespeare drew on the common man's language when in 1605 he inserted, "son and heir of a mongrel bitch" within the manuscript of *King Lear* (act 2, scene 2). As a reference to a female dog, *bitch* (*bicce*) has been used since at least the tenth century and by the fifteenth century it was being generally used to describe an immoral woman. In its current form, "son of a bitch" first turned up in 1712 and quickly became one of the most offensive and commonly used insults in the English language.

Why is a warm spell in autumn called "Indian Summer"?

"Indian Summer" (1778) is a brief warm period following the first autumn frost. Early settlers looked forward to relief from Indian raids during the cold weather so a reprise of summer-like conditions in the fall meant that they were again vulnerable to war parties that were usually only conducted during the summer months.

Why has someone half-mad been "driven around the bend"?

In Victorian England it was the custom to screen those confined to mental institutions and to prevent them from seeing beyond their asylum by designing a bend in the driveway. Anyone driven to such an institution followed the curved road through the trees to the entrance which was "around the bend."

Why is a talent for speaking called "the gift of gab"?

The word *gab* had a long and colourful journey before becoming a slang expression for being able to speak well. *Gab* came from Scotland in the fourteenth century as *gabben*, meaning to speak foolishly. The word had been borrowed from the Viking word *gabba*, which meant to mock or scoff. By 1719, as *gabby*, it had taken the meaning of one who engaged in idle chatter. As a prolonged conversation, *gabfest* appeared in America in 1897. Today, "the gift of gab" is considered an admirable quality for politicians, paramours, and businessmen.

What is the origin of "I wouldn't touch that with a ten-foot pole"?

"I wouldn't touch that with a ten-foot pole" means the subject is trouble. Ten-foot poles were commonly used to push recreational barges along shallow rivers during the nineteenth century in an exercise called punting. They were known as barge poles and were generally replaced by oars and engines. Use of the phrase "I wouldn't touch him with a ten-foot pole" was first recorded in the United States in 1846.

Referring to an act that came before parliament, "they wouldn't touch that again with a barge pole" is the earliest British mention and was recorded in Lady Monkswell's diary from 1893.

Why is a serious response to a situation called "fighting fire with fire"?

"Fighting fire with fire" means to meet a challenge with measures at least equal to the problem being confronted. The expression originates from a method still used to fight forest fires and serious grass fires. Settlers in the New World learned quickly to set fire to a strip of land in the wind path of an advancing prairie fire. By the time the wild fire reached the now-barren burned-off strip, it was stopped when it had nothing to feed on. This procedure is very dangerous when not practised by an expert. American writer Samuel Clemens (1835–1910), better known as Mark Twain, reported hearing the phrase during the 1850s.

If we want the truth, why do we say "read between the lines"?

Sometimes the truth is obscured within the written text of a letter, and so we must "read between the lines." Centuries ago it was discovered that by writing a secret message between the lines of a normal letter with lemon juice, the real message would stay transparent until the document was heated over a flame, which causes the juice to become discoloured, revealing the intended message written between the lines of the ruse.

If your reputation is ruined, why is your name "mud"?

After John Wilkes Booth assassinated President Abraham Lincoln at the Ford Theatre, he broke his leg while leaping from the balcony and onto the stage. During his escape, Booth stopped in at the home of a country doctor for treatment. That doctor's name was Mudd. Although he claimed no knowledge of Booth's crime, Dr. Mudd was sent to prison, and in America, his name became unfairly synonymous with disrepute.

Why, under urgent circumstances, do we say we have to "strike while the iron is hot"?

To strike while the iron is hot means to act quickly before an opportunity is gone. In medieval Europe, blacksmiths worked red-hot iron by hand from a forge. They shaped the heated metal with a hammer before it cooled, so they needed to work quickly, because as the iron cools it becomes brittle and impossible to work with. If the moment is missed, the metal has to be reheated and the process started over.

Why do we say that something flawed "isn't all it's cracked up to be"?

If something "isn't all it was cracked up to be," then it's less than advertised, a disappointment. *Crack* began as the verb "to praise or boast" in the fifteenth century and today is often used as a noun. For example, you might be cracked up by a good wisecrack. In the U.S. South, a cracker is a feeble-minded braggart. And if you've lost it, you've gone crackers. No matter how you look at it, if it isn't all it's cracked up to be, you've been had.

Why do we say that something very obvious is "as clear as a bell"?

In a simpler time when birds could be heard above traffic or construction noise, a single clear note sounded by a church bell could be heard over a wide area and was used to communicate time, to announce a celebration or important event, or even to warn of an impending attack. When the bell sounded, everyone heard the message as clear as a bell.

Why is something in great shape said to be in "A1 condition"?

In their early days, Lloyd's of London used an "A list" to classify sailing ships for insurance purposes. Only vessels meeting strict specifications would go to the top of that list, where they were said to be in A1 condition. When, as a general insurer, the company began covering everything from Mary Hart's legs to Jennifer Lopez's derrière, Lloyd's continued to classify anything first-rate as "A1."

Why do we say "I'll be there with bells on"?

During the frontier days, peddlers travelling between settlements had to move as silently as possible through the hostile forest, but when they approached a homestead or town they would take out their muffled bells and hang them on their horses' necks to announce their arrival. The peddlers' arrival "with bells on" brought news, letters, and goods from the outside world, and was an exciting event for the isolated settlers.

Why, when getting serious, do we say "let's get down to brass tacks"?

In the days of the general store, cloth came in bulk and was sold by the yard. The storekeeper, who quickly became expert at measuring, often used the length of his arm as a measure of each yard being purchased. If the measurement was challenged, the seller would re-measure the cloth against two brass tacks embedded in the counter that were precisely a yard apart. The issue was therefore settled by getting down to those two brass tacks.

Why do we tell someone to "get off his keister" when we mean stand up and do something?

The word *keister* is derived from *kiste*, the German Yiddish word for *strongbox* or *suitcase*. Early Jewish immigrants who arrived with all their belongings in a *kiste* would often sit on them while waiting to be processed through customs. The English-speaking agents didn't realize that it was the suitcase and not their bottoms they were referring to when they told the immigrants to "get off their keisters."

What do we mean when we say someone's from the "wrong side of the tracks"?

In the nineteenth century, railway tracks usually ran right through the centre of town, and it was the prevailing winds that determined which was the right or wrong side to live on. As the town developed, the wealthy built homes on the cleaner, windward side of the tracks, while industrial development and the working class were confined to the other, dirtier side. To be from the "wrong side of the tracks" meant you were from a poor or working-class family.

Why do we say "either fish or cut bait" when we mean "make up your mind"?

There are two main jobs on a fishing boat. One is to "cut bait," which means to prepare or cut "junk" fish for a hook, or for "chum," which is dumped in the water to attract other fish. The second job is to do the actual fishing. So the admonition "Either fish or cut bait" doesn't mean either fish or cut your line; it means make up your mind and decide which job you're going to do, and just do it.

What do we mean by the "sixth sense"?

Humans are credited with five senses: sight, hearing, touch, taste, and smell. So someone with a "sixth sense" is gifted with an unexplained perception outside of the common five. The expression "sixth sense" comes from a study of blind people reported in 1903 in which it was found that, although deprived of sight, some of the subjects could perceive or sense certain objects in a room in a way that defied scientific understanding.

Why is someone with a lot of nerve referred to as being "full of moxie"?

"Moxie" has come to mean fortitude and determination, mainly as a result of successful branding by a patent medicine manufacturer in the 1870s. Dr. Augustin Thompson invented a "cure all" tonic that he called "Moxie Nerve Food." He said he named the drink in honour of a Lieutenant Moxie, who he credited with discovering the active ingredient while exploring near the equator. There are some who dispute the existence of Lieutenant Moxie, and argue that the name really derived from the moxie-berry plant that grows in Thompson's native state of Maine.

In the 1920s, the Moxie name was acquired by a soft drink company that produced a carbonated pop that was marketed for its energizing qualities. The drink caught on as did the modern sense of the word, often used in the phrase "full of Moxie."

Although it has been overshadowed by the likes of Pepsi and Coca-Cola, Moxie continues to be popular in New England, and was recently named the official soft drink of the state of Maine.

Why do we call a working vacation a "busman's holiday"?

Bus is an abbreviation of omnibus, which is what they called the original horse-drawn vehicles used for public transportation. The busman, of course, was the driver, and because the bus was drawn by the driver's own horses, he was very concerned about their well-being. It wasn't uncommon for busmen to frequently come down to the barn during their vacation time to ensure that their horses were being well treated, which gave us the expression "busman's holiday."

Why is a superficial vacation known as a "Cook's tour"?

When Thomas Cook founded the world's first travel agency in 1841 he organized a railway trip for a group of non-drinkers into the British midlands. Soon the safety and security of travelling in groups encouraged the less adventurous to see the world. The more seasoned travellers, enamoured of their ideas of individual adventure, scoffed at these disciplined tours and referred to them sarcastically as "Cook's tours."

Can a person be "on the level" if he's going "against the grain"?

Both "going against the grain" and being "on the level" are expressions from carpentry. When a bladed instrument is used to smooth a wooden surface it only works when applied with, or in the same direction as, the grain, otherwise it's a mess. A level ensures the precision of a frame alignment. Someone going against the grain is doing things wrong, and so is probably not as trustworthy as someone on the level.

Why wouldn't you give a "tinker's dam" if you consider something useless?

A tinker travelled from town to town repairing tin pots, kettles, and pans and got his name from the noise he made while working. His equipment included clay from which he made a mould to hold melted solder for refastening handles and joints. He called this mould a "dam," and because it was only good for one pot, the tinker tossed it when the job was done. That's how a tinker's dam became synonymous with worthless.

Why do we say that a bad idea "won't hold water"?

The expression "won't hold water" comes from the legend of Tutia, a Roman Vestal Virgin who was accused of having lost her innocence. To prove herself not guilty she had to carry a sieve full of water from the Tiber River to the Temple of Vesta. If the sieve held the water she was innocent, but if not she would be buried alive. She passed the test and gave us the expression for failure, "It won't hold water."

What's the difference between "having your back to the wall" and "going to the wall"?

"Having your back to the wall" comes from street fighting and means you're in a desperate situation, and although there is no room to retreat you might still win if you fight off the attack with renewed energy. On the other hand, "going to the wall" means that although you are in an equally desperate situation, you are there willingly, even though there is no chance of winning. Going to the wall comes from the condemned facing a firing squad.

Why is unexpected trouble called "getting into a scrape"?

"Getting into a scrape" means to be in a difficult situation and is as old as England itself. When that country was a primeval forest, it was overrun with wild deer. To avoid hunters, these deer would use their sharp hooves to scrape deep gullies into the ground, where they would huddle for cover. In time these would become overgrown and difficult to detect, so while out in the forest it wasn't uncommon to fall into a scrape.

Why is something ordinary said to be "run of the mill"?

Since the dawn of the industrial age, anything that is unspectacular yet functional has been called "run of the mill." When a raw product is to be mechanically processed, whether through a gristmill or the mill of a mine, it emerges in bulk before the different sizes and qualities have been separated by value. Worth can't be determined until further refining and so everything looks the same — and that's why anything ordinary is called run of the mill.

Why do we say that someone who has overcome the odds has "pulled themselves up by their own bootstraps"?

In the sixteenth century, bootstraps were leather loops sewn into the top, sides, or back of high-fitting boots. These were so difficult to put on that it required the help of a device with a handle and a hook and required so much energy that the vivid image of someone lifting themselves up during the process — although impossible — became a figure of speech for accomplishing what appeared to be unachievable.

Why might you say that someone irrational is "mad as a hatter"?

Years ago, manufacturers of felt hats used mercury to treat the wool, which made it easier to pound the fibres into felt. Mercury poisoning attacks the nervous system, which caused many hatters to develop tremors and then madness. In Alice's Wonderland tea party, she met not only a Mad Hatter but also another descriptive expression, "mad as a March hare." The hare breeds during March, so he might be excused for his absurd antics.

Why does "back to square one" mean starting over?

During the 1930s, the BBC broadcast soccer or football games on the radio. As an aid to listeners they published a map of the playing field, which was divided into numbered squares. The commentators would mention the square number of the action after each description of the play. Square one was near the goal-tender, so that to score you needed to carry the play the full length of the field.

What's the difference between "marking time" and "killing time"?

"Marking time" is a military command for soldiers in close-order drill to stop their forward progress but to keep their feet moving in precision so they can quickly resume marching on command. Marking time means that although your progress has been temporarily stopped you are fully prepared to continue when the time is right. On the other hand, "killing time" means that you're doing absolutely nothing, or, as the proverb says, "You don't kill time, time kills you."

Why do we say a simple procedure is "cut and dried" unless we "hit a snag"?

"Cut and dried" means it's a finished job and comes from the lumber industry. The two processes for preparing wood for sale are to cut it and then dry it. The same industry gave us the expression "hit a snag," meaning we've got a problem. A snag is a tree trunk stuck on the river bottom with one end protruding just enough to slow or stop the log drive, which can't continue until the snag is removed.

Why is a dirty story said to be "off colour"?

In Britain, "off colour" has always indicated that someone might feel under the weather because the colour of their skin has changed from its normal hue to pale. In America the expression "off colour" has a related but different meaning. When someone says something that is considered sexually shocking or impolite, it will often cause those listening to blush from a rush of blood that changes their skin colour to red, so the story that caused the skin colour change is referred to as being off colour.

Could an Irishman go to a "shindig" and take on the whole "shebang" with his "shillelagh"?

A shindig, a shebang, and a shillelagh are all from Irish expressions. *Shindig* comes from the fighting Irishman's habit of digging the steel toe of his boot into his opponent's shins. *Shebang* is from *shebeen,* an Irish reference to an illegal bootlegger. His wooden club took its name from the famous oak trees near the Irish town of Shillelagh — so yes, he could go to a shindig and wipe out the whole shebang with his shillelagh.

**words
and language**

Why do Americans pronounce the last letter of the alphabet "zee" while Canadians say "zed"?

The last letter of our alphabet is from the Greek word *zeta*, which in standard English became *zed*. There were, however, parts of Britain that shortened *zed* to *zee*, and it was from these regions that many people immigrated to the United States. Canada's first immigrants (including the French) were all from regions that used the "zed" pronunciation. In 1828, Webster's first dictionary favoured "zee" as a distinct American sound.

What English words have a *q* without a *u*?

Only one common English word uses *q* without an accompanying *u* and that is *qwerty*, the acronym for the standard keyboard layout. The rest of the words are Arabic, the most familiar being *faqir*; Jewish, *sheqel* (also *shekel*), the main unit of Israeli money, or Chinese, like the musical instrument called a *qin*. France provides *cinq*, which is used in the game of dice.

Why do we pronounce *colonel* as an *r* and spell it with an *l*?

It's a messy story, the result of confusion between two forms of the word that came into English at different times. Its source is the Italian *colonna*. This (along with the English word *column*, with the same meaning) derives from the Latin *columna*, because a column of men was reminiscent of the shape of a pillar. The Italian *compagna colonnella* (literally, "little-column company") referred to the small company of soldiers that marched at the head of a regiment and was commanded directly by the officer in charge. That officer became known as the *colonnello*. This shifted into French as *coronel*, but later changed back nearer the Italian original as *colonel*. Much the same thing happened in English, where *coronel* was the more common form up to about 1630. For a while after this date both forms were in use until *colonel* eventually won. At first the word was pronounced as three syllables, but the middle became swallowed, and under the continuing influence of the *r* spelling the *l* in the first syllable vanished.

Why do Canadians and Americans pronounce the military rank "lieutenant" differently?

Canadians follow British military customs and consequently pronounce the word *lieutenant* as *lef-tenant*. It's believed that this comes from an Old French spelling and pronunciation of *leuf-tenant* (*live–tenant*). The Americans took the French prefix *lieu* as it's now spelled and properly interpreted it as "in place of" because in both cases no matter how it's pronounced, the rank of lieutenant literally means "one who is holding or representing the power of another" — (a superior officer). The word began as a description of someone from wealth who had rented the rank and occupied it for a period of time as a "tenant."

Why do some people say *orientated*, while others say *oriented*?

It depends which side of the pond you're on, the "pond" being British slang for the Atlantic Ocean. Both words come from the French verb *orienteer*, and both are correct. In North America, *oriented* is most frequently used; in Britain *orientated* seems to be the current standard.

What do *razor* and *raze* have in common?

When a man shaves, he uses a razor, so why when soldiers destroy a town do we say they "razed" it to the ground? *Raze* is often employed to describe the results of a fire, not because it has anything to do with flames but simply because there's nothing left. The term's origins began in the fourteenth century when the French word *raser* entered English to describe the morning ritual of shaving. The word meant to scrape, slash, or erase the hair from one's face, just as when an army razes a town it knocks down all of the buildings and levels the settlement to the ground. An anonymous quotation from the Vietnam War puts *raze* into context: "It takes a village to raise a child, but it takes a B-52 to raze a village."

Naughty Anglo-Saxon Words

When the French-speaking Normans conquered England in 1066 and became the ruling caste, they considered the language of the Anglo-Saxon natives to be crude and inferior. It was 300 years before the two languages blended into the new language we call Middle English but even in this time of Modern English, many Anglo-Saxon words are still considered impolite or vulgar in proper circles while the Norman words with the exact same meaning are acceptable. You be the judge!

Norman	Anglo-Saxon
Perspiration	Sweat
Urine	Piss
Desire	Want
Excrement	Shit
Dine	Eat
Deceased	Dead
Fornicate	F*#!
Prostitute	Whore

Is Celt properly pronounced "Kelt" or "Selt"?

The Irish people are descendants of the Celts with a hard *C* (*Kelts*). The word began as the Greek word *Keltoi,* which is what they (and the Romans) called the peoples of Europe who once lived in parts of Gaul, Spain, and Britain. The Celts were to Europe what the Native American Indians are to North America. They were tribal and nomadic without a central capital. As the Romans conquered these nations, the people moved north concentrating mainly in Brittany, the Isle of Man, Wales, Scotland, Cornwall, and Ireland.

The soft *C* (*Selts*) pronunciation is from the French who called these people *Celtique* (*selteek*) and through their political liaisons with France against England, the Scots began using this French pronunciation to describe themselves.

So the Scots are "Selts" while the Irish and the rest are "Kelts". This explains the Scottish Glasgow Celtics (*seltics*) football club but not the Boston Celtics (*seltics*) basketball team. When that team was formed in 1949, the owner, Walter Brown decided to pander to the huge Irish population of his city by naming his team the Celtics but apparently no one picked up that using the soft *C* (*S*) wasn't Irish and so the name remains with a Scottish pronunciation.

Quickies
Did you know...
- that the letter *e* is the most commonly used letter from the English alphabet?
- that one of every eight letters written in English is the letter *e*?
- that in his 1939 novel, *Gadsby*, Ernest Vincent wrote 50,000 words without once using the letter *e*?

How did written punctuation originate?

It wasn't until the end of the fifteenth century that the Italian printer Aldus Manutius introduced the system of markings we call punctuation. The proper use of punctuation marks is a learned skill that has eluded even great writers ever since. Mark Twain once filled the last page of a manuscript with all the various symbols of punctuation and instructed his editor to disperse them within the story as he saw fit.

What does *whelm* mean in *overwhelmed*?

An author facing writer's block is overwhelmed by indecision. The word started out in the 1300s as *whelm*, meaning to overturn or cover. For example, food was preserved by whelming it with another dish, or a capsized ship had been whelmed by the ocean. In the 1600s, *over* was added to intensify the meaning. *Overwhelm* then became figurative for being drowned by circumstances.

What English words rhyme with *orange*, *purple*, and *silver*?

In the English language, there are only two words that end in *gry*: *angry* and *hungry*. There are only three that end in *ceed*: *exceed*, *proceed*, and *succeed*, while *liquefy*, *putrefy*, *rarefy*, and *stupefy* are the only four words ending in *efy*. As for *orange*, *purple*, and *silver*, poets and songwriters should stay away from them, because there are no words in the entire English language that rhyme with them — absolutely none!

Odds & Oddities

The passage of the word *pass*:
Pass started out in Latin as *passus* meaning "step" or "pace" but by the thirteenth century in England it took the meaning "to go by" or "cross over." These are some of the dates and transitions in meaning of the word *pass*:

"Passing time" — 1390
"Pass an exam" — 1429
"Pass the hat" — 1762
"Passing yourself off as something you're not" — 1809
"Pass as in declining to participate" — 1869
"Pass as in transfer a puck or ball during a game" — 1865
"Pass the buck" — 1865
"Pass as in making an amorous move" — 1928

Why do we say that somebody who speaks nonsense is "babbling"?

To babble means to speak foolishness. It is a verb rooted in the French and Scandinavian languages and was used to describe baby talk in the months leading up to a child's first words. Babble has many different forms and circumstances, for example, squabble, blather, and charlatan, all of which, to some degree, mean "chattering and prattling nonsense."

The Latin for *babble* is *blatire*. *Blatire* is the word that *blatant* is derived from. It was coined by English poet Edmund Spenser (1552–1599) in *The Faerie Queene* in 1596 to describe a thousand-tongued beast representing slander.

If *right* means correct, does *left* mean incorrect?

The word *right* surfaced in English as *riht* and meant "straight." To put things right is to straighten them out. *Right* took the metaphorical meaning of "good" or "just," as in the Bill of Rights, because most people were right-handed. The suggestion that *left* is incorrect was understood, like in a "left-handed compliment," which is an insult. *Right* became a synonym for correct, but *left* was evil and so was left alone.

Quickies
Did you know...
- that the word for *left* in Italian is *sinistra* or *sinistro*? In English, definitions of *sinister* include; "suggesting or threatening evil," "presaging trouble/ominous," and "on the left side."
- that the word *gauche* is French for "awkward," "lacking social polish," and "left-handed"?

Why are a barrier and a form of fighting with swords both called "fencing"?

If you fence in or enclose your yard, you are protecting it from outside forces and if you learned how to fence during the Middle Ages you were learning how to fight or protect yourself with a sword. In both cases the word *fence* is an abbreviation of defence. The use of the word *fence* meaning a criminal dealing in stolen goods is from the sixteenth century and implies the defence of the transactions through silence.

Why is a painfully difficult experience called an "ordeal"?

The word *ordeal* for a trial of character began as an *ordel,* which is derived from the old Germanic word *urteil,* meaning "divine judgment" or "that which the gods deal out." It was used to describe an ancient Teutonic mode of trial that involved what we would call torture. If the person accused was innocent, then God would intervene, otherwise the cruel test would continue even on to death. Ordeal has become a metaphor for any test of character or endurance. Once common in Old English, the prefix *or,* meaning "out," only survives today in the word *ordeal.*

Why do we say that a subordinate person is "kowtowing" to another when they are "knuckling under" to their wishes?

We call the finger joints knuckles, but the word used to mean any joint in the body, including the elbows and knees. To "knuckle under" is left over from those days and refers to bending your knees or bowing, signalling submission. *Kowtow* is Chinese and means "to kneel and press your forehead to the ground," which was expected in the presence of the emperor or anyone else you feared.

Why when someone has been banished or ostracized by a group do we say they've been "blackballed"?

Ostracize comes from a Greek word meaning "voting tablet," and the ritual of "blackballing" someone was a democratic process of elimination. A group decided if a suspect member would be banished or allowed to stay by dropping black and white balls into a ballot box. The word *ballot* means "little ball." If the majority were black, the candidate lost and was said to have been blackballed.

Why is a crowning achievement called a "masterpiece"?

Masterpiece suggests great art, but when the word first appeared in German as *meisterstuck*, it referred to a medieval standard of excellence expected from an apprentice before being allowed to join a guild of master craftsmen. After many years under the guidance of a master, the apprentice submitted a piece of work for assessment. If his work or masterpiece passed the test, he would be allowed into the trade as a master craftsman.

Why is "benchmark" used as a reference point for quality and precision?

A *benchmark* is a surveyor's term and, beginning in the nineteenth century, meant a mark cut into a stone or a wall that established the exact level of altitude for a tract of land they were measuring. Today a benchmark is a high standard to strive for, but the surveyors took their meaning from the word *bench* as it relates to a long tract of level elevated land along a shoreline or a sloping hill.

Why is a pretentious person called a "snob"?

A snob is someone who pretends wealth and demands respect he doesn't deserve. Universities only educated children of the nobility until Cambridge opened its doors to commoners in the seventeenth century. These new students were required to register in Latin as *Sine Nobilitate*, which means "without nobility." Abbreviated, this Latin phrase is S.Nob, pronounced "snob," and it took on the meaning of anyone above his station.

Why is a wise counsellor called a "mentor" or a "guru"?

The original Mentor was the name of a wise and trusted counsellor in Greek mythology who was Odysseus's friend and a trusted teacher of Telemachus, Odysseus's son. Mentor was often the goddess Athena in disguise. The word *guru* has the same meaning as *mentor* because it is the Hindi word for "honoured teacher." Guru was first used this way in 1966 by Canadian communications theorist Marshall McLuhan (1911–1980).

The derivative *men* in *mentor* is the same as that in *mental* and means "to think."

Why is someone we consider slow called a "dunce"?

A dunce still means someone we consider out of step, and it derives unfairly from Duns Scotus, the name of a brilliant thirteenth-century Scottish philosopher who, along with his followers (who were called "Duns men"), resisted the thinking within the Renaissance that swept the Middle Ages. As unfair as the sight of a child in a conical dunce cap, Scotus was ridiculed for being different and for daring to express his own thoughts.

Why when things go wrong do we say they've gone "haywire"?

Haywire is used on farms to hold together bales of hay. It's tightly bound and when cut will sometimes whip around in a dangerous erratic manner. But more than this, because haywire is often used as a temporary repair on machinery that has broken down, or to hold together any equipment that's falling apart, it became a rural expression for things or people that aren't functioning properly … they've gone haywire.

Why does the term *barbarian* refer to a rough or wild person?

The early Greek and Roman term for foreigner was *barbaroi*, meaning that they babbled in a strange language (by which root we also have the word *babble* itself). Another possible contributory origin is the Latin word *barba* meaning "beard." A Roman would visit the tonsor to have his beard shaved, and the non-Romans, who frequently wore beards, or *barbas*, were thereby labelled barbarians.

Why are some university graduates and most unmarried men called "bachelors"?

In the eleventh century, a bachelor was a low-ranking knight without the means to raise an army. To indicate this he flew a pointed banner, whereas a full knight had a flag without a tip. The bachelor was a junior, which is why a bachelor's degree refers to the lowest rank from a university. Because most young men were unmarried, they began being referred to as bachelors in the fourteenth century.

Why, when we don't understand someone, do we say they're talking "gibberish"?

An eleventh-century alchemist translated into Latin the original eighth-century writings of an Arabian alchemist named Jabir. If his work had been discovered he would have been put to death, and so he wrote Jabir's formulas in a mystical jargon of his own creation. To anyone other than the author, the Jabir translations didn't make sense. And so anything like it was "Jabirish," which eventually became gibberish.

What are the meanings of common Yiddish words?

Some familiar Yiddish words are: *chutzpah*, "audacity or boldness"; *schmuck*, "a jerk or a foolish idiot" (literally meaning *schmok*, "penis," or "family jewels"); *klutz*, "a clumsy person"; *putz*, "an unclean, stupid person"; *mensch*, "a good and decent human being"; *l'chaim*, "joyful toast to life"; *schlemiel*, "an inept or incompetent person"; *goy*, "a Gentile, a person who is not Jewish"; *tochis*, "rear end," "butt"; *pisher*, "a male infant, a little squirt, someone of little significance" (yes, the word comes from what it sounds like); *shiksa*, "a Gentile woman" (originally this word meant "an abomination"); and *schmooze*, "small talk," usually meaning "sucking up."

Yiddish is a Germanic language and is spoken by about three million people throughout the world. Although the word *Yiddish* is, in fact, Yiddish for "Jewish," it is most likely from the German word *jiddisch*, an abbreviated form of *yidish-taytsh* or "Jewish German." The word came to North America and entered English with immigrants from Central and Eastern Europe at the beginning of the twentieth century.

Mazel tov is well-known for its use at the end of a Jewish wedding ceremony. Often it is thought to be Yiddish, but actually it comes from *mazzāl*, which means "star" in Hebrew. *Mazel tov* is used as "congratulations," but literally means "may you be born under a good star." After telling someone *mazel tov*, it is customary to shake hands.

How did the word *moron* come to mean stupid?

We have all been called a moron at one time or another and understood it to mean we've done something foolish. The reason is that in 1910 Dr. Henry H. Goddard (1866–1957) proposed the word to the American Association for the Study of the Feebleminded to describe an adult with the mental capacity (IQ below 75) of a normal child between eight and 12 years of age. A moron was, in fact, the highest proposed rating of a mentally challenged person. The two lowest ratings suggested were imbecile and idiot. These categories have been dropped by the scientific community and are no longer in use — except as an insult!

Moron is from the Greek *moros*, meaning "stupid" or "foolish."

Why is a person who takes punishment for someone else called a "fall guy"?

Since the 1880s, "taking a fall" has meant to be arrested or imprisoned. To take a fall now figuratively means to be taken down for something you may or may not have done; but a fall guy, like a professional wrestler, has been paid or framed to take punishment. On a movie set, a fall guy is a stuntman who again is paid to literally take the fall, sometimes from high buildings, for another actor.

What is the difference between a "bum," a "tramp," and a "hobo"?

During the Great Depression of the 1930s, Godfrey Irwin published *American Tramp and Underworld Slang*, within which he explained the difference. Bums loaf and sit; tramps loaf and walk; but a hobo moves and works. *Hobo* is derived from *hoeboy*, because many of the young men travelling the rails were from farms and carried a hoe with them so that they could work the gardens of those households that might employ them.

Why is a spineless coward called a "wimp"?

Someone who is weak and indecisive is often called a wimp, which is a short form of the word *whimpering*. The origin of *wimp* is a series of children's books written in the 1890s by Evelyn Sharp, which featured characters called Wymps with a *y*, who loved playing practical jokes on others but who would cry when jokes were played on them. In the 1930s, a corpulent Popeye cartoon character named J. Wellington "Wimpy" kept the word alive.

Why is a small-time player called a "piker"?

Many early highways had entrances that were blocked by a pike, or long pole, which was "turned," or opened, after a toll was paid. These highways were called "turnpikes." Those who walked these roads were sometimes vagrants and very often unsophisticated farm boys on their way to seek their fortunes in the city. If you just "came down the pike" you were naive and often admonished as a "piker."

Why are the names of those out of favour said to be kept in a "black book" or on a "black list"?

The "blacklisting" of artists by the American Congress during the 1950s was a shameful and well-documented reign of terror, but black lists and little black books are still quietly with us, especially among those who see enemies everywhere. It began with King Henry VIII of England, whose infamous black book recorded so-called abuses in monasteries to justify his purge against the Catholic Church.

Why is a speaker's platform known as a "rostrum"?

After a victory at sea the Romans customarily removed the decorative prow or rostrum from defeated enemy ships to be returned to Rome as symbols of their supremacy on the high seas. These *rostra* were displayed on the speaker's platform in the Roman Forum until there were so many that the stage from which a speaker addressed the assembly became known as the rostrum, or the ship's prow.

Why do we call a reaction of coercion and punishment a "boycott"?

The word *boycott*, meaning to ostracize an oppressor, originated in Ireland in the late nineteenth century. As punishment for falling behind in rent, poor tenant farmers in County Mayo were being tossed from their homes by Captain Charles Boycott, who was acting as the agent of an absentee English landlord. The tenants eventually forced Boycott's downfall by refusing to take in the harvest, making the repossessed land useless to its English owner.

Why is the Irish gift of the gab called "blarney"?

Kissing the Blarney Stone at Blarney Castle near Cork, Ireland, is supposed to transfer the gift of gab to the kisser, but the idea that the word *blarney* meant a smooth talker came from the mouth of Elizabeth I of England in 1602. She had insisted that Dermot McCarthy surrender Blarney Castle as proof of his loyalty, but he kept coming up with excuses — so many excuses, in fact, that the Queen once exclaimed in exasperation, "Odds Bodkins, more Blarney talk!"

Why are BC, AD, BCE, and CE all used to give calendar dates to historic events?

In 525 AD the Christian church introduced a calendar using the year of Christ's birth, 1 AD, or "Anno Domini," as the starting point. Earlier events were BC, or "Before Christ." Uncomfortable with these references, non-Christians replaced BC with BCE for "Before the Common Era" and AD with CE, the "Common Era."

What do the words *algebra*, *sofa*, *sash*, and *sequin* have in common?

Algebra, *sofa*, *sash*, and *sequin* are among the hundreds of common English words that originated within the Arabic languages. A few others are: *magazine*, *alcohol*, *jar*, *cotton*, and *mattress*. *Racquet* comes from an Arabic word for *hand*, which is how tennis was originally played. The words *alcove*, *chemist*, *coffee*, and *chess* are also included among the everyday Arabic words that enrich our language.

war and
the military

Why is a victory gained at too great a cost described as "pyrrhic"?

In 279 BC, at the battle of Asculum in Apulia, King Pyrrhus of Epirus commanded an army that defeated the Romans commanded by Publius Decius Mus. Both sides had fought savagely all day and were unwillingly separated at nightfall. King Pyrrhus had been wounded in the arm by a javelin, and 15,000 men from both sides had died on the battlefield when an officer approached and congratulated the King on his victory. Pyrrhus, who had lost most of his army and almost all of his friends and generals, replied that another victory such as this would utterly undo him. This incident is the origin of the phrase "a pyrrhic victory."

What is the origin of the "Rough Riders"?

Theodore (Teddy) Roosevelt, future president of the United States, raised a regiment of cavalry in 1898 to fight in the Spanish-American War. Shortly after they were formed, the public and media dubbed them "Rough Riders" for reasons Roosevelt was never able to explain. At the battle of San Juan Heights (Kettle Hill and San Juan Hill), near Santiago, Cuba, they participated in a famous charge that overwhelmed the Spanish troops. Another group that distinguished themselves in the charge was the 2,000 Buffalo soldiers, who were African-American.

One of the officers for the Buffalo soldiers was General "Black Jack" Pershing, who later led the American Expeditionary Force in France during the First World War.

What does a soldier mean when he says there's "fire in the hole"?

"Fire in the hole" showed up in the film Saving Private Ryan during a scene on Omaha Beach when soldiers set off an explosive device called a Bangalore torpedo. The phrase is also the title of a quarterly magazine produced by the U. S. Navy Seals Museum. There's some dispute as to its origins. Some suggest that the term comes from naval gunnery in the days when you touched a match to priming powder or a fuse to discharge a ship's cannon. The more widely accepted explanation is that the phrase is uttered when a controlled explosion is imminent at a mine or a construction site.

Who first used the expression "thousand-yard stare"?

The "thousand-yard stare" actually started out as a "two-thousand-yard stare." That was the title an artist named Tom Lea gave to a 1944 painting of a Marine on a Pacific island of Beliliou, site of the brutal Battle of Peleliu. The painting depicts a soldier with an unfocused gaze that reveals he's been exposed to more horror and stress than he can handle.

Who was the civilian general who led Canada's troops at Vimy Ridge?

Lt. General Sir Arthur Currie is one of Canada's greatest war heroes. A real estate developer, he entered the military reserve after his business failed, and went to France at the start of the First World War. In 1917, he led the planning for an assault on Vimy Ridge, which allied armies had failed to capture on several previous occasions. Although the loss of life was terrible — 3,598 Canadians killed and 10,602 wounded — by standards of the First War, the operation was a huge success.

Currie went on to become the first Canadian-born commander of the Canadian Corps.

Why does "wreaking havoc" mean causing chaos?

The word *havoc* is used several times by Shakespeare to describe brutal confusion. During the fourteenth century, the vocal cry of "Havoc!" was a common practice of soldiers sacking an occupied enemy town or settlement. It meant that a full blown riot of pillaging was in progress and the cry was one of encouragement. The word was initiated by the French who cried "Havot!" meaning "plunder at will." Richard II outlawed the cry and the practice of "havoc" with the death penalty for offenders in the British military.

Why are some soldiers called "guerrillas"?

Guerrilla warfare is conducted by small unofficial paramilitary groups of indigenous men usually fighting oppressors in occupied territory. They use surprise to sabotage and harass the enemy. The word grew out of Spanish resistance to Napoleon in 1809. The word *guerra* is the Spanish word for "war" and *guerrilla* literally means "little war." A guerrilla is a citizen soldier in such a war.

Why is willful destruction called "sabotage"?

During the Nazi occupation of France, the underground guerrilla freedom fighters often used sabotage as a means of disrupting the enemy. The word *sabotage* means to deliberately destroy property and is derived from *sabot* — a wooden shoe. The legend is that during a labour dispute, the workers brought the factory to a halt by tossing their shoes into the machinery. Whether or not this is true, the word *sabot* became the source of the word *sabotage* for the actions of those who created havoc for the occupying Germans.

Why, when there's no turning back, do we say, "The die is cast"?

When you say, "The die is cast," you are quoting Julius Caesar. In 49 BC, the Roman general stood and thought long before crossing the Rubicon River into Italy with his army, a move that would break Roman law and start a civil war. When he made his decision and moved forward, he said, Alea jacta est (the die is cast), meaning, as when throwing dice, that the outcome is in the hands of fate, and there is no turning back from the consequences. Another phrase with a similar meaning came out of this same event: Crossing the Rubicon means taking a step or action that sets you on an irrevocable path.

Who were the Minutemen?

Minutemen were the elite militia soldiers in the British colonies during the seventeenth and eighteenth century. From 1645 on, towns throughout the colonies were required to maintain militias, which are often drawn on to fight campaigns against the French or aboriginals. Approximately a quarter of the men of these militias, the most enthusiastic and able, were chosen and trained as Minutemen, to be ready to fight on short notice.

At the start of the American Revolution, a Minuteman named Paul Revere set out on his famous ride to warn militias in Massachusetts that the British were coming.

Where did we get the expression "Over the top"?

During the First World War, a charge over the protective battery that ran alongside a trench was called "going over the top." Such a charge usually resulted in many casualties, as did most operations during that tragic conflict. Since the casualty rate was very high, it took remarkable bravery to go over the top. Some considered it excessively brave, and the phrase has come to be associated with excess.

Where did the word *assassin* come from?

While mounting a jihad against the invading Christian Crusaders in the 1300s, Hassan ben Sabah controlled his command of radical killers with a potion that gave them dreams of an eternity in a garden where young women pleased them to their heart's content. The potion was from hashish, and these young killers became known as hashish eaters, which in Arabic is *hashashin*, or as the Crusaders pronounced it, "assassin."

Why do the military say "Roger" then "Wilco" to confirm a radio message?

During the Second World War, the United States Navy used a phonetic alphabet to clarify radio messages. It began, Alpha, Baker, Charlie, Dog, and went on to include Roger for "R." Because "R," or "Roger," is the first letter in received, it confirmed that the message was understood. On the other hand, "Wilco" is a standard military abbreviation for "will comply."

Why is a secret enemy amongst us referred to as a "fifth column"?

Any secret force within an enemy's midst during wartime is called a fifth column. The phrase comes from the Spanish Civil War, when the general leading the 1936 siege of Madrid with four columns of infantry was asked if four were enough. He replied that he had a fifth column hiding inside the city. Since then a fifth column has meant a secret organized force amongst the enemy or ourselves.

What does the D stand for in D-Day?

Although D-Day has become synonymous with the Allied landing on June 6, 1944, in Normandy, it was used many times before and since. The D in D-Day simply stands for "day," just as the H in H-Hour stands for "hour." Both are commonly used codes for the fixed time when a military operation is scheduled to begin. "D minus thirty" means 30 days before a target date while "D plus fifteen" means 15 days after.

How did a crushing public humiliation become known as a "Roman holiday"?

The Etruscans of ancient Italy ritually honoured their dead war heroes by sacrificing the lives of all prisoners seized in battle. After conquering the Etruscans, the Romans borrowed and embellished the ritual by having the prisoners kill each other. They turned the slaughter into public gladiatorial games and declared the spectacle a Roman holiday, which became an expression synonymous with any cruel and crushing public destruction.

Why do we say, "It's cold enough to freeze the balls off a brass monkey"?

Early warships fired iron cannonballs from a stack piled next to the cannon. To keep them in place, they used a square piece of rust-proof brass with indentations to secure the bottom layer of balls. This plate was nicknamed "the monkey." When it got cold enough, the mischievous brass monkey would shrink, causing the balls to fall out and roll all over the deck. It was "cold enough to freeze the balls off a brass monkey."

Why is someone who doesn't live up to expectations called a "flash in the pan"?

On a pioneer flintlock rifle the hammer struck a flint to create a spark that ignited a small amount of priming powder in what was called the pan. This ignition then set off the main charge of gunpowder, causing a small explosion that fired the bullet through the barrel. When the powder in the pan didn't ignite properly it created a flash, but the rifle wouldn't fire. It looked good, but it was only a "flash in the pan."

Why is a single-minded person said to be "zeroed in"?

Before the modern era, rifle gun sights were aligned to hit a target at a known distance. Therefore, with the guesswork removed, any adjustment from a set position would be zero. The same principle applies to artillery batteries, which adjust their fire to a fixed point or "ground zero," a term still used with satellite- and laser-guided bombs and missiles. Like the single-minded person, they're zeroed in.

How did a telegram bring the United States into the First World War?

In 1917, the British intercepted a cable from the German foreign minister to their Mexican ambassador proposing an alliance whereby the Mexicans would reacquire Texas, Arizona, and New Mexico if that country would join Germany in an attack from the south on the neutral Americans. The British made the telegram public on March 1, and the outcry forced the United States into the war a month later.

What was the cost in human life to liberate each Kuwaiti citizen during Operation Desert Storm?

After Saddam Hussein invaded Kuwait, an American-led military force liberated the tiny country in 1991 — but at what cost? There were 491,000 Kuwaiti citizens, who made up only 28 percent of the country's population. The rest, or 72 percent, were immigrant labourers. Estimates are that 150,000

Iraqis were killed during the war, while 141 American, 18 British, 2 French, and 44 Arab soldiers gave their lives. This means it cost one life to liberate every three Kuwaitis.

What are the origins and military significance of the phrase "Go for broke"?

"Go for broke" came from the world of professional gambling and is over 100 years old. It means to risk everything, no matter what the outcome. "Go for broke" was the motto for the segregated Japanese-American volunteers of the 442nd Battalion during the Second World War. At first considered enemy aliens, these soldiers fought so well that they became the most decorated unit in American military history.

What is the unique story behind the Victoria Cross?

The United Kingdom's Queen Victoria created the Victoria Cross in 1856 to recognize individual acts of gallantry by soldiers and sailors of the British Empire. The new medal came on the heels of, and was inspired by, the heroics of the Crimean War fought by Britain, France, the Kingdom of Sardinia, and the Ottoman Empire against Russia between 1854 and 1856. To this day each Victoria Cross is forged from the melted-down metal of Russian cannon captured during the Crimean War. Unlike some other British medals, the Victoria Cross can be awarded to any member of the military regardless of rank. To date, at the time of this writing, 1,355 people have received the medal.

Who were the first and last Canadian recipients of the Victoria Cross?

On August 9, 1945, navy pilot Lieutenant Robert Hampton Gray became the ninety-fourth, and last, Canadian to win the Victoria Cross. He was awarded the medal posthumously for bravery during an attack on a Japanese destroyer on the final day of the Second World War. The first Canadian to receive the medal was Lieutenant Alexander Roberts Dunn, who won his for bravery during the Charge of the Light Brigade in 1854 at the Battle of Balaclava in the Crimean War.

Canada's last living Victoria Cross recipient was Ernest Alvia "Smokey" Smith, who died at his home in Vancouver in August 2005. Smith, who won his medal in Italy in October 1944, single-handedly saved his company from a German counterattack by three tanks, two self-propelled guns, and 30 infantrymen.

Why is someone of key importance to a team leader called a "right-hand man"?

The term *right-hand man* refers to someone indispensable to the person in charge and derives from the military. Today, when soldiers line up on a parade square, they are copying the alignment employed when armies used to face, then approach, each other in lines for mortal or pitched combat. The tallest or "right-marker" is the first called into position, and all others line up in a sequence of diminishing height to his left. The right-marker is the anchor and reference for all verbal commands off whom the other soldiers react both on the parade square and during battle.

A line of soldiers is called a "pitch."

Why do we say that someone is too old to "cut the mustard"?

The phrase "too old to cut the mustard" was popularized by a hit song during the 1940s when military expressions were uppermost in the minds of returning servicemen. Simply put, it means that one's "salad days" are in the past. Mustard is a mispronunciation of the military word *muster*, which means "inspection." If a soldier doesn't "cut or pass muster," he or she doesn't make the grade. In effect, the soldier fails to pass inspection.

Why is the truth referred to as "the real skinny"?

The word *skinny* came to mean "emaciated" around 1605, and during the Second World War, it began to suggest something that was true. The expression means "let's cut to the bare bones of a situation without any embellishment." In combat there is no time for anything except the "naked truth," so eventually a creative and expedient new slang, "the real skinny," arose.

"Skinny-dip" has the same derivative as "the real skinny" and first appeared in the 1950s.

Where do we get the expression "bang for the buck"?

"Bang for the buck" means getting the most for the amount you have paid. The phrase is a Cold War military expression with sinister suggestions of atomic and other explosive devices. Before the Berlin Wall came down in 1989, the United States and its allies in the West were engaged in a series of confrontations and skirmishes with the former Soviet Union and its satellite states. "Bang for the buck" described how efficiently the American defence (and offence) budgets were being spent.

As poet and playwright T.S. Eliot (1888–1965) wrote in "The Hollow Men" in 1925, "This is the way the world ends/Not with a bang but a whimper."

What is Tecumseh's Curse?

The great Shawnee Chief Tecumseh, who died fighting with Canada against the United States in the War of 1812, placed a curse on the American presidency. He proclaimed that every president elected in a year that ends in a zero would die during his term. Since then, every president elected in such a year has died in office, with the exceptions of Franklin D. Roosevelt, who died of natural causes in his fourth term, and Ronald Reagan, who was shot, but survived. Here is a complete list of presidents affected by the curse:

- William Henry Harrison, elected in 1840, died of pneumonia one month into his presidency.
- Abraham Lincoln, elected in 1860, was assassinated in 1865 at the beginning of his second term.
- James A. Garfield, elected in 1880, was assassinated in 1881.
- William McKinley, elected for his second term in 1900, was assassinated in 1901.
- Warren G. Harding, elected in 1920, died of Ptomaine poisoning in 1923.
- Franklin D. Roosevelt, elected for his third term in 1940, died of a cerebral hemorrhage in 1945 at the beginning of his fourth term.
- John F. Kennedy, elected in 1960, was assassinated in 1963.
- Ronald Reagan, elected in 1980, survived an assassination attempt while in office.

animals

How are things going if you're living "high on the hog"?

Living high on the hog meant originally that you ate what were regarded as the superior cuts of meat, the ones on the higher parts of the animal — pork chops, hams, etc. — as against the belly, feet, knuckles, jowls, and the like. Someone who lives high on the hog is therefore, in the extended sense, pretty well off.

Why is someone worn out "at the end of his rope"?

This expression evolved from the phrase "at the end of his tether." Such a phrase would have been used to describe a dog or a horse being tied or tethered. The old phrase was meant to convey a sense of self-restraint, while the new suggests that one has reached or exceeded one's defined boundaries.

What happened when rabbits were introduced into Australia?

Rabbits were introduced to Australia with the country's first colonists in 1788. By 1907 they had spread so widely that the government of the state of Western Australia constructed a rabbit-proof fence that stretched for 1,833 km to contain them. The fence was too late, however, as some rabbits had already crossed to the other side. In 1950, control was attempted by introducing a virus called myxoma, but survivors developed a resistance and populations were soon back to plague levels. Rabbit fleas were also tried to weaken the rabbits and give the virus chance to take hold again, but that failed as well. In recent years, immunocontraceptives are being tested in the hope that reproduction rates will fall and the population will shrink.

How any animals are killed on roads each year?

Roads and highways are killing and injuring millions of animals around the world. And people get killed and injured too. The Alberta government documented over 11,000 collisions in 2002, injuring 422 people and killing nine. In the same year, Michigan reported 63,000 deer collisions. These statistics only hint at the problem: Many collisions go unreported, animals crawl off the road to die and many never get counted because they are too small or scavengers like ravens clean them up before someone counts them.

Why do we say when someone has a raspy voice that he has a "frog in his throat"?

The expression "frog in your throat" doesn't come from sounding like a frog because you have a cold or sore throat. It originates from an actual Middle Ages medical treatment for a throat infection. Doctors believed that if a live frog was placed head-first into a patient's mouth the animal would inhale the cause of the hoarseness into its own body. Thankfully, the practice is long gone, but the expression "frog in your throat" lives on.

Why does March come "in like a lion and out like a lamb"?

When March weather roars "in like a lion," the adage suggests that the end of the month will leave like a lamb. This is because during early March, the constellation Leo is rising in the east, crossing the meridian on March 20. Therefore, the lion is associated with spring. At the same time the constellation Aries the ram (or the lamb) is setting in the west. So every March is "in like a lion and out like a lamb."

If you're wrong, why do we say you're "barking up the wrong tree"?

"Barking up the wrong tree" comes from hunting raccoons. Hunters use dogs to track down the little masked bandits, who will run into underbrush and, if cornered, climb a tree. When the dogs find that tree, they park under it barking and baying until the brave human arrives with the gun, only to often find that the raccoon has outsmarted the dogs by crossing the branches to another tree … and freedom.

Why when either humans or animals are on a rampage do we say they've "run amok"?

Running amok metaphorically means that someone is in some way dangerously out of control. An elephant that breaks free at a circus might also be described as running amok. *Amok* is a Malaysian word meaning "a state of murderous frenzy." Sixteenth-century explorers said that it was terrifying to see someone running amok, a condition brought on by drug use among some of the Malay.

When creating or correcting something, why do we say we're "licking it into shape"?

When bear cubs are born, like many other newborn animals, they are covered by an amniotic membrane. To ancient people who observed the birth from a considerably safe distance, these cubs looked shapeless until their mothers would lick away the membrane to reveal the perfectly shaped body of the baby bear. Dating from Roman times, this belief gave us the expression for making something right by licking it into shape.

Why are hot summer days called "the dog days"?

Sirius, the "dog star," is within the constellation Canis Major and is the brightest in the heavens. The ancient Egyptians noted that the Dog Star's arrival in July coincided with the annual flooding of the Nile, which was important for a good harvest. The Romans believed that, because of its brightness, the Dog Star Sirius added to the heat of the summer sun, and so they called July and August "the dog days."

Quickies
Did you know...
• that the popular dog name Fido is from *fidus*, the Latin word for faithful?

Why is "until the cows come home" considered a long time?

If left to their own devices, cows in pasture will regularly show up at the barn for milking twice a day: once in the morning and once in the evening. The expression "'til the cows come home" first appeared in the sixteenth century when most people were familiar with the cycles of farm life. It was often used when a party went on long into the night — it would have to end in the morning when the cows came home and needed milking.

Why do we say that someone who has wasted his life has "gone to the dogs"?

In prehistoric China, for hygiene and safety reasons dogs weren't allowed inside the city walls. It was also forbidden to dispose of garbage within the city, and so the designated dump outside the walls was where the stray dogs found food. When undesirables and criminals were banished from the city and forced to compete with the dogs for food at the garbage dump, it was said they had "gone to the dogs."

Why do we say a hysterical woman is acting like she's "having kittens"?

In medieval times and during the American era of witch trials in Salem, whenever an unfortunate pregnant woman began to have premature pains or extreme discomfort, the authorities suspected that she had been bewitched. Because witchcraft and cats were synonymous, they feared that she was about to have a litter of kittens and that the creatures were scratching to get out from the inside. They would say her hysteria was because she was "having kittens."

Why do we use the word *wildcat* to describe a risky venture?

Whether it's a strike or an oil well, the word *wildcat* describes anything that is considered risky and has a good chance of failing. It comes from a time before regulations when state banks like the Bank of Michigan issued their own money. That bank's notes had a panther on the face and were called "wildcats." When the bank went down, so did a lot of fortunes. From then on, all high-risk ventures were described as wildcats.

Why do we call a computer problem a "bug"?

According to Grace Hopper, who led the team that developed the first large-scale computer for the American Navy in 1945, the word was coined when, after tracing an unexplained problem for days, they finally found the cause to be a two-inch bug — a moth — that had gotten stuck in the relay system. From then on, all unexplained computer problems were called bugs.

Why when astonished would someone say, "Well, I'll be a monkey's uncle"?

During the famous Scopes trial in 1925, a Tennessee schoolteacher, John T. Scopes, was accused of breaking that state's law by teaching Darwin's theory of evolution rather than the Biblical origins of mankind. The trial was a sensation and astonished many who had never heard that humans might be related to the apes, and from this came the expression, "Well, I'll be a monkey's uncle."

Why is there a tool called a monkey wrench?

The word *wrench* began in Old English as *wrencan* and means "to twist or wring" and was applied to implements of torture. In 1794 it was recorded as "a tool with jaws for turning." The first hand device for tightening and loosening nuts and bolts was called a "spanner" in England and was patented in 1835 by Solymon Merrick. The monkey wrench was invented in the United States in 1858 and was adjustable and designed for reaching confined areas. The tool is properly called a "Monky" wrench after its inventor Charles Monky who sold the patent for $2,000 which he used to buy a house in Williamsburg, Kings County, New York.

Today, the monky wrench has generally been replaced by the adjustable-end wrench.

What makes a monarch butterfly unique?

The monarch is the only North American butterfly known to migrate. Scientists believed monarchs migrated for quite a long time, but it wasn't until 1975 that Cathy and Ken Brugger found the butterfly's wintering grounds in Mexico's Sierra Madre. There they discovered that the aboriginal peoples who lived in the area thought the butterflies represented spirits of dead children or the souls of lost warriors.

Logging and other kinds of human interference are threatening the survival of the Mexican monarch butterfly colonies. Climate change may be imperilling them, as well.

What is the difference between reindeer and caribou?

There are many who consider reindeer and caribou the same animal. And in fact they share the same genus and species name: Rangifer tarandus. The distinction that is usually made is that reindeer are domesticated deer, while caribou are not. But those looking to make further distinctions point to a number of different traits; for example, reindeer are shorter and stouter than caribou. Also, reindeer have thicker fur than their caribou cousins. The naysayers attribute such differences to the domestication of reindeer and insist that while there are some differences, the two deer are virtually the same.

Why do we say a "leopard can't change his spots"?

Much like "you can't teach an old dog new tricks," we sometimes say "a leopard can't change his spots" to underline that mature people can't alter who or what they are. Such a person's character is too indelible. The phrase about the leopard's spots comes from Jeremiah 13:23 in the Bible: "Can the Ethiopian change his skin or the leopard his spots?"

Why are Siamese cats so fussy?

If you have ever wondered why Siamese cats are always "talking" or bossing you around, it may be because they are descendants of royalty. Cats were revered in Siam where they were often selected to become receptacles of the souls of departed royals and senior government officials. When such a regal person died, a chosen cat would be taken to a temple where priests and monks would attend to their every need.

The first Siamese cats came to Europe and North America in the late nineteenth century from the Kingdom of Siam, which became Thailand in 1939. There are three popular lines of Siamese cats: seal points, chocolate points, and blue points.

Why do we say someone is "happy as a clam"?

"Happy as a clam" seems to assume that the mollusk is indeed happy. This notion was probably inspired by the observation that if a clam is held sideways and looked at straight on it appears to be smiling. However, the expression is incomplete. It began as "happy as a clam at high tide." High tide is, of course, the time when clams can feed. High tide is also a time when clams are safe from clam diggers which, obviously, would make them very happy.

The word clam is derived from the same Scottish word that means "vise" or "clamp."

Why is an untamed animal referred to as "feral"?

Anything living in a natural wild state (plants and animals) can be called feral including those that revert from domestication such as a pack of dogs. In this savage state animals are considered dangerous. The words *fierce* and *feral* are from the same Latin root *ferus* meaning "wild and untamed."

Feral once meant "brave and proud" in reference to an outstanding individual but that use died out in the sixteenth century and evolved into the animal reference a century later.

How did we get the expression "loaded for bear"?

"Loaded for bear" means you are well armed to meet any problem. In the days of muskets, the gunpowder charge could be adjusted depending on the size of the animals you expected to encounter in the wilderness. So if you were hunting bear, or simply entering their territory, you went into the bush well armed with an extra charge loaded into your musket. This expression originated in Canada.

Anyone familiar with Canadian wildlife knows that a simple walk in the bush can become a life-and-death confrontation with a dangerous animal. The bear is very territorial, viciously protective of its cubs, and extremely difficult to take down. Today "loaded for bear" means carrying a powerful rifle as well as a sidearm and a knife.

**a horse
is a horse ...**

What is the difference between a mule, a donkey, a burro, and an ass?

The mule is the result of crossing a female horse and a male donkey. If the crossbreeding is of a male horse with a female donkey the result is called a hinny. All mules are born sterile. An ass is a wild animal related to the horse but smaller. A donkey is simply a domesticated ass. A male donkey is called a jack while the female is a jenny. A jackass is simply a male ass. A burro is a small donkey introduced to America by the Spanish. Its size makes it well suited as a pack animal. Asses originated in Africa and were first domesticated over 3,000 years ago.

Why are horses always mounted from the left side?

All riding horses are trained to be mounted on the left side. The animal adjusts for the weight and can be spooked and resistant if an attempt is made to change this. This left-side mounting is centuries old and dates back to a time when men wore swords on their left side to be easily drawn for combat by the right hand. Stepping in a stirrup with the left foot and raising the sword-less right leg over the horse was more practical than the reverse where the sword could cause a problem being lifted across the animal.

Why when we have no choice at all do we say it's a "Hobson's choice"?

Thomas Hobson lived between 1544 and 1631 and was the owner of a livery stable in Cambridge, England. He was a very stubborn man whom Seinfeld might have called the "Livery Nazi" because, regardless of a customer's rank, he would rent only the horse nearest the stable door. Hobson became famous for never renting horses out of order, so "Hobson's choice" came to mean, "Take it or leave it."

Why do we say, "Never look a gift horse in the mouth"?

It's considered rude to examine a gift for value, and the expression "Never look a gift horse in the mouth" means just that. The proverb has been traced to St. Jerome, who in 400 AD wrote a letter advising a disgruntled recipient to accept the gift in the spirit given without looking for flaws. It was then, and is still, common practice to look into a newly acquired horse's mouth, where you can tell its age by the condition of its teeth.

Why when someone has done something crudely do we say they "rode roughshod" over the situation?

To ride roughshod over something means to have done something without regard or consideration for finesse or good manners. Roughshod refers to the once common practice of leaving the nails stuck out of a horse' shoes to keep the animal from slipping if it were going across country or through the bush. If roughshod horses passed over a garden or manicured lawn, the area would be torn up and completely destroyed.

Why is sloppy work called "slipshod"?

If a horse's hoof is protected by a shoe, it's said to be shod. So it is when a human foot is protected or covered by a shoe. The *slip* in *slipshod* is an abbreviation of *slipper,* so the word *slipshod* means "wearing slippers." The image of a person in a bathrobe wearing slippers isn't one that promotes confidence in their attitude towards work. That's why, since 1815, slipshod has been used to describe the work of a careless or slovenly person.

Why what does it mean to be "long in the tooth"?

Horses get "long in the tooth" as they age because their gums recede. Horse buyers use this fact to help them determine if the horse they want to buy is the age the seller says it is. The phrase was first noted in print in an 1852 work called the The History of Henry Esmond by William Makepeace Thackeray. However, Thackeray was not commenting on a horse, he was describing Thomas Esmond's cousin, who was a middle-aged lady.

Why are wild horses called "mustangs"?

A mustang is a half-wild horse descended from the Arabian horses brought to the Americas by Spanish explorers in the sixteenth century. The word *mustang* comes from the Mexican-Spanish word *mestengo*, meaning "stray animals that are ownerless." Today's mustangs are the offspring of generations of runaways and those horses stolen or recaptured by aboriginals. By 1800 there were millions of mustangs on the North American prairies, but as European settlers moved west, they killed and stole from the aboriginal stock until today, because they are still hunted, there are fewer than 1,000 of these magnificent living symbols of independence still running free.

It is bitterly ironic that after four decades the Mustang car has more respect than its living namesake.

How fast could you mail a letter using the pony express?

The pony express was 18 months of high adventure for as many as 183 daring riders. On over 300, seven to 16 day journeys, riders would travel over 1,864 miles from St. Joseph, Missouri — the easternmost extent of the American railways in 1860 — to Sacramento, California, or back again. The youngest pony express rider was only 11 years old. His nickname was "Bronco Billy." One who was destined for fame was William F. Buffalo Bill Cody. Several riders died during their runs, including one who simply disappeared — his horse turned up, but he wasn't on it — and another who froze to death.

**the
human condition**

Why is a receding hairline said to reveal a "widow's peak"?

A widow's peak is hair that comes to a point at the top of the forehead. Today the term generally applies to men with receding hair, but it began as a reference to women with just such a pointed hairline. The reason it is called a widow's peak is because it resembles the pointed crest of a sixteenth-century mourning hood worn by widows when their husbands passed away. It was believed that if a woman developed a hairline resembling the front of that mourning hood, her husband would soon die. For a time, similar hair growth on a man was called a widower's peak and was equally bad news for the wife. The mourning hood was called a biquoquet.

Where do we get the word *stereotype*?

Stereotype was coined by a famous French printer named Firmin Didot at the end of the 1700s. His word described the process of duplication that involved making a papier-mache, plaster, or clay mold from a tray of lead type characters (a newspaper page, for example) and using it to cast metal plates for use on a printing press. The word began to be used by one group to paint simplistic, distorted, and often offensive characterizations of individuals in another group during the 1920s.

How did feminists come up with the expression "male chauvinist pig"?

The word chauvinism originally meant excessive patriotism and came from the name of Nicolas Chauvin, a French general who was known for his extreme devotion to Napoleon Bonaparte. "Male chauvinism" became a description of a man preoccupied with masculine pursuits during the 1950s, and the word pig, borrowed from a slur on policemen, was added by the women's movement in the 1970s.

Why is a sophisticated person called "highbrow"?

While English was evolving through foreign influences, the meaning of brow changed many times. First it was a reference to what we now call the eyelids, then shifted into the area that we call the eyelashes. Next, because the Anglo Saxons didn't have a word for the ridges above the eyes they called them eye brows. By the sixteenth century the brow was accepted as the lower part of the forehead which shows emotion. By the late nineteenth century "highbrow" started meaning a person with superior intellect or taste while a "lowbrow" was the opposite. It was believed that intelligent people had higher foreheads than those more challenged. To "browbeat" means to bully, but originally meant to look down your nose with a stern arrogance.

Why is "sowing wild oats" a reference to irresponsible youth?

"Feeling his oats" (1831) is the American variation with the same meaning of being young and wild as the English derivative "sowing wild oats" (1564). The seed reference to sexual promiscuousness is obvious but the domesticated oat grain is different from the wild, which when discovered by range horses will cause them to become giddy and erratic. Sowing wild oats instead of domestic is a mistake which the farmer will regret.

Why do we use the phrase "Keep your eyes peeled" as a warning?

"Keeping your eyes peeled" means stay awake! Your lids are the skin or covering of your eyes and just as fruit and vegetables are peeled for usefulness, your eyes need to be wide open to avoid trouble. The earliest known use of the expression was in the newspaper, The Political Examiner in 1833. "Young man! Keep your eye peeled when after women."

What is the difference between misogyny and misogamy?

There is a great deal of difference between misogyny and misogamy. Misogyny is the hatred of women while misogamy is the hatred of marriage. On the other hand, misandry is the word used to describe a woman who hates men. If some-one decides that they hate everybody they are a misanthrope.

Why is idle, speculative conversation called "gossip"?

Gossip is usually made up of groundless rumour and innuendo and is generally a conversation based upon the private lives of others, especially celebrities. Gossip is from the Old English word for godparent which was *godsibb*. Godsibb is a combination of *God* plus the word *sib*, which at the time, meant any relative. *Sibb* is the derivative of the current word *sibling*. By 1362, *sibb* had expanded to include any close acquaintance and *Godsibb* began meaning any of the women invited to attend and assist in childbirth. These women spent much of the time waiting for the birth by engaging in idle chit chat which gave rise to the use of Godsibbs as a reference to women exchanging trifling rumours. By 1566, *Godsibb* had begun to mean anyone involved in spreading rumours through trite or casual conversation about the affairs of others and the word itself subsequently morphed into the word gossip by the early nineteenth century.

How did "420" become a code for marijuana?

"Four-twenty" is a code name for users of marijuana. There are several myths why this is and these include; (1) there are 420 active chemicals in the drug; (2) April 20 is National Pot Smokers Day; (3) April 20 is Hitler's birthday; (4) 4:20 p.m. is tea time for pot-smokers in Holland; (5) April 20 is the anniversary of the Columbine school shootings; (6) The California State Police dispatch code for marijuana is 420. But none of these is correct! In 1971, a group of about a dozen pot-smoking students of San Rafael High School created 420 as a discreet reference to marijuana so that they could talk about getting high in front of their teachers and parents without them knowing. 4:20 was the time of day the students would meet by the campus statue of Louis Pasteur to light up. This small group called themselves the Waldos and their 420 code spread through an entire generation who are now in their fifties. It should be mentioned that today, 4:20 p.m. every April 20, has become an international "burn time" or moment of rebellion for hardened pot smokers.

Quickies
Did you know...
- that one out of every five Americans between 20 and 49 years old have tried cocaine? One in 150 use it regularly.
- that the odds are one in 428 that you were arrested for a marijuana related crime in 2006?
- that 75 percent of North American homes forbid the smoking of cigarettes?

divorce

How old is divorce?

Divorce is quite likely almost as old as marriage. European observers of indigenous peoples in the Americas, Africa, and elsewhere recorded that in some cultures people "married" just by moving in together and "divorced" simply by going their own separate ways. Common causes for these separations seemed to be: the wife had borne no children, was bad-tempered, or neglected her domestic duties, or the husband was abusive, was a poor provider, or stayed away from home too long.

What were legal grounds for divorce in ancient Egypt?

An Egyptian could divorce a spouse for adultery, infertility or strong personal dislike. The wife could take with her any property she had taken to the marriage, but she could legally challenge her ex-husband for some of the goods that had come into their possession during the marriage. The Egyptians took a seriously dim view of adultery. A person found guilty of adultery, in addition to being divorced, could also be publicly flogged. Women were more likely to receive this punishment, but men could also be subjected to it. Generally, the Egyptians tried to discourage divorce.

Why was divorce considered a serious matter in ancient societies?

If a husband divorced his wife and her natural family would not or could not take her in, then the responsibility of providing for her — and possibly her children — fell upon the community. Some societies took better care than others of women and children who had no form of support, but all expected a man to live up to his responsibilities as a husband. If he did not, he'd better have a very good reason.

What was the ancient Greek method of divorce?

If an Athenian husband wanted to divorce his wife, he simply expelled her from his house. However, he had to have just cause. A husband who divorced a wife who had fulfilled her obligation to bear legitimate children, especially sons, and whose conduct was irreproachable, was considered immoral. Theoretically, a wife who wished to divorce her husband simply had to leave his house and go back to her family. However, if the husband wanted, he could use force to prevent her from leaving.

How did the ancient Romans view divorce?

In Rome's early days the people took a very dim view of divorce. There were strict laws, supposedly written by Romulus, the legendary founder of Rome, forbidding divorce except for three reasons. A husband could divorce his wife if she: poisoned their children, committed adultery, made duplicates of his keys.

Why did Roman attitudes about divorce change?

As Rome became richer, more powerful, and more decadent, many of the old ideals of morality were lost. Many Roman husbands and wives engaged in numerous affairs and divorced each other for the most trivial reasons. One husband divorced his wife because she had gone to the arena without his permission. Men could climb the social ladder or advance themselves politically through a series of strategic marriages and divorces. The ambitious general Gaius Marius, for example, greatly enhanced his career by divorcing his wife of many years so he could marry into the aristocratic Caesar family. To divorce a spouse, a Roman simply had to give the person a letter stating that they were now divorced.

Seven Reasons a Husband Could Divorce His Wife in Ancient China
- She didn't obey his parents.
- She committed adultery.
- She had borne no children.
- She had a jealous disposition.
- She had an obnoxious disease.
- She talked too much.
- She had been caught stealing.

Three Ways a Wife Could Avoid Divorce in Ancient China
- She had mourned his deceased parents for three years.
- The family had prospered financially during the marriage.
- The husband couldn't find a family to take her in.

What were grounds for divorce among the Aztecs?

The very advanced Aztec civilization in what is now Mexico had a highly developed code of law that included rules for marriage and divorce. A man could divorce his wife if she were childless, bad-tempered, or lazy. A wife could divorce her husband if he physically abused her, didn't provide for the children's education, or generally neglected his family.

Quickies
Did you know...
- that in China if a married man's parents didn't like his wife or thought she was a lazy worker, they could order him to divorce her and find someone they considered satisfactory?

Why could getting married during the Middle Ages take a long time?

Many young people married in the church but without parental consent. The church thus found itself in the awkward position of having to defend a marriage that was sacred in the eyes of the church, while at the same time trying to placate parents who wanted marriages annulled. By spreading the process out over a period of time, church officials could investigate the backgrounds of the prospective bride and groom, families could come to terms, and messy separations, annulments, and divorces could be avoided.

Whose divorce in 32 BC plunged the Roman world into civil war?

Octavian, nephew of the late Julius Caesar, ruled the western part of the Roman Empire, while Marc Antony ruled in the east. Antony was married to Octavian's sister, Octavia. In 32 BC Antony divorced Octavia so he could marry Cleopatra, the queen of Egypt. This insult to his family's honour was all the excuse Octavian needed to declare war on Marc Antony. Octavian's forces defeated those of Antony and Cleopatra, who subsequently committed suicide. Octavian, as Augustus Caesar, became sole master of the Roman Empire.

Why did Napoleon divorce Josephine?

Josephine was six years older than Napoleon, and had children from a previous marriage. But she had no children with Napoleon, and he wanted an heir. At first they thought the problem lay with Napoleon, because Josephine had already had children.

Then Napoleon's mistress became pregnant. Napoleon decided that Josephine was too old to conceive. He told her France needed an heir, and then divorced her in a solemn ceremony. This, incidentally, made the ruling families of Europe very nervous as they knew Napoleon would now be searching for a new wife and none of them wanted the common-born Bonaparte for a son-in-law.

Whom did Napoleon choose for his new bride?

Napoleon married Marie Louisa, 19-year-old daughter of Emperor Francis I of Austria, whose army Napoleon had humiliated on the battlefield several years earlier. Maria gave birth to a son, Napoleon Francois-Joseph Charles, whom Napoleon gave the title King of Rome. After Napoleon's fall and exile, the boy lived with his mother. He died at the age of 21, probably from tuberculosis.

How do Gypsies perform a divorce?

Gypsy customs vary considerably from place to place and are often shrouded in secrecy. In the past, divorce was allegedly quite rare among them. However, one nineteenth-century non-Gypsy writer claimed to have witnessed what he described as divorce over the sacrifice of a horse. A wife who had been accused of adultery laid her head on an "unblemished" horse. The horse was then turned loose to roam free. It was watched carefully, and its behaviour determined the degree of the woman's guilt. One person in the Gypsy band was appointed priest, and the horse was brought forward to be charged with the crime and put on trial. Upon being found guilty, the horse was stabbed in the heart and allowed to bleed to death. The husband and wife stood on either side of the dying horse, held hands, and said words to repudiate each other. They walked around the dead horse three times, making the sign of the cross each time. Then they stood at the horse's tail, shook hands, and turned to go their separate ways. The woman had to wear an iron token as a symbol of her divorced state and wasn't allowed to marry again. If she did, she could be put to death.

Why did the divorce rate rise in the 1970s?

There were great economic and social shifts in the 1970s. The husband could often no longer be the sole "bread winner" in the family, unless he was willing and able to work ever longer hours. The wife had to go to work at an outside-the-home job, in addition to keeping her traditional role as housekeeper. This caused severe strains on relationships in many households, especially those in which the husband considered it unmanly if he could not financially support his family alone.

What contributed to a decline in the divorce rate in the 1990s?

By the 1990s the idea of a husband and wife as dual breadwinners was much more acceptable than it had been a generation earlier. A husband did not have to feel ashamed because his wife had a job, and more husbands were willing to share in domestic duties. There were also more socially acceptable alternatives to traditional marriage. Many couples simply moved in together.

How did a greater acceptance of unwed mothers affect the divorce rate?

At one time an unwed young woman who became pregnant was a centre of intense shame for her family. This often resulted in the mother-to-be and the child's father getting married because they "had to". Such couples were prime candidates for divorce. As the twentieth century neared its end, changes in the general perception of single mothers, thanks largely to the feminist movement, made alternatives to a "shotgun wedding" available to these women. Many opted to remain single, rather than enter into a marriage that had poor prospects of success.

How has living longer affected the divorce rate?

Centuries ago, when a bride and groom made their wedding vows and promised to love, honour, and obey each other, "till death do us part", they were looking ahead at what would probably be a relatively short period of time. A few people lived to ripe old ages, but the average person wasn't likely to live past the mid-forties, and many died in their 30s. Today many people live into their seventies and eighties and beyond. This is long past the time when their children have moved out of the home. Many older couples who, in spite of marital difficulties, have stuck it out "for the sake of the kids," split up after the last chick has left the nest.

When was the first divorce in what is now the United States?

The first recorded divorce was on January 5, 1643, when the Quarter Court of Boston in the Massachusetts Bay Colony granted a divorce to Anne Clarke. The court found that her husband, Dennis Clarke, was guilty of abandoning Anne, with whom he'd had two children, and of being involved in an adulterous relationship with another woman, with whom he'd also had two children. Clarke refused to return home to his wife, so the Puritan court's final decision read: "Anne Clarke, beeing deserted by Denis Clarke hir husband, and hee refusing to accompany with hir, she is graunted to bee divorced."

What American state's divorce rate rose suddenly in the nineteenth century?

It was the state of Utah, largely settled by Mormons who at that time were polygamous. One of the conditions for Utah being granted statehood in the American Union was the abandonment of polygamy. That meant a lot of ex-wives-to-be! In the 1870s, one Utah law firm was so overwhelmed with divorce cases that it built a type of pioneer dispensing-machine that produced the required legal documents for $2.50 a set. The spouses involved had only to sign the papers to make them fully legal.

What was a "Wife Sale"?

A wife sale was a pre-1857 form of illegal divorce in England. The husband would put a halter around his wife's neck and lead her to a prearranged location where she would supposedly be sold by auction, and would go to live as the wife of the man who was the highest bidder. As cruel and degrading as this appears, it was done with the wife's consent, and the highest bidder was rarely a complete stranger. He was usually a man whom the woman preferred to her husband.

Who described a wife sale in one of his classic novels?

In *The Mayor of Casterbridge*, written in 1866, English novelist Thomas Hardy described a wife sale. Unlike most real wife sales, this one was a drunken, spontaneous action initiated by the husband.

What was "advertising a wife"?

When a couple divorced, or if the wife "deserted" the husband, the husband might still be held responsible for any debts she might have. To free himself of this responsibility he would "advertise" her. He would place an ad in the local newspaper, stating that he would no longer be financially responsible for her. Such ads often had such statements as "My wife has left my bed and board without just cause", and were considered extremely humiliating to the woman. In small communities a woman who had been advertised was quite likely to be shunned, and would often have to move to another town.

What was meant by "denial of wifely services"?

For many people the first thought that comes to mind is the wife refusing to have sex with the husband. That was a legitimate cause for divorce, but not one that most husbands would admit to. There were, however, other "wifely services" that were just as important. These included cooking, cleaning, doing the laundry and caring for the children. A wife accused of negligence in providing these services could be divorced, and was generally considered an object of shame. There were even instances of husbands who tolerated their wives infidelity rather than lose their housekeeping services.

How does divorce affect global warming?

Some scientists claim that the high rate of divorce increases energy consumption. When there is a divorce, people who were living in one household are now living in two. That means two refrigerators, two TV sets, two dwelling places to light, heat and air condition, etc. A study of one American community showed that because of the many divorces there the town had 11,000 housing units that would not have been required if the couples had stayed together.

customs

Why do we cover our mouths and apologize when we yawn?

The yawn is now known to be the body's way of infusing oxygen into a tired body, but suggestion is the only explanation for its contagiousness. To ancient man, who had witnessed many lives leave bodies in a final breath, a yawn signalled that the soul was about to escape through the mouth and death might be prevented by covering it. Because a yawn is contagious, the apology was for passing on the mortal danger to others.

Why are Christian men required to remove their hats in church?

Removing clothing as an act of subjugation began when the Assyrians routinely humiliated their captives by making them strip naked. The Greeks amended this by requiring their new servants to strip only from the waist up. By the Middle Ages, a serf had to remove only his hat in the presence of his superiors. Following these gestures of respect for the master is the reason Christian men remove their hats in church and why Muslims leave their shoes by the mosque door.

Why do the British excuse bad language with "pardon my French"?

To the English, "pardon my French" usually means "you can put it where the sun doesn't shine." It's a non-apologetic apology. The expression is as old as the historic wars waged between France and Britain, and we can be certain the French have similar expressions about the English. Hatred aroused during war frequently leads to bigotry that instills a necessary passion within those who do the killing.

There are dozens of English expression defaming the Dutch and Scots for the same reason. To say "pardon my French" means "I'm about to say something vulgar … like something you would expect from a Frenchman."

Examples of French customs that the British found revolting are: French kissing (kissing with the tongue) and French lessons (a euphemism for prostitution — oral sex).

If most people use a fork in their right hands, why is it set on the left at the table?

When the fork surfaced in the eleventh century, the only eating utensil was a knife, which was used by the right hand to cut and deliver food to the mouth. The left hand was assigned the new fork, which is why it's set on the left. In the mid-nineteeth century, forks finally reached the backwoods of America but without any European rules of etiquette, so settlers used the right hand for both utensils.

When did men start shaving every morning?

In many cultures shaving is forbidden. The reason we in the West lather up every morning can be traced directly back to Alexander the Great. Before he seized power, all European men grew beards. But because young Alexander wasn't able to muster much facial hair, he scraped off his peach fuzz every day with a dagger. Not wanting to offend the great warrior, those close to him did likewise, and soon shaving became the custom.

Why does being "turned down" mean rejection?

To be "turned down" comes from an antiquated courting custom followed by our very proper ancestors. When all meetings between young men and women required chaperones, and because aggressive romantic suggestions were forbidden, a man carried a courting mirror, which, at a discreet moment, he would place face up on a table between them. If the woman favoured his advances, the mirror went untouched, but if she had no interest she would turn down the mirror and the suitor.

Why do we roll out a red carpet for special guests?

The red carpet treatment dates back to the 1930s, when a carpet of that colour led passengers to a luxurious train, the Twentieth Century Limited, which ran between New York and Chicago. The Twentieth Century was the most famous in America and was totally first class with accommodation and dining car menus that were considered the height of luxury. Walking the red carpet to the train meant you were about to be treated like royalty.

Why is a bride's marital "hope chest" called a "trousseau"?

The personal possession such as jewellery, linens, and household items collected as parental gifts and brought to a marriage by a bride is called a trousseau. It was intended to enhance her dowry. The word has a French root, *trousse* meaning "bundle." The word does have other applications. For example, it is used to describe a container for a variety of small items as in a doctor's portable handbag.

What are the rules of etiquette regarding divorced people remarrying?

If both the bride and groom have been married before, they usually pay most of the cost of a simple wedding themselves. If only the groom has been previously married, the bride's family can host a traditional first wedding celebration. If only the bride had been married before, the couple can have a larger-than-usual second wedding celebration for the benefit of the groom's family, but the bride's father does not give her away, as that is done only at a bride's first wedding. The bride's parents are not obliged to pay for her second wedding. Second weddings are usually less formal than first weddings. The bride can wear a suit or dress of any colour, and no veil. The groom wears a suit and tie. Children from previous marriages may attend.

Five points of etiquette concerning divorce
- A divorced woman does not wear her diamond engagement ring on the fourth finger of her left hand. Unless she wishes to save the ring for her children's use later, she may have the stone reset into a bracelet or necklace.
- A divorced couple does not return wedding gifts.
- Friends of the divorced couple should not pry or take sides, but should try to be supportive of both individuals.
- If children are involved, the families of both spouses should be respectful of the other family's right to spend time with them.
- One parent should not be critical of the other parent in front of the children.

Why do we put candles on a birthday cake?

The Greeks borrowed celebrating birthdays from the Egyptian pharaohs and the cake idea from the Persians. Then early Christians did away with birthday parties for a while until the custom re-emerged with candles in Germany in the twelfth century. Awakened with the arrival of a birthday cake topped with lighted candles, which were changed and kept lit until after the family meal, the honoured child would make a wish that, it was said, would come true only if the candles were blown out in a single breath.

What subtleties are hidden in the Japanese custom of bowing?

A Westerner probably won't notice the sophisticated use of the bow in Japanese culture. There are four bows, each with a different meaning. The simplest, at an angle of five degrees, means "good day." A bow of 15 degrees is more formal and means "good morning." As an appreciation of a kind gesture the angle is 30 degrees, while the most extreme, a bow of 45 degrees, conveys deep respect or an apology. During a recent five-year period, 24 residents of Tokyo died while bowing to each other.

What is the origin and meaning of the Latin male gesture of kissing the fingertips?

Latinos and Europeans use hand gestures differently than North Americans. Kissing one's fingertips before directing them toward the object of esteem can be an appreciation of anything from a good wine to a good soccer play. It simply means something is beautiful. The custom comes from the Romans, who kissed their fingertips and then directed them to the gods when entering or leaving a temple.

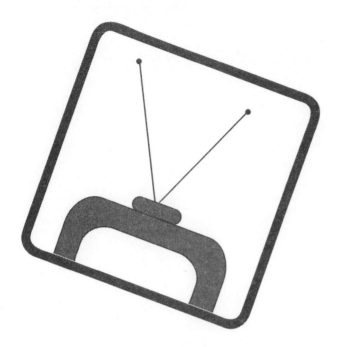

show business

How many movies are made annually in Hollywood?

There hasn't been a movie made in Hollywood since 1911, when, because of its ramshackle sets and the chaotic influence of hordes of actors and crews, the town tossed out the Nestor Film Company and wrote an ordinance forbidding the building of any future studios. Even so, the magic of the name was already established, and so the industry we call Hollywood grew up around that little town in such places as Burbank, Santa Monica, and Culver City — but not in Hollywood.

Why do we call Academy Awards "Oscars"?

Since 1928, the Academy Awards have been issued by the American Academy of Arts and Sciences for excellence in filmmaking. The statuettes were nick-named "Oscar" in 1931 by Margaret Herrick, a secretary at the academy who, upon seeing one for the first time, exclaimed, "Why it looks just like my uncle Oscar." Her uncle was Oscar Pierce, a wheat farmer.

How did Hollywood get its name?

"Hollywood" is a synonym for fantasy for some and decadence for others, yet the dream capital acquired its name from strangers on a train and became a gesture of love between a husband and a wife. In 1887, Mrs. Harvey Wilcox, whose husband owned the California land, overheard the woman next to her on a train refer to her summer home as "Hollywood." Mrs. Wilcox liked the name Hollywood so much that her husband gave it to their California property.

In movie credits, what are the actual jobs of the gaffer, the key grip, and the best boy?

Filmmaking requires precision teamwork, and each credit is well earned. In movie language, a gaffer is the chief electrician; it evolved from the German word *granfer*, meaning "grandfather." A grip requires strength, because he or she builds and dismantles scenery and handles other physical chores that require a strong grip. A best boy is the gaffer's or grip's assistant.

What are the origins of the Tony and the Emmy awards?

The Tony Awards are named in honour of the prominent Broadway personality Antoinette Perry, whose nickname was Tony. The Tony Awards began in 1947, the year after her death. When the Emmy Awards were introduced in the 1940s they were called Immies, after the word image in "Image Orthocon Tube," an important part of a television camera. Over time the Immy became an Emmy.

Why is the "straight man" in a comedy team called a "foil"?

To most of us the noun *foil* is a thin sheet of aluminum food wrap which was introduced in 1946, but the word has a number of other meanings derived from the Latin *folia* meaning "leaf." The straight man as a foil or "one who enhances another by contrast," entered the language in 1581 and comes from the jeweller's practice of backing a gem with a metal foil to make it shine brighter.

How did the Romans use "thumbs up" and "thumbs down" in the Coliseum?

Ancient Roman spectators in the Coliseum did use their thumbs to show their decisions on whether a losing gladiator should live or die, but not in the manner we see expressed today. It was the movies that gave us the simple "thumbs up or thumbs down." The thumb symbolized the weapon of the victor. "Up" meant "lift your sword and let him live." But if the verdict was death, then the thumb was thrust forward and downward in a stabbing motion.

What is the weight of the Academy of Motion Picture Arts and Sciences' prized Oscar?

Recipients of the Academy Award, commonly known as the Oscar, always seem to be surprised at its weight. The Oscar was designed in 1928 by Cedric Gibbons (1893–1960), Metro-Goldwyn-Mayer's chief art director. The statuette depicts a knight standing on a reel of film and holding a crusader sword. Originally, Oscar was made of gold-plated bronze. Today the base of the 24-karat gold-plated britannium statuette is black marble. Oscar is 13.5 inches tall and weighs 8.5 pounds.

Why would a movie director use the pseudonym Alan Smithee?

When a film director doesn't want his name on a bad film, the credit will be given to Alan Smithee, a fictitious name created specifically for this purpose. It began during the shooting of the 1967 film *Death of a Gunfighter* starring Richard Widmark and Lena Horne. The director, Robert Totten was fired by the studio and replaced with Don Siegel. When the disastrous film was released two years later neither director wanted to be associated with the final print. Both demanded to be removed from the credits. Because of this, the Directors Guild decided to establish a fake name to hide unhappy directors from being embarrassed, especially when the final cut had been taken from them by the studio. They settled on Smith before realizing that there might be a real director with that name someday and so they added the two *e*'s with the first name Alan and came up with "Smithee." It then became the name to appear in the credits if any director did not want his own name associated with a film.

Why is a sexy, seductive woman called a "Vamp"?

You can thank Theodosia Burr Goodman for sexually exploitive women being called "Vamps". As a great silent film star she used the name Theda Bara, which is an anagram for "Arab Death." She starred in over 40 films with titles like; *The Unchastened Woman*, *When Men Desire*, *The She Devil*, *When a Woman Sins*, *Cleopatra*, *The Vixen*, *Sin*, *The Devil's Daughter*, and *Siren of Hell* but it was from her 1915 performance in *A Fool There Was*, in which she played a seductive vampire that the abbreviation "Vamp" emerged; not only as a nickname for the beautiful Miss Bara, but as a continuing reference to any unscrupulous seductress.

When a man gifted with charm seizes an opportunity, why do we say, "He's in like Flynn"?

The Australian actor Errol Flynn had an amazing prowess with the ladies, and of course the tabloids built this into a legend. During the Second World War, servicemen coined the phrase "in like Flynn" either to brag about their own conquests or to describe someone they envied. Flynn said he hated the expression, but his own boast that he had spent between 12 and 14 thousand intimate nights ensured its survival.

Quickies
Did you know...
• that Errol Flynn was the great-great-great-great-grandson on his mother's side of a crewman of the HMS Bounty? Flynn portrayed that ship's captain, Fletcher Christian, in the film *In the Wake of the Bounty* (1933).

Why is a glitzy sales presentation called a "dog and pony show"?

In the late 1800s, shows featuring small animals began touring little North American farming towns that weren't on the larger circuses' itineraries. These travelling shows were made up of dogs and ponies that did tricks. Some, like the Gentry Brothers Circus, were very successful, using up to 80 dogs and 40 ponies in a single show. Over time the expression "dog and pony show" became a negative description for anything small-time and sleazy, like a low-budget sales presentation that's heavy on glitz and light on substance.

**he said,
she said:
celebrity split-ups**

How long did the marriage of Ernest Borgnine and Ethel Merman last?

Broadway star Ethel Merman married movie tough guy and Academy Award winner Ernest Borgnine in 1964. After 32 days, Merman filed for divorce. *The Tonight Show* host Johnny Carson joked, "And they said it wouldn't last." While writing her memoirs, Merman said, "The chapter on my marriage to Ernest Borgnine consists of one blank page."

Why did Elizabeth Taylor's two marriages to Richard Burton end?

Richard Burton and Elizabeth Taylor were two of the most popular and talented movie stars of their day. Their marriage crowned what appeared to be a classic Hollywood romance that began on the set of *Cleopatra* in which Taylor played the Queen of Egypt, and Burton played Marc Antony. But both had serious problems with drugs and alcohol, and Burton was a notorious womanizer. At the time of their first divorce, Taylor told a friend, "I love Richard Burton with every fiber of my soul. But we can't be together. We're too mutually self-destructive. Their second marriage ended when Burton told Taylor he wanted a divorce so he could marry Suzy Hunt, an ex-model who was half his age.

How many times has Elizabeth Taylor been married and divorced?

The legendary Hollywood actress has been married eight times to seven husbands:

- Conrad Hilton — May 6, 1950, to January 29, 1951 — divorced
- Michael Wilding — February 21, 1952, to January 26, 1957 — divorced
- Michael Todd — February 2, 1957, to March 22, 1958 — widowed
- Eddie Fisher — May 12, 1959, to March 6, 1964 — divorced
- Richard Burton — March 15, 1964, to June 26, 1974 — divorced
- Richard Burton (again) — October 10, 1975, to July 29, 1976 — divorced
- John Warner — December 4, 1976, to November 7, 1982 — divorced
- Larry Fortensky — October 6, 1991, to October 31, 1996 — divorced

12 Hollywood Celebrities Married Five Times or More
- Zsa Zsa Gabor — 9 husbands
- Elizabeth Taylor — 8 husbands (one of them twice)
- Lana Turner — 8 husbands (one of them twice)
- Mickey Rooney — 8 wives
- Robert Evans — 7 wives
- Hedy Lamarr — 6 husbands
- Tony Curtis — 6 wives
- Boris Karloff — 6 wives
- Gloria Swanson — 6 husbands
- Martin Scorsese — 5 wives
- David Carradine — 5 wives
- Kenny Rogers — 5 wives

He Said, She Said: Celebrity Relationships Gone Bad

Who?

Zsa Zsa Gabor, Hungarian actress; and George Sanders, British actor.

Where and When?

Married, April 2, 1949, Las Vegas. Divorced, April 2, 1954.

Why?

Sanders was jealous of his wife's numerous affairs, including flings with John F. Kennedy and Porfirio Rubirosa, a notorious playboy from the Dominican Republic. Yet when Sanders had to travel abroad to make films, he refused to take Zsa Zsa with him. It was he who finally filed for divorce.

What did they say?

Zsa Zsa Gabor: "Getting divorced just because you don't love a man is almost as silly as getting married just because you do."

George Sanders: "Married life with Zsa Zsa was one of the great humiliations of my life. I suffered severe mental anguish and countless embarrassments."

Who?

Mike Tyson, boxer; and Robin Givens, Actress

Where and When?

Married, February 7, 1988, Chicago. Divorced, February 14, 1989, Dominican Republic.

Why?

Givens accused Tyson of being abusive and manic depressive. Tyson accused Givens and her mother, Ruth Roper, of being gold diggers who were after his money and were trying to seize control of his life and career.

What did they say?

Robin Givens: "(Mike) has, throughout our marriage, been violent and physically abusive and prone to unprovoked rages of violence and destruction."

Mike Tyson: "It was like a sting game. They worked on my emotions because they knew I was in love."

Who?

Joan Collins, British actress; and Peter Holm, Swedish pop star.

Where and When?

Married, November 6, 1985, Las Vegas. Divorced, August 25, 1987, Los Angeles.

Why?

Collins accused Holm of being unfaithful, of being violent and of being a parasite on her. Holm said Collins owed much of her success to him, and was trying to get out of a substantial pre-nuptial agreement.

What did they say?

Joan Collins: "(Holm) demonstrated a capacity for violence and irrational behaviour ... (Holm is) the most combative person I've ever met." She added that he threatened to shoot her.

Peter Holm: "Joan is consumed by Alexis (her sleazy character on *Dynasty*), that's why she's doing this. She really loves me and I love her and we'll get back together, I know it." They didn't.

Who?

Sonny Bono, singer, songwriter; and Cher (Cherilyn Sarkisian), singer, actress.

Where and When?

Married (? The time and place of Sonny and Cher's wedding has always been a mystery. At different times they claimed to have been married in Tijuana, Mexico, in 1964, and in Los Angeles in 1966, '67 and '69). Divorced, June 27, 1975, Santa Monica.

Why?

Cher complained that Sonny tried to control every aspect of her life, even telling her what movies she could see and forbidding her to play tennis with her friends. Sonny said that he had made Cher a star, and she was ungrateful for what he had done for her.

What did they say?

Cher "(Sonny) is a Sicilian dictator husband."

Sonny: "Forget it. I've worked for ten years and if you think I'm going to let you go, just to walk off now, you are crazy."

Famous Quotes

"A wife lasts only for the length of the marriage, but an ex-wife is there for the rest of your life."
— *Woody Allen*

"Ah, yes, divorce … from the Latin word meaning to rip out a man's genitals through his wallet."
— *Robin Williams*

"I'm an excellent housekeeper. Every time I get a divorce, I keep the house."
— *Zsa Zsa Gabor*

"A lot of people have asked me how short I am. Since my last divorce, I think about $100,000 short."
— *Mickey Rooney*

Who?

Ann Landers (Esther Friedman), newspaper advice columnist; and Jules Lederer, founder of Budget Rent-a-Car.

Where and When?

Married, Sioux City, Iowa, July 2, 1938. Divorced, Chicago, October 9, 1975.

Why?

Jules said he was tired of being "Mr. Ann Landers". He told his wife over dinner in a restaurant that he was having an affair. She accused him of infidelity and mental cruelty.

What did they say?

Ann Landers: "That was quite a bomb for him to drop between the soup and the salad."

Jules Lederer: "(She) hadn't always conducted herself as a true, kind and affectionate wife."

Who?

Halle Berry, actress; and Eric Benet, musician.

When and Where?

Married at a secluded California beach January 24, 2001. Divorced, January 2005.

Why?

While Berry's career was soaring and his own career was sputtering, Benet became involved with another woman. At first Berry would not believe the rumours, but finally accepted them as true.

What did they say?

Halle Berry: "At first I didn't believe the stories. I felt like they'd either been made up or exaggerated. There's so much inaccurate reporting that I didn't take them seriously enough. So I defended him. I stood by my man. I thought what we had together was beyond cheating or lying. I refused to believe the stories then and I was in denial for a long time. I didn't think anything had gone wrong. I felt it was all in the imagination of the other women."

Eric Benet: "Ultimately what was the end of us was she just couldn't trust me anymore. You can't blame her for that."

Who?

Rita Hayworth, actress and Orson Welles, actor and producer.

When and Where?

Married, September 7, 1943, Santa Monica, California. Divorced, Los Angeles, November 10, 1947.

Why?

The couple had a child, and Welles did not adapt well to fatherhood. He embarked on a series of affairs, and kept away from his family as much as he could. By the time Rita filed for divorce, the two were not speaking to each other.

What did they say?

Rita Hayworth: "Goddamn it! I'm not Mrs. Orson Welles. I'm Rita Hayworth!"

Orson Welles: "I could have patched it up in a day, but I had reached the end of my capacity to feel such a total failure with her. I had done everything I could think of, and I didn't seem able to bring her anything but agony."

Who?

Debbie Reynolds, actress; and Eddie Fisher, singer.

When and Where?

Married, September 26, 1955 at Grossinger's Catskills Resort, New York. Divorced, February 19, 1959.

Ten Divorce Movies
- *The Gay Divorcee* (1934, starring Fred Astaire and Ginger Rogers)
- *The Parent Trap* (1961, starring Hayley Mills and Maureen O'Hara)
- *A Man for All Seasons* (1966, starring Paul Scofield)
- *Divorce American Style* (1967, starring Dick Van Dyke and Debbie Reynolds)
- *Kramer vs. Kramer* (1979, starring Dustin Hoffman and Meryl Streep)
- *Shoot the Moon* (1982, starring Albert Finney and Diane Keaton)
- *Irreconcilable Differences* (1984, starring Ryan O'Neal and Shelley Long)
- *The War of the Roses* (1989, starring Michael Douglas and Kathleen Turner)
- *Mrs. Doubtfire* (1993, starring Robin Williams and Sally Field)
- *The First Wives Club* (1996, starring Bette Midler, Goldie Hawn, and Diane Keaton)

Why?

The couple had been romantically involved for months and because of Reynolds' squeaky clean image there was considerable pressure on them to get married. As husband and wife, they soon realized it was a bad match. Both devoted much time to their careers and little to each other. When Reynolds recording of the song "Tammy", made for the movie *Tammy and the Bachelor*, became a big hit, Fisher had a bout of professional jealousy. Reynolds filed for divorce when Fisher told her he was in love with Elizabeth Taylor.

What did they say?

Debbie Reynolds: "He's a needy, dependent person. I don't know what to compare him to — he's like an elevator that can't find the floor."

Eddie Fisher: "As I later discovered, Debbie Reynolds was indeed the girl next door ... But only if you lived next door to a self-centered, totally driven, insecure, untruthful phony."

Who?

Mary Tyler Moore, actress, and Grant Tinker, advertising executive.

When and Where?

Married Las Vegas, June 1, 1962. Divorced December 30, 1980.

Why?

Both cited irreconcilable differences. Mary was edgy and restless after her long-running TV show went off the air — at her own decision. She was smoking and drinking heavily. Then came two severe blows; her sister died in a medication mishap, and then Ritchie, Moore's son from an early marriage, was killed in a shooting accident. Moore and Tinker mutually believed their time together had come to an end. They separated for awhile, and then agreed to a divorce. It was one of the most civilized divorces in the entertainment world's history.

What did they say?

Mary Tyler Moore: "Grant wasn't just my best friend, he was my only friend."

Grant Tinker: "Relationships wear out and come to an end, just like shows."

Who?

Anita Bryant, singer; Bob Green, former disc jockey turned evangelist.

When and Where?

Married June 25, 1960. Divorced Miami, Florida, August 15, 1980.

Quickies

Did you know...
- that early in her career Mary Tyler Moore was the Hotpoint Pixie in TV ads on the *Ozzie and Harriet Show*? At the time she was married to Richard Meeker. She became pregnant and lost the Pixie job. She gave birth to Richie, but soon divorced Meeker.

Why?

A life-long Christian fundamentalist, Bryant had become a controversial figure in a right-wing crusade against the "anti-American evils" of homosexuality, atheism and divorce. A backlash against her stance made her an object of ridicule. She later claimed that husband Bob had pressured her into the campaign, and that she really had little understanding of gay people or things like gay rights. For years she had believed it was her Christian duty to obey her husband. Green insisted that she, as his wife, owed him unquestioning obedience. After a long period of being manipulated and controlled, Anita filed for divorce, to the horror of her former fundamentalist colleagues.

What did they say?

Anita Bryant: "Bob gave me no respect, no trust, no affection, no love life, no recognition as a worthwhile human being."

Bob Green: "Blame gay people? I do. Their stated goal was to put (Bryant) out of business and destroy her career. And that's what they did. It's unfair."

Who?

Brad Pitt, actor; Jennifer Aniston, Actress.

Where and When?

Married, Malibu, California, July 29, 2000. Divorced, March 2005.

Why?

Both were so busy with their careers that they had little time for each other. There were rumours that Pitt was involved with co-star Angelina Jolie on the set of *Mr. and Mrs. Smith*, though both stars denied it.

What did they say?

Brad Pitt: "There is so much pressure from day one to be with someone forever — and I'm not sure that it really is in our nature to be with something for the rest of our lives. Jen and myself don't cage each other with this pressure of happily ever after. We work it out as we go along."

Jennifer Aniston: "Everybody always asks if we're happy. Give me a break. We're married two years. In Hollywood years, that's forever."

Who?

Johnny Carson, TV talk show host; Joanna (Holland) Carson, model.

Where and When?

Married, Los Angeles, September 30, 1972. Divorced, March 8, 1983, Los Angeles.

Why?

Joanna claimed that Johnny put more time and energy into *The Tonight Show* than he put into their marriage.

What did they say?

Joanna Carson: "I want you to get the hell out of my life."

Johnny Carson: "You got it."

What did Joanna Carson demand in the divorce settlement from Johnny Carson?

She demanded $220,000 a month temporary alimony, until the court could decide on a permanent sum. This included: $107,000 a month for household bills; $4,945 in salaries for her servants; $1,400 for groceries for herself; $690 for household supplies; $800 for the monthly telephone bill; $220 to put gas in her cars; $2,695 a month for travel and vacations; $1,085 for limousine bills; $12,365 a month to buy presents for her friends; $3,955 a month for clothing; $37,065 a month for jewelry and furs; $120 a month for stationery; $5915 a month for security; and $270 a month to feed her cat. In addition she wanted $500,000 to pay her lawyers and $176,000 for her accountants and appraisers. She added another $2,500 a month in support for her grown-up son from a previous marriage. On top of that she wanted half of all of Carson's money and assets.

What was Joanna Carson awarded by the court?

A Bel Air mansion, a condominium and two apartments in New York City, a 1976 Rolls Royce and a 1976 Mercedes Benz, all the clothing, jewelry, and furs purchased during the marriage, 75 solid gold Krugerrands, 50 percent ownership of several of Carson's companies, large numbers of stocks and bonds, $216,000 cash from a tax refund, $388,000 cash from accounts receivable, $337,000 from Carson's salary for doing the annual *Tonight Show* anniversary specials, portions of Carson's pensions from AFTRA and the Screen Actors' Guild, 50 percent of the money Carson would receive for re-runs of *Tonight Show* episodes in which he starred during the marriage, plus $35,000 a month alimony for five years. If Carson died before the five years were up, the alimony would continue to be paid by his estate.

Quickies
Did you know...
- that the document drawn up to settle the Carson divorce case was longer and more detailed than the document for the First World War Armistice with Germany, the Second World War Japanese and German Instruments of Surrender, the 1782 Treaty of Paris that ended the American Revolutionary War, the 1814 Treaty of Ghent that ended the War of 1812, and the United Nations Charter combined?

theatre
and the arts

Who was Mona Lisa in da Vinci's famous masterpiece?

Although it's known as the *Mona Lisa*, Leonardo da Vinci's famous paint-ing was originally titled *La Giaconda*. Painted on wood, it's a portrait of Lisa Gherardini, the wife of a Florentine merchant. X-rays reveal that Leonardo sketched three different poses before settling on the final design. The painting of Lisa has no eyebrows because it was the fashion of the time for women to shave them off.

How did classical ballet get on its toes?

Dancers have been performing classical stories set to music since the fifteenth century. However it wasn't until 1872 when the graceful Italian dancer Maria Taglioni introduced toe dancing that modern ballet was born. It took nearly another quarter century and the development of sturdier shoes before other dancers could learn and dance pointe and follow Taglioni's innovation.

Why do we refer to a tired story or joke as an "old chestnut"?

Quickies
Did you know...
- That the short revealing dress worn by ballerinas was called a tutu from a French reference to a baby's backside?
- That in Russia, where ballet is a supreme art form, *Bolshoi* ballet means "grand" ballet?

If a joke or expression works, especially for a comic or a public speaker, it is usually overused and is consequently called "an old chestnut." The expression comes from a British play, *The Broken Sword*, or the *Torrent of the Valley*, written by William Dimond (1780–1837) and first produced in 1816 at London's Royal Covent Garden Theatre. Within that play a principal character continually repeats the same joke about a cork tree, each time with a subtle variation, including changing the tree from cork to chestnut. Finally; tiring of the joke, another character, Pablo, says: "A chestnut! I've heard you tell that joke 27 times and I'm sure it was a chestnut!"

The impact moment when the phrase likely entered the English language was during a dinner party somewhat later in the nineteenth century. At the dinner the American actor William Warren the Younger (1812–1888), who at the time was playing the part of Pablo, used the "chestnut line" from the play to interrupt a guest who had begun to repeat an old familiar joke. Coincidentally perhaps, the younger Warren's father, also named William, was an actor, too, who for a time was associated with Philadelphia's Chestnut Street Theater.

What is a "curtain call"?

A "curtain call" happens at the end of a play, when actors appear together to take a bow, thank the audience and receive applause. These days, curtain calls are an expected part of any theatrical performance, but the practice has relatively recent origins. The first play to receive a curtain call was performed in 1884.

Why when someone takes credit for another person's achievement do we say she "stole his thunder"?

In the early 1700s, English playwright John Dennis introduced a metallic device that imitated the sound of thunder. The production it was created for failed, and the thunder device was forgotten until months later, when, while attending another play at the same theatre, Dennis heard the unmistakable sound of his invention. He made such a public fuss that all of London picked up the phrase, "they've stolen my thunder."

**literary
language**

What is the difference between a "ghost writer" and a "hack writer"?

A ghost writer is a craftsman who writes speeches or books for another person who gets the credit as author. Although well paid, they're called "ghosts" because they're invisible. In the fourteenth century, while there were warhorses and draft or workhorses, an ordinary rented riding horse was known as a "hackney" or a "hack." The word hack came to mean anything for hire, including writers who did commercial work of any kind to support their efforts at art.

Why are some books called "potboilers"?

The term "potboiler" was coined in 1864 in reference to a formula book which is written and published simply for the money. In order to eat it was necessary to keep the pot of food boiling and to do this the stove needed fuel. A formula book was like adding a log to the fire that ensured the survival of the author and his family.

Who was Pansy O'Hara in *Gone with the Wind*?

Margaret Mitchell was a first-time writer when in 1936 she submitted a manuscript of Civil War stories told to her by her grandfather under the title *Tomorrow Is Another Day*, featuring a Southern belle named Pansy O'Hara. The publisher convinced her to change the book's name to *Gone with the Wind*, a line from a nineteenth-century poem by Ernest Dowson, and, after a bitter argument, to change "Pansy" to "Scarlett."

Quickies
Did you know...
- that North Americans purchase about five million books every day? That's about 57 books each second. 127 new titles are published every day.
- that Mark Twain's *The Adventures of Tom Sawyer* was the first book ever written on a typewriter? The year was 1875 and the typewriter was a Remington.
- that it took Leo Tolstoy four years (1865–1869) to write *War and Peace*? His wife hand-copied the massive manuscript seven times.
- that using candlelight and quill pens, it took Noah Webster 36 years to complete his first American dictionary?
- throughout history, there have been more than two and a half billion Bibles made? If placed together they would fill the New York public library 468 times. The Bible has 810,697 words containing 3,566,480 letters.

Why is relaxing a tense situation called "breaking the ice"?

Overcoming an awkward moment in either business or social circles sometimes requires a little levity to "break the ice" in order to make progress. The expression originally meant to smash the melting ice that hindered commerce during the long winter freeze. It was first used literally in its figurative modern way in 1823 when, in *Don Juan*, Lord Byron (1788–1824) wrote in reference to the stiff British upper class: "And your cold people are beyond all price, when once you've broken their confounded ice."

Who were detective Sherrinford Holmes and Ormand Sacker?

When Arthur Conan Doyle began writing mystery novels, he chose one of his medical school instructors, Dr. Joseph Bell, as his sleuth's model and named him Sherrinford Holmes. His assistant, Watson, took his name from one of Bell's assistants, but not before being briefly named Ormand Sacker. Incidentally, in none of the stories does Holmes ever say, "Elementary, my dear Watson." That was used only in the movies.

Who said, "It is better to live rich than to die rich"?

James Boswell, a famous English diarist of the eighteenth century, attributed this quote to Samuel Johnson, whose daily life he recorded for ten years in a series of books called *The Life of Samuel Johnson*. Johnson is said to have provided more quotable quotes to the English language than anyone else besides William Shakespeare. He is also credited with producing the first dictionary of the English language. He achieved all this and much more even though he was deaf in the left ear, almost blind in the left eye, and dim of vision in the right eye. He also survived smallpox.

What is the origin of "It's all Greek to me"?

Once again we have a phrase introduced by Shakespeare. "It's all Greek to me" comes from dialogue within *Julius Caesar* when, during the conspiracy leading to the assassination, Casca recounts to Brutus and Cassius how Caesar had rejected the crown. When asked if the senior senator Cicero had said anything, Casca relates that he did but Cicero spoke in Greek and although those understanding smiled and nodded, he (Casca) couldn't interpret what was said because "it was Greek to me!"

What is "the be-all and end-all"?

Shakespeare introduced the expression, meaning "the ultimate or most important solution," as dialogue for *Macbeth*, who thinks about killing Duncan and wonders "that this blow might be the be-all and the end-all" (*MacBeth* Act I Scene vii). Macbeth then says he would risk his status in the afterlife if it were true. Today, Shakespeare's second "the" is usually dropped but "the be-all and end-all" still means "the ultimate."

What does it mean to "gild the lily"?

To gild something is to cover it with a thin layer of gold. Because a lily is already in a state of natural perfection, gilding it would only be excessive. The expression is a misquote of Shakespeare's *King John*, during which the king's barons describe his second redundant coronation, "As throwing perfume on the violet or to gild refined gold to paint on the Lily."

Why, when something doesn't make sense, do we say "it's neither rhyme nor reason"?

When you say that something is "neither rhyme nor reason," you are quoting Sir Thomas More. After reading something a friend had written, Sir Thomas told him that he would have to rewrite it in order to make his point clear. After his friend reworked the manuscript, More read it again, and this time he approved, commenting: "That's better, it's rhyme now anyway. Before it was neither rhyme nor reason."

**between
the lines
of nursery
rhymes & fairy tales**

Who was Mother Goose?

The image of a kindly old woman fascinating children with rhymes has been with us for so long that the exact origins are unknown. The term *Mother Goose* first surfaced in print during the seventeenth century and referred to any fanciful rhyme or collection of rhymes that amused children. It wasn't until about 1765 that a collection of traditional stories was published by John Newbery under the title *Mother Goose's Melody: or Sonnets for the Cradle* that the kindly woman's name became associated with a collection of stories by an assortment of authors and fables from folklore.

What's the origin of the phrase "goody two-shoes"?

A "goody two-shoes" is an unbearably self-centred little girl and comes from a nursery rhyme, "The History of Little Goody Two-shoes." "Goody" was a common nickname for married women and came from the word *goodwife*. In the nursery rhyme, Goody owned only one shoe. When given a pair, she ran around showing them to everyone, even those less fortunate than she, smugly announcing, "Look! Two shoes." The phrase came to mean a self-centred brat.

"The History of Little Goody Two-shoes," inspired by an actual person, was written by Oliver Goldsmith and published in 1765 by John Newbery. The real Goody's full name was Margery Meanwell, and she lived in Mouldwell.

What is the hidden meaning in the nursery rhyme "Baa Baa Black Sheep"?

"Baa Baa Black Sheep" was a Middle Ages protest song against heavy taxes. The common man was required to give one third of his income to the Crown, a third to his local nobility, and the final third was all he could keep.

> "Baa Baa, Black Sheep, Have you any wool? Yes sir, yes sir, three bags full:
> One for my master, [The King], one for my dame, [Local nobility]
> And one for the little boy [Himself], that lives in the lane!"

How is the nursery rhyme "Ring Around the Rosie" connected to the Black Death?

Many of the verses now called nursery rhymes weren't always meant for children, but were popular commentaries on what were then current events. "Ring Around the Rosie" has more than one version. "Ring around the rosie, pocket full of posies" refers to the flowers people carried or even wore around their necks for protection from the Black Death and to cover the foul odour that came from the dead and from the sick. "Hush-a, hush-a, we all fall down" simply means "we all drop dead." There were also versions in which "hush-a, hush-a" was replaced with "ashes, ashes" or "achoo, achoo."

Why do we say people have "skeletons in their closets" if they hide their past?

The expression about skeletons in a closet comes from a fairy tale about Bluebeard the pirate, who, legend has it, murdered all his many wives. When he gave his new wife the keys to the house, he forbade her to open a specific closet at the end of a long hall — which, of course, she did the moment he left on business. When she unlocked the door and looked inside, she was horrified to find all the skeletons of Bluebeard's previous wives.

What was the inspiration for Hush a Bye Baby?

This playful lullaby started as a nursery rhyme after European settlers took notice of how Native American mothers placed their babies to be rocked gently by the wind in the lower branches of trees. The words were first published in 1765 and immediately began being sung to babies as they rocked in their mothers' arms just like those in the trees.

Hush a bye baby, on the tree top
When the wind blows the cradle will rock;
When the bow breaks, the cradle will fall,
And down will come baby, cradle and all.

Was Pussycat, Pussycat a real cat?

During the reign of Elizabeth I of England, an old cat owned by one of the Queen's ladies in waiting, was allowed to roam Windsor Castle at will. Once during a formal moment with Elizabeth settled regally on her throne, the cat dashed underneath where she was sitting and its tail brushed the monarch's leg startling her and interrupting the proceedings. After a tense moment, the Queen expressed her amusement by decreeing that the cat could continue visiting the throne room so long as it kept the mice away.

When word of the incident became gossip among the people, someone came up with the rhyme:

"Pussycat pussycat, where have you been?"
"I've been up to London to visit the Queen."
Pussycat pussycat, what did you dare?"
I frightened a little mouse under her chair … meow!"

Who was Georgie Porgie?

It is thought that during the seventeenth century, George — or in this case Georgie — was the English Duke of Buckingham. He was known as a voracious womanizer but because he was a close friend of the King, Charles II, he was always protected from the wrath of jealous husbands. When the men in parliament stepped in and prevented the King from intervening on Georgie's behalf, the frightened Duke went into hiding … "Georgie Porgie ran away."

> "Georgie Porgie pudding and pie
> Kissed the girls and made them cry
> When the boys came out to play
> Georgie Porgie ran away."

Why is Old Mother Hubbard associated with King Henry VIII?

This nursery rhyme is from the sixteenth-century reign of Henry VIII and was a way of making fun of the political buffoonery of the monarch and his court without being treasonous. Old Mother Hubbard is Cardinal Wolsey who angered the King when he failed to arrange for his divorce from Queen Catherine of Aragon in order to marry Ann Boleyn. The doggie is the King and the bone is his divorce. The cupboard is the Catholic Church.

> "Old Mother Hubbard
> Went to the cupboard
> To get poor doggie a bone
> The cupboard was bare
> So the poor little doggie had none."

house and home

Why is a reclining chair called a chaise lounge?

When the French produced a long reclining chair for casual comfort, they simply called it a "long chair" or *chaise longue*. When imported to the United States, the Americans misunderstood *longue* as meaning "lounge" and that's how the chair became incorrectly known as a chaise lounge.

Why do dinner knives have rounded tips?

Up until 1669, dinner knives had sharp points just like steak knives but that year, French Cardinal Richelieu impulsively had them removed from the court. He claimed that his motive was disgust with people picking their teeth with the points, but there were many who believed he had acted to cut the odds of assassination. Other European Royal Courts saw the wisdom in this and had their pointed dinner knives rounded at the tip … just in case.

Why is a large cup called a "mug"?

A mug is a large drinking cup with a handle and is most commonly used to drink coffee, although it's not unknown to beer drinkers. A "mug" is also slang for the face. In the eighteenth century, drinking vessels were shaped and painted to look like the heads of pirates or local drunks or even despised public officials or politicians. Now called "Toby jugs," these cups with faces became known simply as mugs.

Why are drinking glasses sometimes called "tumblers"?

In 1945, Earl Tupper produced his first polyethylene plastic seven-ounce bathroom tumbler, so called because it could fall or tumble without breaking. But a "tumbler" drinking glass had already been around for centuries before Tupperware. It was specially designed with a round or pointed bottom so that it couldn't stand upright and had to be drunk dry before it could be laid on its side — otherwise it would tumble and spill.

Quickies
Did you know...
- the word *table* came from the Latin word *tabula* which means "board"?
- that the words *plate* and *platter* are from the Old French word *plat*, meaning "flat"?
- that *bowl* is from the Anglo-Saxon word *bolla* meaning "'round"?
- that a dish was so-called by the Romans because, like a discus, it's round?
- the word *cup* is from the Sanskrit word *kupa* which means "water well"?
- that a saucer was originally used exclusively for serving sauces before it became a cup stabilizer?
- that *glass* is from the Celtic word *glas* meaning "green" because the first impure glass was coloured green?
- that a "doily" was devised as a circular linen napkin to protect the tablecloth and is named after its English inventor?

Why is a woman's private room called a "boudoir"?

A tastefully decorated bed chamber is often called a boudoir. The reason is that Louis IV of France needed to accommodate his many jealous mistresses and so he had several lavish intimate rooms designed for these women so that when upset, they could retire and be alone. He called such a room a boudoir from the French word *bouder*, meaning to "sulk" or "pout".

Why did people start growing grass lawns around their homes?

Lawns became the fashion in Britain during the early nineteenth century due to the popularity of games played on grass. These games, such as croquet, lawn bowling, badminton and golf weren't the exclusive interest of the rich and so the common people began replacing rock gardens and shrubbery with grass lawns of their own to play and practice these games.

**wealth,
money,
gold, and finance**

How did "hard up" come to mean short of cash?

If you're "hard up" you are in need of financial help. You're facing a stormy future unless immediate, urgent problems are dealt with. "Hard up" began as an urgent cry to all hands during the seventeenth century to turn a sailing ships bow away from the wind when faced with a sudden and powerful head on gale. Putting the helm "hard up" could prevent disaster. The expression started being used to describe one who was in need of money around 1821.

Why is a person who spends money recklessly called a "spendthrift"?

Combining *thrift* with *spend* seem incongruous to describe an extravagant spender until you realize that it was originally applied to a prodigal who wasted his inheritance. He/she lavishly and foolishly was spending the estate or fortune left to him/her by a parent who had accumulated the wealth through thrift. They were spending the consequences of their parents' thrift.

Why do we call luxurious living a "posh" existence?

In the days of their empire, British tourists travelled by ship from England to the warmer climates of India and the Mediterranean. Wealthy passengers on these voyages demanded cabins shaded from the sun, which meant being on the port side on the way out and the starboard side on the way home. Tickets for these cabins were marked "POSH," which stood for Portside Out, Starboard Home, and *posh* stuck as a word that signified luxury.

Why is sneaking money away from an individual or a business called "embezzlement"?

"Embezzlement" is a violation of trust. It comes from an old French word that means torment, destroy, and gouge. People who embezzle tend to be professionals who manage the property and funds of others, such as accountants, lawyers, and stockbrokers, or family members and close friends.

Quickies
Did you know...
- that James Marshall's 1848 gold strike at Sutter's Mill started the California gold rush, but his claim dried up and he died a penniless alcoholic?
- that Lucky Strike cigarettes were named in 1856 after the California Gold Rush?
- that the name California means "hot furnace" in Spanish?

If both the United States and England were $1 billion in debt, which country would owe the most money?

The United States and England calculate both one billion and one trillion differently. One billion in the United States is one thousand million, while in England it is one million million. One trillion in the United States is one million million, while one trillion in England is one billion million. In both cases the British quantity is larger, so if both countries owed $1 billion, England would have the greater debt.

Why are American dollars favoured by counterfeiters?

Counterfeiters like currencies that people are not too familiar with but will accept anyway. American dollars are used all over the world, and people outside the United States may not know what to look for to ensure they are genuine.

Credit cards are popular targets for fraud for the same reason. Thousands of companies offer credit cards, making it impossible for anyone to be sure that a card is real by appearance alone.

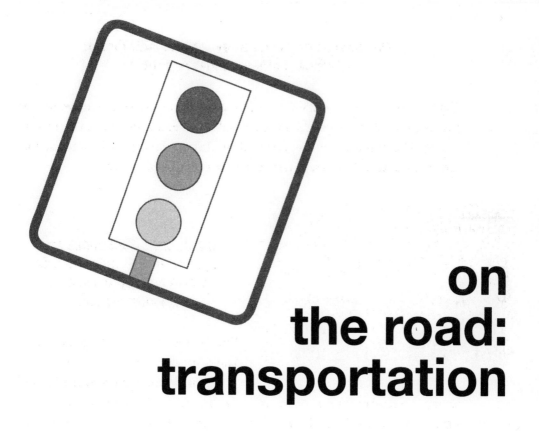

on the road: transportation

Why is a tough, all-terrain vehicle called a "Jeep"?

In 1937, the Army introduced a general purpose four-wheel drive vehicle which, when abbreviated, became G.P. At the same time the very popular Popeye cartoon had introduced Eugene the Jeep as a weird little pet for Olive Oil; it communicated by calling "jeep." The young men in the service put the little G.P. and the cartoon character together and called the vehicle a Jeep.

What is the meaning of the word *Humvee*?

Humvee is a trademark for a durable wide-bodied military vehicle with four-wheel drive that was developed by American Motors in 1983 to replace the Jeep. The name Humvee is a rough military acronym that came out of the 1991 Gulf War. It means high-mobility multipurpose wheeled vehicle. Substantially larger than the Jeep, the Humvee was able to replace several other vehicles, as well. Since 2000, General Motors has been selling civilian versions of the vehicle.

How did a driver check the gas tank in the Model T?

To check the gas with the optional gas gauge offered for the 1922 Ford Model T, a driver had to find a place to pull over and stop the car. He then had to step out and lift up the front seat cushion to so he could see the gas tank. The gauge was a wooden ruler marked off in gallons. The driver opened the gas tank, stuck the ruler in and took a reading, just like we check oil today. Then he packed everything up and got back in the car to begin looking for a gas station.

Windshield wipers were another extra on the Model T.

Studebaker offered the auto industry's first gas gauge with its 1914 product line. The company closed its doors in 1966.

What's the difference between a truck, a tractor semi-trailer, and a full tractor-trailer?

Those huge vehicles overwhelming the highways are called tractor semi-trailers because the back portion sits on wheels while the front end supports the tractor. A full trailer rides on its own wheels with axles on the front and back and is connected to the tractor by a drawbar. Sometimes a full trailer is attached to a semi, which is attached to the tractor. A truck doesn't have any attachments.

How did the famous Italian automobile brands FIAT and the ALFA get their names?

FIAT, or Fabbrica Itailana Automobili Torino, was formed in a 1903 takeover of Ceirano, which had been founded in 1901 to make cars under Renault licence using a deDion engine. Ceirano's assets included a racecar driver named Vincenzo Lancia. In a similar 1910 move, a group of Milanese businessmen took over a factory set up to produce Darracq 4-cylinder taxicabs. This group was called Anonima Lombarda Fabbrica Automobili, or ALFA.

What city first used stop signs?

Stop signs first showed up in Detroit, Michigan, in 1915. They were black on white and smaller than modern signs. Until then traffic-control devices were generally manual, using such devices as semaphores (flags), policemen in traffic towers, and hand-turned stop-and-go signs. In the 1920s, black-on-yellow signs were introduced, while white-on-red signs appeared in 1954.

Mounting height has also evolved. Early signs were about three feet off the ground. Modern signs are more than six feet high.

What does "MG" stand for on the classic British sports car?

The MGB is the best-known classic British sports car and was introduced in 1962 as an update of the original MGA, which first appeared in 1955. There were approximately 375,000 MGBs built before the company went out of business in 1981. The MG stands for Morris Garages, a retail outlet that was established in 1911 and that began selling MG-badged Morris Specials in the 1920s.

Where did the Rolls-Royce automobile get its name?

Charles Rolls (1877–1910), a salesman, and Henry Royce (1863–1933), an electrical engineer, got together in 1906 to produce a car that would be sold exclusively by Rolls. They agreed the car would be called a Rolls-Royce. The first model was the Silver Ghost, which they produced until 1925. The company continued in private ownership until 1971 when financial problems in its aircraft division led to a takeover by the British government. Today, Rolls-Royce is owned by the German automobile maker Bayerische Motoren Werke (BMW).

Rolls-Royce is highly regarded for its engines. They powered many of the Spitfires and Hurricanes used in the Battle of Britain during the Second World War.

Why is the rubber covering of a car wheel called a "tire"?

The word *tire* is taken from the word *attire*, because, like clothing, it was introduced as a dressing or covering on a wheel. First used to describe the iron rim of a wooden carriage wheel during the thirteenth century, it was spelled *tyre*. This shifted to *tire* during the seventeenth century and although this became the standard spelling for North America it shifted back again to *tyre* in England with the introduction of a ring of rubber, either inflated or otherwise, that came with the bicycle wheel during the 1870s.

The rubber tire (tyre) was invented in 1845 by Scotsman Robert W. Thomson.

Why do we say "right away" when solving an urgent problem?

If something requires immediate attention we assure a prompt response with the adverb, "right away." This comes directly from the cries of railroad engineers who, when fast approaching an obstacle such as a cart or farmers cow on the train track, would shout, "right of way!" meaning "I can't stop, so if you don't move at once, we'll collide."

sailing
on the high seas

Why are ships referred to as feminine?

Most vehicles, including boats, cars, and airplanes are referred to as "she" by the owners or crew. One explanation is that in ancient times, ships were protected by guardian goddesses with the appropriate female figurehead on the prow. Although some feminists believe that this custom signifies the masculine domination and possession of all things feminine, most men or women who own or work onboard a ship consider the expression as one of affection and protection such as in a nurturing mother. The sea can be cruel and the ship protects you like a mother.

What is the name of the world's biggest cruise ship?

Cunard's $800 million *Queen Mary 2* began taking passengers in January of 2004. Currently, she is the largest cruise ship in the world, at 151,000 tons, but it does not look like she will hold that record for very long. Royal Caribbean International has already placed an order for a $1.24 billion ship that will weigh 220,000 tons when it is delivered in the fall of 2009.

The *Queen Mary 2* has a capacity for about 2,600 passengers. Royal Caribbean's new ship will carry about 6,400.

Where is the "Graveyard of the Atlantic"?

More than one stretch of deadly water has been called the "Graveyard of the Atlantic." Cape Hatteras has laid claim to the title. Indeed, it has been said that the whole North Carolina coast is a maritime graveyard. But the granddaddy of them all is Sable Island. This 26-mile strip of sand 100 miles off the coast of mainland Nova Scotia had its first documented wreck in 1583 when Sir Humphrey Gilbert's ship, *Delight*, ran aground there. Between that time and 1947, when the freighter *Manhasset* became Sable Island's last major victim (not including the yacht *Merrimac*, in 1999), 350 vessels came to grief in the waters around Sable — and those are only the recorded wrecks. No doubt many a ship written off as "lost" met its fate in these notorious waters.

Why was the *Titanic* said to be unsinkable?

The *Titanic* was the most majestic ship of its time; 11 storeys tall and as long as four city blocks. Her interior was divided into 16 watertight compartments that could be separated by emergency doors activated by the flick of an electrical switch in the bridge. The *Titanic*'s owners and officers knew that if more than five of the watertight compartments were breached, the ship would sink. But the odds against such an occurrence were astronomical.

Five Reasons for the Great Loss of Life on the *Titanic*

- There were 1,028 too few spaces available in the *Titanic*'s lifeboats to accommodate all of the people onboard.
- The launching of the available lifeboats was badly handled, with none of the boats being assigned a full capacity of people. There had been no lifeboat or life jacket drill.
- Few of the people in lifeboats did anything to help people struggling in the water.
- The nearest ship, the *Californian*, only 20 miles away, was unaware of the *Titanic*'s situation. People on the *Californian* thought the *Titanic*'s distress flares were celebratory fireworks.
- The North Atlantic water was freezing cold and even people wearing life jackets could survive in it for only a few minutes. When the ship *Carpathia* arrived to search for survivors, its crew picked up 705 people in lifeboats. No survivors were plucked from the sea. There is some doubt about the exact number of people who perished. The Americans peg the death toll at 1,517; the British estimate it to be 1,490.

What happened to the *Titanic* at 11:40 p.m.?

At that time Seaman Frederick Fleet, on lookout duty in the crow's nest, signalled to the bridge that an iceberg was dead ahead. First Officer William Murdock ordered a hard turn to starboard, pulled the engine room telegraph to full-speed-astern, and hit the switch to close all the watertight doors. But it was too late. Thirty-seven seconds after Fleet gave his signal the *Titanic* brushed against a submerged protrusion of the iceberg. Steel plates on the liner's starboard side buckled like cardboard as the ice slashed a gash below the waterline, long enough to flood six of the vessel's compartments, including the number five and number six boiler rooms. The *Titanic* was doomed.

Why are sailors' carvings on whalebone called "scrimshaw"?

> **Quickies**
> *Did you know...*
> • that the most popular christened name of private boats in North America is *Obsession*?
> • that the top 10 most popular boat names for 2007 were: *Black Pearl, Liberty, Second Wind, Amazing Grace, Aquaholic, Knot on Call, Second Chance, Wanderlust, The Dog House,* and *Carpe Diem or Seas the Day*?

"Scrimshaw" is a slang term thought to have originated among New England whalers in the early 1800s. It describes the art works sailors created while carving whalebone and teeth during the many hours of spare time they had during whaling voyages that lasted for years. The hobby created a class of craftsman called scrimshanders. Their creations included umbrella handles, knives, and various fittings like hinges, with images of ships, wives and girlfriends, and whaling scenes scratched onto their surfaces.

President John F. Kennedy, who was assassinated in 1963, collected scrimshaw and helped bring it back into the public eye.

Why is a rigid, immovable position said to be "hard and fast"?

If a person can't be moved through any debate or argument, they are said to be holding "hard and fast." This is another nautical term and simply means that a ship is firmly stranded on shore, making it very difficult to move. The figurative use of the expression with its application to anything immovable was well known before the nineteenth century.

Why do sailors fear "deadheads"?

"Deadhead" has a surprising number of meanings. The one most likely heard today describes the followers of a 1960s band called the Grateful Dead. Many of these fans have devoted years of their lives to following the band from one show to the next. The dangerous deadhead is feared by sailors at sea. It is a log, or perhaps the remains of a wrecked wooden ship, that floats just below the surface of the water ready to collide with an unwary vessel.

How can you tell a person's character by the "cut of their jib"?

A person's general character can be quickly determined by their overall appearance and manner or by "the cut of their jib." You can tell whether or not you would deal with a person by this first impression. The jib of a sailing ship is a triangular sail between the fore topmast and the jib boom. A sailor could determine the nationality and seaworthiness of a ship and crew and quickly form an opinion of it by the shape and style or "cut of its jib." The use of the idiomatic expression to describe a person began in the early nineteenth century.

Why is the British national flag called a "jack" as in Union Jack?

Any national flag which incorporates a union within its design is a jack. Therefore, the American Stars and Stripes is also a jack. In 1634, the union flag symbolizing the crowns of England and Scotland was introduced by combining the crosses of St. George and St. Andrew. The cross saltire of St. Patrick was added in 1801 after the union of the parliaments of Ireland and Great Britain. The term *jack* was first used to name the small union flag on a ship. (Sailors have long been called "jacks" or "Jack Tars.")

When challenging the truth, why do we say "tell it to the marines"?

The expression, "tell it to the marines" means "that doesn't sound true" and began in the longer form, "He may tell that to the marines, but the sailors won't believe him." The first marines were foot soldiers assigned to serve on board ships during the reign of England's King Charles II in 1664. The hardened sailors had little respect for the young marines. They were more gullible than the worldly sailors, so if a tall tale was suspect, you might get a marine to believe it but never a sailor. Legend has it that the expression came from the King himself.

Why does "working out the kinks" mean getting into shape?

After a period of inactivity, or not paying attention to a problem, we may need to "work the kinks out" before becoming ship-shape or up to speed. In baseball, spring training's purpose is to "work out the kinks" so the team can function at its best. *Kink* is a Dutch word for twists or knots and was picked up in the seventeenth century by the British navy as meaning unravelling the multitude of ropes necessary for making a sailing ship seaworthy.

Why are sailors called "Tars"?

There was a lot of canvas on the old sailing ships and this canvas was water and weather proofed with coats of tar turning it into tarpaulin. Sailors of the time often wore coats of this tarpaulin and the nickname "tar," first recorded in 1647, became a natural extension of this practice. Another more imposing use of tar at sea was the punishment of being "tarred and feathered" which was imposed by Richard I in 1189 for sailors caught stealing.

What is the difference between a boat and a ship?

The United States Navy defines a boat as "any vessel that can be hoisted aboard a ship." Generally a boat is smaller because it's built to sail inland waters whether by sail, oar, or motor power; a ship is built larger for open seas. Any floating vessel under 100 feet in length is considered a boat while anything longer is a ship.

Exceptions: Submarines are called boats because the first ones were so small; ore carriers and ferryboats, no matter how large, are labelled boats because they follow specific routes. Ships majestically sail the high seas!

Ten High Seas Movies
- *Mutiny on the Bounty* (1935 starring Charles Laughton and Clark Gable)
- *Pirates of the Caribbean* (2003 starring Johnny Depp)
- *Das Boot* ("The Boat" Russian, 1981)
- The Hunt for Red October (1990 starring Sean Connery)
- *Titanic* (1997 starring Leonardo DiCaprio and Kate Winslet)
- *The Poseidon Adventure* (1972 starring Gene Hackman and Ernest Borgnine)
- *A Perfect Storm* (2000 starring George Clooney and Mark Wahlberg)
- *Dead Calm* (1989 starring Nicole Kidman and Sam Neill)
- *The Caine Mutiny* (1954 starring Humphrey Bogart)
- *Captain Blood* (1935 starring Errol Flynn)

Why is a ship's bathroom called the "head"?

There was no space on early sailing ships for such luxuries as bathrooms, urinals or toilets. When a crew member wanted to relieve himself, he went to the front or "head" of the ship and did his business while sitting in the rigging over the water. Eventually, holes were built into the sides of the ship's bow (head) for this purpose with a pail of water nearby for flushing into the sea.

Why do we say that someone is "on the spot" when they're facing big trouble?

To be "on the spot" means you're in serious difficulty, and it comes from the pirates of the Caribbean. The spot is the ace of spades, a card that pirates ceremoniously showed to a condemned person indicating that they were about to be executed as a traitor. To be put on the spot has become much less dire, and instead of being a signal that you're being put to death, it has evolved into meaning, "Explain yourself or you're out of here."

How did "spick and span" come to mean very clean?

Today, Spik and Span is a trade name for a well-known cleanser, but the expression began in the fourteenth century as the nautical term "spick and span new," to describe a freshly built or refurbished ship. A *spick* was a spike, while *span* was a Viking reference to new wood, but also means any distance between two extremities (such as the bow and stern of a ship). The wooden ship was so clean that even the spikes looked new.

Why does "chewing the fat" mean gossip or casual conversation?

During the twentieth century, "chewing the fat" came to mean passing time with informal small talk. The phrase originated with the grumbling of nineteenth-century British sailors whose lean diet was often nothing more than the fat from barrels of salt pork. Their whining while chewing the tough meat would expand to include complaints about every other hardship at sea and became known as "chewing the fat."

Why when dreaming of better times do we say, "When my ship comes in"?

During the nineteenth century, Bristol, England, was the busiest seaport in the world, and while local sailors were at sea, tradesmen would extend credit to their wives until the very day their husband's ship returned to port. Because the ship meant her family's livelihood, women referred to their husband's vessel as "my ship," and when asking for credit would promise to pay the tab "when my ship comes in."

Why do we say that someone burdened by guilt has an "albatross" around his or her neck?

An "albatross" is a figurative stigma for shame. It refers to a guilt that never leaves you and becomes the defining characteristic of a moral burden. The albatross is a bird that symbolized good luck to sailing ships because it signalled that land was nearby. The bird's change in fortune resulted from Samuel Taylor Coleridge's 1798 poem *The Rime of the Ancient Mariner* that tells of a captain who killed an albatross after which there was a prolonged calm that stranded his ship. As a consequence, the captain was forced by the crew to wear the dead bird around his neck.

Coleridge (1772–1834) himself had his share of dire straits, battling drug addiction, marital difficulties, and personal setbacks through much of his middle years.

What did the Kon Tiki expedition seek to prove?

One of the boldest ocean voyages of the twentieth century was led by a Norwegian named Thor Heyerdahl in a balsa wood raft called the Kon Tiki. He built the raft to specifications set out by ancient South American craftsmen. A radio was the only modern convenience he allowed himself. His goal was to prove that people living in western South America could have colonized the Polynesian islands on the other side of the Pacific Ocean thousands of years ago.

The voyage lasted 101 days and covered 4,287 miles, ending when the Kon Tiki was wrecked on a coral reef short of its ultimate destination of Tahiti. A 1951 book about the voyage paints wonderful images of life lived so near to the ocean surface.

What is the meaning of the nautical phrase "before the mast"?

In his book *Two Years Before the Mast*, the American lawyer and author Richard Henry Dana (1815–1882) reveals his experiences as a young man at sea aboard the brig *Pilgrim* in 1834. The mast of a sailing ship was the boundary between the quarters of officers and crew. Dana kept a diary of the wretched treatment and conditions experienced by a common seaman living "before the mast," and from his notes he compiled his book, published in 1840.

Why were sailors so superstitious?

Life-and-death situations always give rise to superstitions, so early sailors took no chances and followed many good-luck rituals beyond prayer. One such ritual was to "step a mast," or place a silver coin from the year a ship was built under its main mast to keep the wind "happy." As a backup, horseshoes were nailed to the mast to keep storms at bay. Sighting a dolphin brought good luck, but killing them could be disastrous. Killing a gull was unforgivable, since it was believed that these birds carried the souls of sailors lost at sea.

What makes a ship a "tramp steamer"?

Today a "tramp steamer" is more accurately described as a "tramp freighter," since steam engines have long been replaced by diesels. In either case, just like human "tramps" who wander the streets, these ships navigate the oceans of the world without a fixed schedule, looking for ports of call that will offer the best price for their cargoes.

Tramp steamers were often the way adventurous people got to exotic places during the first half of the twentieth century. A number of famous writers, American playwright Eugene O'Neill (1888–1953) and British novelist Malcolm Lowry (1909–1957) to name two, shipped aboard tramp freighters when they were young and later wrote about their experiences.

How do large ships anchor in deep water?

Because of the oceans great depth, a harbour anchor is of no use to a ship at sea. In its simplest form, a sea anchor is a canvas sack attached to a metal ring. Tying it to the stern of a boat and dragging it through the water creates resistance, which slows the boat down. In a strong gale, sea anchors can make the difference between life and death.

Why does the word *careen* describe dangerous driving?

We describe a "careening" car as one that lurches or swerves from side to side in a dangerous manner, because the word *careen* is the nautical term for keel. Sailing ships leaning precariously while sailing into the wind must careen or steer from side to side. These ships needed to have their bottoms repaired regularly and scraped to rid them of barnacles. When no dry dock was available, the captain would find a suitable beach, and then run his ship aground at low tide. The vessel was then "careened" or tipped over, exposing the keel and allowing sailors to clean and restore one side of the hull. Once both sides were finished, and the tide returned, the ship would float off the beach and sail back to sea.

Why is a gentle wind called a "breeze"?

In 1626 in a guide for young seamen, the English captain and explorer John Smith (1580–1631) recorded the first use of the word *breeze* in a list of winds in order of their severity. These included a calm, a breeze, a gale, a gust, a storm, a spout, a tornado, a monsoon, and a hurricane. Captain Smith spelled *breeze* as *brese* and had taken it from the Spanish word *briza*, meaning "a light wind."

Where is the "Graveyard of the Great Lakes"?

Each of the Great Lakes — Superior, Michigan, Huron, Erie, and Ontario — has one or more "graveyards." The most notorious of them is Long Point. This slim peninsula jutting 20 miles from the Canadian shore of Lake Erie is surrounded by treacherous shoals. The deep channel between Long Point's shoals and the American shore is very narrow, which in the nineteenth century made collisions a major danger. One such accident in August, 1852, resulted in the sinking of the passenger steamer *Atlantic*, with a loss of 350 lives.

holidays
and celebrations

Why is a special day called a "red letter day"?

In the Middle Ages, simple survival meant working long and hard from sunrise to sunset, so any break, such as for a religious festival, was a very special day. Called "holy days," these feasts were marked on the calendar in red, giving us the expression "red letter day." Around the fifteenth century, "holy days" became "holidays," meaning simply a day off work, still marked on the calendar in red.

Why do we say "let's have a ball" when looking for a good time?

A "ball" was a medieval religious celebration held on special occasions such as the Feast of Fools at Easter. It was called a ball because the choirboys danced and sang in a ring while catching and returning a ball that was lobbed at them by a church leader (called the ring leader). Although tossing balls during large circular dances became a common folk custom, the only ball at a dance today is the name.

Why do Canadians celebrate Victoria Day?

To most Canadians, May 24 signals the start of gardening season, but it's also a memory of what was once called Empire Day, when the people living on 20 percent of the Earth's land surface owed allegiance to the British Crown. For 64 of its 300 years, the Empire was presided over by Queen Victoria. Canada has celebrated Victoria Day on May 24 since 1845. Nowadays, the May 24 holiday celebrates the birthday of the current monarch.

What's the story behind Kwanza?

Kwanza is a seven-day celebration beginning the day after Christmas. It was created in 1966 by Maulana Karenga, chairman of African studies at California State University, and is based on an African winter harvest. *Kwanza* means "first fruits" in Swahili and celebrates African heritage. On each night of Kwanza, one of several candles is lit and gifts reflecting creativity and community are exchanged.

Kwanza is based on seven principles: *umoja* means unity, *kujichagulla* means self-determination, *ujima* means collective work and responsibility, *ujamaa* means cooperative economics, *nia* means purpose, *kuumba* means creativity, and *imani* means faith.

Why is Easter a higher Christian holiday than Christmas?

With the rise of Christianity, the church decided that death days were the real birthdays because the deceased was being reborn in paradise, and so the date of a person's demise was recorded as their birth, or rebirth, day. The birthdays of saints are celebrated on their death days. It was through this logic that Christ's death day, or Easter, became more important than Christmas.

Why is Thanksgiving celebrated six and a half weeks earlier in Canada than in the United States?

It took 200 years after the pilgrims first celebrated Thanksgiving in 1621 before it became an annual holiday in the United States. It was Sarah Hale, the author of "Mary Had a Little Lamb," who convinced Abraham Lincoln to create the annual celebration in 1863. Canada went along in 1879, but because of a shorter growing season changed the date in 1957 from the end of November to the second Monday in October.

How did pumpkin pie become associated with Thanksgiving?

There was no pumpkin pie at the first Thanksgiving, but because the plant's season coincides with the celebration and because it was Native Americans who taught the Pilgrims the pumpkin's value, the melon has become a traditional Thanksgiving dish. At first pumpkin was customarily served stewed as a custard or sweet pudding and was presented in a hollowed-out pumpkin shell. The first reference to pumpkin pie appeared in a book entitled *The History of New England* written by Edward Johnson in 1654.

How accurate is the Groundhog Day forecast?

In German folklore, if it's sunny when he emerges from hibernation, a ground-hog will be frightened by his own shadow and return to his lair; therefore crops shouldn't be planted because there will be another six weeks of winter. In fact the groundhog comes out hungry and ready to mate, but if he's still dozy and his senses are dulled, he goes back to sleep. As a forecaster, the groundhog is only accurate 28 percent of the time — about the same as the weatherman.

What is the origin of Boxing Day?

Beginning in the Middle Ages, Boxing Day was known as St. Stephen's Day in honour of the first Christian martyr. Although unknown in the United States, Boxing Day is still observed in Britain, Canada, New Zealand, and Australia. It's called "Boxing Day" because on the day after Christmas, the well-off boxed up gifts to give to their servants and trades people, while the churches opened their charity boxes to the poor.

Why is a major celebration called a "jubilee"?

A jubilee is "a season of rejoicing" and comes from the ancient Hebrews. Fifty years after the Jews were freed from Egyptian bondage, they created a semi-centennial festival that lasted a full year within which all land would be left fallow and returned to its original owners. All debts were paid off and all slaves were emancipated. Declared a year of rest, the jubilee's arrival every 50 years was announced by the trumpeting of rams' horns throughout the land. A ram's horn in Hebrew is *yobhel*, which led to the English word *jubil* or *jubilee*.

Today there are silver jubilees (25 years), golden jubilees (50 years), diamond jubilees (60 years), and platinum jubilees (75 years). In 1897, Britain's Queen Victoria celebrated her diamond jubilee throughout the British Empire.

When is Mother-in-Laws' Day?

According to a resolution passed by the United States House of Representatives in 1981, the fourth Sunday in October is set aside to honour mothers by marriage. Although the United States Senate hasn't adopted the resolution making the occasion official, the greeting-card industry continues to lobby for Mother-in-Laws' Day and each year about 800,000 cards are sent to spouses' mothers.

When is Grandparents' Day?

In 1969 a 65-year-old Atlanta man named Michael Goldgar returned home from visiting an aunt confined to a nursing home and realized that most of the elderly were treated as burdens by their children and grandchildren. He thought of earlier times when the elderly were a source of wisdom and the nucleus of a family. Goldgar began a seven-year campaign, including 17 trips to Washington, D.C., at his own expense before President Jimmy Carter (1924–) signed legislation making Grandparents' Day the Sunday after Labor Day. As a result, more than four million cards are sent each year to grandparents.

How did the word *carnival* come to mean a self-indulgent celebration?

In the Christian calendar, Lent, a reverent and disciplined observance of Easter, begins on Ash Wednesday. In the Middle Ages the faithful were forbidden to eat meat during Lent, and so the day before Ash Wednesday became known as Fat Tuesday, when everyone would overindulge in a Mardi Gras of what was about to be forbidden. In Church Latin, *carne vale* literally means "farewell to meat."

Why is a decorated parade vehicle called a "float"?

The more elaborate the parade; the more elaborate the floats. Certainly, because the wheels are generally covered by the trappings on the parade vehicle they appear to float like a boat but this isn't how they got the name. The tradition began with decorated flat bottom floating barges which were pulled along a canal by horses during elaborate festivals.

Who invented the pre-Christmas anti-holiday, Festivus?

A 1997 episode of *Seinfeld* introduced the world to the pseudo-holiday of Festivus, and since then, the day has enjoyed a surprising and growing popularity. Celebrated on December 23, Festivus features an aluminum pole (in place of a Christmas tree) and such Festivus dinner activities as "the Airing of Grievances" and "the Feats of Strength." (The latter tradition requires that a celebrant wrestle the head of the household to the floor and pin him or her.) Although it was *Seinfeld* that first brought Festivus to the masses, the holiday had been an annual tradition of the O'Keefe family for years. *Reader's Digest* columnist Dan O'Keefe created Festivus in 1966. His son, Daniel, would grow up to become a writer on *Seinfeld*, and worked Festivus into a storyline.

christmas

What's the story behind "Silent Night"?

On Christmas Eve in 1817, when Father Joseph Mohr of St. Nicholas Church in Arnsdorf, Austria, found that a mouse had chewed through the bellows of his church pipe organ, he rushed to the home of music teacher Franz Gruber. The two men quickly wrote a musical piece, hoping it would save the Christmas Mass. With Father Mohr playing guitar, they sang their song in harmony to a small Austrian congregation who became the first to hear the most beloved carol of them all —"Silent Night."

"Silent Night" was performed by troupes of Tyrolean Folk Singers, but by 1848, when Father Mohr died penniless at the age of 55, "Silent Night" had fallen into obscurity. In 1854, King Frederick William IV of Prussia heard the song and was so moved, he became responsible for its revival.

What does "Auld Lang Syne" mean?

Much of the planet sings "Auld Lang Syne" at Christmas and New Year's without having a clue what the words *auld lang syne* actually mean.

The lyrics for the song were written by Scots poet Robbie Burns, who wrote much of his work in Gaelic. The phrase *auld lang syne* directly translates to "old long since," which can more accurately be read as "times gone by."

How did turkey become the traditional Christmas dinner?

Up until the nineteenth century, mincemeat pie was the common Christmas feast in both North America and Europe, with preferred birds being pigeon, peacock, guinea hen, and goose. Turkey was introduced from America to Europe by the Spanish in the sixteenth century and caught on big time in 1843 after Ebenezer Scrooge sent a turkey to Bob Cratchet in the Charles Dickens story A Christmas Carol.

What happened to the man who outlawed Christmas?

In 1643, the English Puritan parliament frowned on the pagan rituals of Christmas and banned its celebration after William Prynne published his anti-Christmas manifesto. Clergymen were imprisoned for so much as preaching on December 25. After several years of rioting against the ban, King Charles II arrested Prynne and had him pilloried then had both his ears cut off while the manifesto was burned in front of him. The king re-established Christmas celebrations, but not before having Prynne expelled from Oxford and the legal profession.

What was the original meaning of merry in "Merry Christmas"?

Today, merry, as in "Merry Christmas," suggests gaiety, a mood for celebration, but its original meaning was quite different. For example, the carol we sing as "God Rest Ye, Merry Gentlemen," should read "God Rest Ye Merry, Gentlemen." The word was at least 400 years old when it was first written down in 1827, and at that time merry didn't mean joyous, but rather, peaceful or pleasant.

Was Rudolph the only name of the red-nosed reindeer?

In 1939, when Robert May, a copywriter for Montgomery Ward, wrote a promotional Christmas poem for that Chicago department store, its principal character was "Rollo" the Red-Nosed Reindeer, but the corporate executives didn't like that name, nor did they approve of May's second suggestion, "Reginald." It was May's four-year-old daughter who came up with "Rudolph," and the title for a Christmas classic.

What is the oldest Santa Claus parade in the world?

In 1905, the world's first Santa Claus Parade was held in Toronto. It was a small affair that year, amounting to a solitary Santa walking from the city's Union Station up Yonge Street to the Eaton's department store. The parade quickly grew and, despite financial difficulties that nearly derailed the event in the 1980s, the Toronto Santa Claus Parade is still a popular annual tradition that is broadcast around the world.

Ten Christmas Movies
- *A Christmas Carol* (1951 starring Alastair Sim)
- *Miracle on 34th Street* (1947 starring Maureen O'Hara and Natalie Wood)
- *It's A Wonderful Life* (1946 starring James Stewart and Donna Reed)
- *National Lampoon's Christmas Vacation* (1989 starring Chevy Chase)
- *A Christmas Story* (1983 starring Peter Billingsley)
- *The Nightmare Before Christmas* (1993 Tim Burton animated)
- *Holiday Inn* (1942 starring Bing Crosby and Fred Astaire)
- *Home Alone* (1990 starring Macaulay Culkin and Joe Pesci)
- *White Christmas* (1954 starring Bing Crosby and Danny Kaye)
- *The Polar Express* (2004 animated with Tom Hanks)

Does Mrs. Claus have a first name?

Yes. In fact, she seems to go by different names depending on where you live. In Switzerland, she is known as "Lucy," in Austria, "Nikolofrau," and in the Netherlands, "Molly Grietja." Movies and stories have often given her a name. Angela Lansbury played her as "Anna" in the 1996 TV movie *Mrs. Santa Claus*, while Katherine Lee Bates (better known as the lyricist responsible for "America the Beautiful") named her "Goody" in the story "Goody Santa Claus on a Sleigh Ride." In the Rankin and Bass TV special *Santa Claus is Coming to Town*, Mrs. Claus answers to the name "Jessica." Despite the many names she goes by, there appears to be only one Mrs. Claus, so there's no need to worry about any indiscretions on the part of Santa.

How many letters to Santa does the post office process each year?

Canada Post, claiming that Santa Claus lives near the magnetic North Pole, which lies within Canadian territory, has a special postal code for Santa's home: H0H 0H0. Approximately one million letters come to this postal code each year from Canada and around the world, and Canada

Post claims that they answer each letter in the language in which it was written. Meanwhile, the post office in North Pole, Alaska, processes roughly 120,000 letters to Santa each year. Numbers are more difficult to track in the United States, since post offices in different communities have their own letters-to-Santa programs. But Santa isn't the only gift-bringer with a lot of reading to do in December. In the United Kingdom, the Royal Mail receives 750,000 letters to Father Christmas each year.

How much would all the gifts cost in "The Twelve Days of Christmas"?

Because the golden rings are pheasants and not jewellery, the most expensive item in "The Twelve Days of Christmas" would be seven swans a-swimming, at US$7,000, followed by ten lords a-leaping and nine ladies dancing. The current price of a partridge in a pear tree is $34, which is the hourly rate for eight maids a-milking. So when everything is added up, the tab is $15,944.20.

What is "wassailing"?

Most of us only know the term *wassailing* from the song, "Here We Come a-Wassailing." The tradition of wassailing has vanished over the years, leaving many to wonder what the song is referring to. The word *wassail* comes from the Anglo-Saxon phrase *waes hael*, meaning "good health"— a phrase offered as a toast when drinking. At Christmastime, wassailers would journey from door to door singing carols in exchange for drinks from a punch bowl. Another tradition had things working the other way around: the wassailers would carry a punch bowl from door to door, offering drinks in exchange for a monetary expression of appreciation. Either way, there was a great deal of drinking to "good health."

What were the bizarre ingredients of history's most exotic Christmas pies?

An early English saying was, "The devil himself dare not appear in Cornwall during Christmas for fear of being baked in a pie." Records show that living creatures from blackbirds to pheasants, from foxes to rabbits, and in one case even a dwarf, were cooked into Christmas pies at temperatures not hot enough to kill them. Then, as a festival highlight, the crust was broken, and the enclosed creatures would fly, hop, or run among the guests.

How much weight does the average person gain over Christmas?

In the Middle Ages, Christmas banquets started at three in the afternoon, with appetizers and fortified mulled wine followed by ten main courses, and lasted until midnight. Today, over the holidays, North Americans consume 24 million turkeys and 112 million cans of cranberries. We drink 108 million quarts of eggnog and 89 million gallons of liquor. The average weight gain over the Christmas holidays is four to six pounds.

religion
and superstition

Why do we say that someone who falls asleep quickly is "out like a light"?

"Out like a light" originated in the early 1900s. It reminds us that electricity is a fairly recent invention. People used to marvel on how quickly light came and went with nothing more than the flick of a switch, just as many people marvel at those who fall asleep without any tossing and turning. The phrase also describes fighters who drop like a stone after a knockout punch in the boxing ring and drunkards who pass out on the floor.

What is a "dead ringer"?

Ringer comes from horseracing in the nineteenth century. Sometimes an unscrupulous owner would run a poor horse in a number of races to develop long odds against it winning. When a major race came around, the poor horse would be replaced by a good horse that looked exactly the same, called a "dead ringer," and people in the know would gamble a lot of money on it and enjoy a big win.

A more ghoulish, but firmly discounted, explanation of dead ringer is that it refers to someone who was been accidentally buried alive, which wasn't all that uncommon in the eighteenth and nineteenth centuries, but was fortunate enough to have a string tied to his wrist that was attached to a bell. If he pulled on the string, the bell would ring, and a grave digger would come to dig him up.

What is the "Evil Eye"?

Virtually every culture throughout history has believed in the danger of falling under the spell of a withering glance or the "evil eye." Folklorists believe that the ancients became fearful of losing possession of their souls after seeing their own reflection in another person's eyes. The word *pupil* is from *pupilla*, the Latin for "little doll." In Roman times, professional sorcerers with the evil eye where hired to cast spells on a person's enemy.

The Egyptian use of mascara by both men and women was devised to absorb sunlight which minimized the reflection of another into the eye and not for cosmetic purposes. During the Middle Ages those with unsettling looks even when caused by medical problems like cataracts were often put to death.

An evil eye is sometimes called the "hairy eyeball" because the eyebrows and eyelashes are scrunched together during an angry glance or stare.

Where did we get the expression, "For the love of Pete"?

This phrase and others like it (for example "For Pete's sake") are euphemisms for the phrases "For the love of God/Christ" or "For God's/ Christ's sake" and hail from a time when those phases were considered blasphemous. Nowadays phrases like "For the love of God" are commonly used, but the euphemisms are still used as well. Why Pete? Most likely it is a reference to the Catholic Saint Peter.

Other phrases with similar origins are "Zounds" (archaic British slang), a contraction of "Christ's wounds"; "Oh my goodness" and "Oh my gosh" for "Oh my God; and "Gosh darn it" for "God damn it."

What is the Holy Grail?

Today we often refer to anything elusive and sought-after as a "Holy Grail" because from the Crusaders to the present the search for the original Holy

Grail has consumed Christendom. The "grail," or bowl, in question was used by Christ at the last supper and disappeared after his crucifixion. Legend has it that the Holy Grail surfaced in England during medieval times and finding it became an obsession of King Arthur.

Part of the legend is that Joseph of Arimathaea used the grail to catch the blood of Christ at the crucifixion.

The Old English *greal* is from the Latin word *crater*, meaning "bowl."

What's the difference between a "priest" and a "monk"?

In the Roman Catholic Church, a priest is ordained to represent Christ in performing the sacraments. Priests usually work from a church under the direction of Bishop. They minister or attend to the needs of believers. Monks take vows of obedience. If they are ordained as well, they are called Fathers, if not, they are Brothers. A monk's principal duty is to pray. Depending on the religious order that a monk belongs to, he may or may not be active in the world outside of the monastery. Monks who work in the community are often called friars.

Why is someone living a good life said to be on the "straight and narrow"?

Someone on the "straight and narrow" is living a legal, moral, and disciplined life and was referred to in *The Pilgrim's Progress* by English writer John Bunyan (1628–1688). In that inspirational book, Pilgrim, the representative of everyman, must follow the "straight and narrow." The phrase has a biblical origin in Matthew 7:14: "Broad is the way that is the path of destruction but narrow is the gate and straight is the way that leadeth to the house of God."

How did the "Quakers" get their name?

One of the founders of The Religious Society of Friends, a movement begun in Britain during the seventeenth century, was George Fox. Fox was a "firebrand" and was imprisoned many times for following his beliefs; chiefly that no one should take any oath of allegiance other than to God. During one of his trials Fox chastised the magistrates telling them that they should "quake" at the word of God. From that point on the Society of Friends became known as "Quakers."

Refusing to swear oaths was one reason for their persecution but Quakers championed such noble causes as the abolition of slavery, the equality of women, the humane treatment of the mentally ill and prisoners, and the end to all war.

The state of Pennsylvania was established as a haven for Quakers in the New World by William Penn.

In 1689, the British Toleration Act of Parliament was passed and made life tolerable for the Quakers. It ensured freedom of conscience and made it illegal for anyone to disturb another's form of worship.

How many saints are there?

The first official canonization took place in 993 AD when Pope John XV (died 996 AD) declared Bishop Ulrich of Augsburg a saint. Butler's Lives of the Saints, published in 1759, had 1,486 entries. The revised edition in 1956 listed 2,565. Currently, an up-to-date version of the book is in the works, so the exact number of saints is unknown.

Pope John Paul II (1920–2005) canonized 12 people, which brought the total number of saints named during his pontification to more than 300, which is about half the number of saints named in the past 400 years.

During the first 800 to 900 years of Christianity, there was no formal recognition of sainthood. The number of martyrs and others of exceptional faith from that time are the main reason for the Feast of All Saints or All Saints Day held on November 1 and the vigil of which is called All Hollows Day or Halloween.

Who is Canada's patron saint?

Canada has two patron saints. Since French Catholics were the first Europeans to settle Canada, they brought their religion and customs with them, including the assignment of patron saints. St. Anne, the Virgin Mary's mother, shares patronage of Canada with Mary's husband, St. Joseph. St. Anne is also the patron saint of housewives, cabinet makers, and all women in labour. Her Roman Catholic feast day is July 26. St. Joseph shares his patronage of Canada with Mexico, China, Belgium, and carpenters. In 1870, Pope Pius IX (1792–1878) declared St. Joseph the universal patron of the church. St. Joseph's feast day is March 19.

Why do Muslims pray five times a day?

Muslims pray five times a day in response to an order from God. Prayers must be said just before sunrise, after the sun peaks at noon, in the late afternoon, just after sunset, and between sunset and midnight. The ritual of prayer involves a series of actions that go with the words of a prayer. Everyday thoughts must be put aside before praying; otherwise no benefit will be realized. Everyone from the age of seven is encouraged to take part in prayer.

In the beginning, before life became too busy, Christians also prayed five times a day!

Why do people pray with a string of beads?

The rosary, or "wreath of roses," first appeared in fifteenth-century Europe, but the practice of reciting prayers with a string of beads or knots goes back about 500 years before the dawn of Christianity. The word *bead* comes from the Anglo-Saxon word *bidden*, meaning "to ask." The principle for both Christians and Muslims is that the more you ask or repeat a prayer the more effective it is, and so the rosary is an aid in keeping count.

Why is an excessive enthusiast called a "zealot"?

A zealot is a supreme fanatic, often a bigot, and perhaps unfairly is best known in history as a radical Jewish political movement called the Zealots. This sect joined with several other Jewish groups to launch a rebellion in Palestine against the Roman Empire in the first century AD. Known for being aggressive, intolerant, and violent, the Zealots captured Jerusalem in 66 AD and held it for four years. When Rome finally recaptured the city, it was destroyed. The sect also captured the fortress of Masada and held it for several years against thousands of troops until the Romans set it on fire in 73 AD, leaving a handful of survivors to tell the tale.

The word *zealot* comes from the Greek *zēlōtēs*, which means "a fervent follower." It is a synonym of the Hebrew word *kanai*, which means "one who is jealous on behalf of God."

Where do we get the expression "earn brownie points"?

The original "brownies" are little Scottish elves (wee brown men) who are believed to fix things and help out around farms when everyone is asleep. They were the inspiration for the name Lord Baden-Powell's sister, Agnes, gave to the branch of Scouts that serves younger girls from six through eight years of age. Brownie points are those accumulated by the girls for good deeds. Enough Brownie points earns a reward or significant badge of honour. The first modern use of "brownie points" was in 1951 when scoring them was offered as a strategy of good deeds for men to stay out of trouble with their wives.

When someone survives disaster, why do we say he's "cheated the devil"?

The first recorded instance of "cheating the devil" can be found in the Hebrew Talmud. The devil offered a farmer two years of a flourishing harvest with the condition that the devil would get the crops grown underground for the first year, and those grown above the ground the following year. During the devil's below-the-soil year, the farmer grew wheat and barley. In the above-the-soil year he grew carrots and turnips, and thereby cheated the devil.

Where were tarot cards first made?

The first tarot cards were hand-painted for Italian nobility in the fourteenth century. They were used for games and fortune telling, and were called *carte du trionfi* or triumph cards. They were renamed tarocchi cards in the 1500s to distinguish them from a popular game being played with regular playing cards. They became known as tarot cards in sixteenth-century France. A tarot deck consists of 22 face cards and 56 suits.

What does a husband have to say to divorce his wife under Islamic law?

According to Sharia law, a husband has only to tell his wife "I dismiss you" three times and they are divorced. This, however, is an oversimplification. There are differences in Islamic divorces depending on whether one is Shiite or Sunni, and depending on which Islamic nation the couple resides in. In some Islamic nations women have more rights in matters of marriage and divorce than in others. For Muslims living in secular nations, Sharia law has no legal application, and divorce must be in accordance with local legislation.

How did ancient Hebrew Scriptures view divorce?

In the earliest writings a wife is a piece of property, like a dog or a donkey. The husband could divorce her for something as trivial as burning his supper. As time passed, it became necessary for the husband to justify the divorce and obtain a "bill of divorcement." This quite likely gave him time to reconsider what might have been a rash act. Eventually, Judaism regarded divorce as something tragic. One ancient author wrote: "the very altar shed tears when a man divorced the wife of his youth."

Where in the New Testament does Jesus speak about divorce?

In Mark 10:2–12, Jesus flatly denounces divorce: "What therefore God has joined together, let no man separate." However, in Matthew 19:1–9, Jesus makes an allowance for "unchastity." As with so much else in the Bible, over the centuries these passages have been the subject of much controversy and interpretation.

What does the Old Testament say about divorce?

In Deuteronomy 24:1–2 it says that "When a man hath taken a wife, and married her, and it come to pass that she find no favor in his eyes, because he hath found some uncleanness in her: then let him write her a letter of divorcement, and give it in her hand, and send her out of his house. And when she is departed out of his house, she may go and be another man's wife."

How did the Council of Trent affect divorce in the Roman Catholic countries of Europe?

In the seventeenth century, the Council of Trent forbade divorce for Catholics. A couple could get a judicial separation, known as "divorce a mensa et thoro", but the marriage itself could not be dissolved. This helped turn some nations toward Protestantism. However, countries like Spain, Portugal, and Italy remained staunchly Catholic. For people in those countries divorce was next to impossible.

politics

Why do we say "deep six" when we mean to eliminate or destroy something?

During the Watergate scandals, John Dean said that John Erlichman told him to shred some sensitive documents and then deep six the briefcase by throwing it into the river. "By the deep six" is a nautical term referring to sounding the water's depth and means six fathoms (36 feet). In the navy, to deep six something meant to dispose of an item by tossing it overboard into deep water where it couldn't be found.

What is an Orwellian situation?

George Orwell's great gift to the world was the image he painted of government out of control, in his novel *1984*. Since its publication, the excesses of "Big Brother" have been recalled innumerable times by people fearful that their governments are going down similar paths. Situations these critics call Orwellian include illegal wiretapping and other invasions of privacy, detention without trial, bureaucratic language that masks truth, and news management.

What Canadian resource do Americans need more — oil or water?

The Alberta tar sands have attracted the interest of the United States, and though Canada already accounts for 16 percent of U.S. oil consumption, new technology may someday diminish the Americans' need for carbon-based fossil fuels. Water is another matter. Each day 4,755 billion gallons of water are funnelled through water pipes, turbines, and irrigation systems in the United

States. This massive activity represents about 12 times the average daily flow of the Mississippi River. The average per person need in the United States is 2,700 gallons, or 370 billion gallons in total each and every day. With American thirst for water increasing by 19 percent per year, Canada's water will become more than a mirage, it will be a necessity.

Why are Conservatives called "Tories"?

By definition, Liberals want to change things while Conservatives want to maintain the status quo, so it should be no surprise that the word *Tory* is from the Celtic words for "the king's party" and "partisans of the king," both of which were derived from the Irish word *toruigh*, meaning "to ambush." Formed in 1679, the Tory Party became the Conservative Party in 1832, but their opponents continue to call them Tories.

Taob-righ is Celtic for "king's party"— *Tuath-righ* for "partisans of the king" — *Tar-a-ri* for "come o king."

What is an "incumbent"?

"Incumbents" are politicians who have been representing your community and want to do more. Incumbents usually start with an edge because their party can often time the election, they are more well-known than their opponents, and they probably have more campaign money. These advantages mean incumbents tend to win unless they've done something to really upset their constituents.

Where did the phrase "spin doctor" come from?

The term "spin doctor" first appeared in the New York Times during Ronald Reagan's campaign for re-election in 1984. Spin is the twist given a baseball by a pitcher throwing a curveball to deceive the batter, while a doctor is someone who fixes a problem. Therefore, a "spin doctor" is someone who, faced with a political problem, solves it by putting a twist on the information to bend the story to his or her own advantage.

Why did Abraham Lincoln's son withdraw from politics?

In 1865, Robert Lincoln rushed to his father's deathbed. Sixteen years later, as Garfield's secretary of war, he was with that president when he was shot by an assassin. In 1901, Robert arrived in Buffalo for the American Exposition just in time to see President McKinley murdered. After that, Robert Lincoln vowed never again to be in the presence of an American president.

How many former American presidents are not buried in the United States?

As of 2008, there are four former American presidents not buried in the United States. Ulysses S. Grant is not buried but is entombed in New York (a body is only buried when it's placed in the ground and covered with dirt). The others are Presidents Jimmy Carter, Bill Clinton, and the current president's father, George Herbert Walker Bush, who are all still alive.

Quickies
Did you know...
• that Ronald Reagan was the only president of the United States who had ever been divorced?

What colour is "Alice Blue"?

President Teddy Roosevelt's 16-year-old daughter popularized "Alice Blue." It's a light blue with a hint of gray to match her eyes. During a time of cartwheel hats and the Gibson Girl look, the press nicknamed the pretty young woman's dress the "Alice Blue Gown," which became the title of a very popular song written by J. MacCarthy and H. Tierney for their 1919 musical *Irene*. During the 1980s the aircraft carrier USS *Theodore Roosevelt* had many of its prominent areas painted "Alice Blue."

Why are some politicians called "lame ducks"?

A lame duck is a powerless American politician. After an election in a parliamentary system, such as that found in Britain or Canada, the House reconvenes and the winners immediately form the new government. In the American system, however, the newly elected congress doesn't take control for months, leaving those who have lost still in charge. During this time, because they can't pass anything meaningful, the powerless politicians are as useless as lame ducks.

What were Winston Churchill's "black dogs"?

Winston Churchill had a gift for coming up with just the right words to describe situations, for instance he was honest about his bouts of depression, which he called "black dogs." Although he is often credited with inventing the expression, he may have learned it from one of his favourite writers, Samuel Johnson, who lived in the 1700s. Today, it is one of the slang terms the British use to describe the disease.

Other Churchillian turns of phrase include, "I have always felt that a politician is to be judged by the animosities he excites among his opponents," and "success is the ability to go from one failure to another with no loss of enthusiasm."

Why was the Japanese Emperor called the "Mikado"?

Gilbert and Sullivan's *Mikado* (1885) is a reference to the emperor but the word literally means "the honourable gate" and refers to the door to the palace. It was unthinkable for the Japanese to mention their rulers name so references were directed to the august entrance that concealed his existence.

Poo-Bah is also from the *Mikado* and was the title given to "The Lord High Everything Else" and now means (as it did in the play) a pompous buffoon with unearned authority. The indirect reference to authority wasn't unique to the Japanese. *Pharaoh* in Egyptian means "Great House" while the former Ottoman Empire's seat of government was called "The High Gate" (*la sublime porte*).

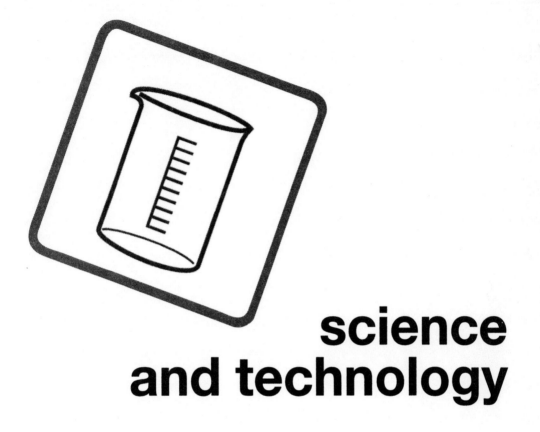

science
and technology

Why is Earth the only planet not named from Greek or Roman mythology?

Earth got its name long before the sixteenth century (the time of Copernicus, when humans started considering that we are on just another planet). *Earth* comes from the ancient Germanic languages and originally meant "the soil that was the source of all life." Earth is the English name, but hundreds of languages all refer to our fertile soil, our Planet Earth, as a nursing mother. *Terra Mater* means "Mother Earth."

In Roman mythology, the goddess of the Earth was Tellus, the fertile soil. Seventy-one percent of the Earth's surface is covered with water. Earth is the third planet from the sun and the fifth largest.

Why do we call our nearest terrestrial neighbour the "moon"?

Because the ancients used the moon to help measure time and predict recurring monthly events such as tides it was known in Sanskrit as *me* which means "measurement." Before that, the beautiful white orb was known in the Indo-European language as *menes*, which was also the word for month. By the Middle Ages, this reliable forecaster of earthly events had linguistically evolved to *mona* and eventually *moon*.

How far can we travel with current spacecraft propulsion technology?

With current methods of powering spacecraft, we are trapped in our solar system. The farthest distance flown by any man-made craft is the 12 light hours travelled by *Voyager 1* between 1977, and the present. The closest solar system to ours is Alpha Centauri, which is 4.35 light years from Earth. If *Voyager 1* heads in that direction, it will need about 100,000 years to get there. Even using the most advanced propulsion systems available today, we would only reduce the time to about 40,000 years.

Was there ever a planet named Vulcan, as in the *Star Trek* series?

In 1845, scientists believed that the only explanation for Mercury's confusing and erratic orbit of the sun would be the presence of gravitational pull from an unseen nearby planet, which they named "Vulcan." Eventually Albert Einstein, through his theory of relativity, explained Mercury's behaviour, thus eliminating the hypothetical planet Vulcan — until it was resurrected by Gene Rodenberry in *Star Trek*.

How frequent are total solar eclipses?

Total solar eclipses are rare events, happening only once every few years, because the sun, moon, and earth must line up precisely, so the sun is completely blocked out by the moon. The most recent one was best viewed in the African country of Ghana, and took place on March 29, 2006. The previous one was in 2003 and was best viewed from Antarctica. The last one visible in Canada took place on February 26, 1979. The next one is due in August of 2008, and Canadians in the northern territory of Nunavut will have the best view.

Where does red rain come from?

Strong winds at high altitudes can carry pollutants, organisms, and other materials for great distances. Huge sandstorms in the Sahara Desert lift massive quantities of sand into the air, where it is carried on Sirocco winds to fall as red rain on many countries in Europe, including Spain, Portugal, France, and Britain, and across the Atlantic where it sometimes falls on Caribbean islands and on the eastern seaboard of the United States. Black rains from soot and yellow or green rains from concentrations of pollen have also been reported in many parts of the world.

Why do local telephone numbers never start with the number one?

The original dial telephone sent out a signal "click" for each number dialled. One click for 1, two "clicks" for 2, et cetera. The zero was reserved for the operator. "One" was never used because early switching systems read every signal as beginning with one click, regardless of the number you were dialling, and so technically, no phone number could start with 1. It continues today simply as tradition.

Quickies
Did you know...
- that, famous as the inventor of dynamite, Alfred Nobel (Nobel Prizes) also invented plywood?
- that the speed of sound changes at different altitudes? At sea level its 760 miles per hour while above 36,000 feet it's reached at 660 miles per hour.
- that the speed of light is 186,282.3959 miles per second?
- that the word *astronaut* is from two Greek words — *astron* meaning "star," and *nautes* meaning "sailor"?
- that the name of the first Russian space station, *Mir*, means "peace" or "world" in Russian?

Why is an alias or electronic nick-name called a "handle"?

An alias intended to conceal a user's real name or identity within an electronic message is called a "handle." Consider that *handle* is an extension of the word *hand* and is used to describe something you can get your hands on. Clearly, though an alias can be used to avoid revealing personal data, a figurative "handle" offers a way of getting hold of someone without disturbing that anonymity. The term was popular with ham radio operators and resurfaced during the CB radio craze of the 1970s and is now used on the Internet.

In the jargon of the 1870s, titles such as "sir" or "Madame" were introduced to common English as "handles."

Shortwave radio operators are called "hams" from the call letters of an amateur wireless station set up by three members of the Harvard Radio Club whose last names began with the letters H, A, and M.

What was a "computer" before the electronic age?

The word computer first appeared in the seventeenth century as the job title of a person who did calculations as an occupation. Although slide rules were sometimes called computers, it wasn't until the 1940s, with the development of massive electronic data machines, that the human occupation of computing became obsolete. These mechanical devices became known as computers.

What hand controls the most keys on a standard keyboard?

When a typists hands take the standard position taught around the world, the left hand controls 15 letters, including the most frequently used, E, A, T, R, and S, while the right hand controls only 11, although it also controls the comma and the period. The left hand makes about 56 percent of the strokes leaving 44 percent for the right. *Reverberates*, *effervesce*, and *stewardess* can be typed entirely with the left hand. *Monopoly*, *homonym*, and *lollipop* can be typed using only the right hand. The delete/backspace keys come under the right, which equalizes the workload between the two hands for an average typist.

The computer terms *byte*, *pixel*, and *modem* are abbreviations of what combinations of words?

Each word is a contraction of two words. *Byte* is a contraction of the words *by eight* and means eight bits. Half a byte is four bits (or a nibble, depending how you look at it). The word *pixel* is an abbreviation of *picture cell*, while *modem* is a combination of the first letters in the words *modulate* and *demodulate*.

What's the difference between Blu-Ray and HD-DVD?

For the average videophile there are two differences between these DVD technologies. Blu-Ray uses a blue laser and can store 25 GB of data on a single-layer disk or 50 GB on a dual-layer disk. HD-DVD uses a red laser, like the original DVDs, and stores 30 GB of data. Sony began using Blu-Ray in its PlayStation3 while Microsoft went with HD-DVD in its X-Box 360 videogame console. Both technologies offer much sharper pictures than standard DVDs, which are themselves much better than VHS tapes.

But the death of HD-DVD has come about faster than I expected. Blu-ray is now your one and only choice because of Toshiba's decision, announced on February 19, 2008, to discontinue the development, manufacturing, and marketing of HD-DVD players and recorders.

How were microwave ovens discovered?

Masters of the culinary arts may have disdain for the microwave oven, but for most modern kitchens they are essential. The cooking use for microwaves was discovered by accident in 1945 when an American scientist named Percy Spencer (1894–1970) noticed that a candy bar in his pocket had melted while he was testing a magnetron, a tube that generates microwaves for use in radar systems. After experimenting with popcorn and a famous boiled egg, Spencer proved that microwaves could cook things.

Percy Spencer worked for the Raytheon Company, and it was that firm that manufactured the first microwave ovens in 1947. They were mainly sold to restaurants because they were the size of small refrigerators and were too expensive for the general public.

Do only the most intelligent graduate from university?

A proper education is an advantage to any mind, but intelligence doesn't guarantee a formal education. Albert Einstein left school at 15 after his teacher described him as "retarded"; Thomas Edison dropped out at eight. Up to 50 percent of North Americans born with a genius IQ never graduate high school. They can take comfort in these words from Emerson: "I pay the school master, but it's the schoolboys who educate my son."

How many people live on Earth?

On February 25, 2005, the United Nations Population Division issued revised estimates and projected that the world's population will reach 7 billion by 2013 and swell to 9.1 billion in 2050. Most of the growth is expected to take place in developing nations. Nearly all humans currently reside on Earth: 6,411,000,000 inhabitants as of January 2005.

Two humans are presently in orbit around Earth on board the International Space Station. The station crew is replaced with new personnel every six months. During the exchange there are more, and sometimes others are also travelling briefly above the atmosphere.

In total, about 400 people have been in space as of 2004. Most of them have reported a heightened understanding of the world's value and importance, reverence for human life, and amazement at the Earth's beauty not usually achieved by those living on the surface.

Quickies
Did you know...
- that there are 7,000 species of grass? As our most important plant it constitutes one quarter of the earth's vegetation.
- that rice fields are flooded to control weeds and have nothing to do with plant nutrition?

fashion
and clothing

How did the bowler hat become an English icon?

The caricature of an Englishman used to include an umbrella, a briefcase, and a bowler hat. Although this is an outdated image, it still recalls a class system that defines the British character. The first bowler was designed in the mid-1800s by London hatters James and George Lock as a protective riding hat for Thomas William Coke. The headgear became synonymous with property owners and consequently the gentry or well-to-do. The hat got its name from Thomas and William Bowler, the hat-makers who produced Coke's prototype.

Americans call this hat a derby, probably because it was so prevalent within the wealthy compound at major horse races.

Winston Churchill (1874–1965) was one of the last of his generation to make the bowler high fashion.

London's trademark black high-roofed taxicabs were designed so that gentlemen wouldn't have to remove their bowlers.

Is there a reason why the zipper on a man's trousers is called a fly?

The zipper or metal clasp on a man's jeans isn't the fly. This use of the word *fly* for the opening on trousers came from the flapping wing of an insect (fly) and was used to describe such things as a tent flap (1810) and so, in 1844, the cloth covering for the buttons was also called a fly but not the zipper!

Why are Levi denims called "jeans"?

In the 1850s, when Levi Strauss ran out of tent canvas for the pants he was selling to California gold miners, he imported a tough material from Nimes in France called *serge de Nim*. Americanized, *de Nim* became *denim*. The word *jeans* is from the French word for Genoa, where the tough cloth was invented. Jeans became popular with teenagers after James Dean wore them in the movie *Rebel Without a Cause*.

Why is a school jacket called a "blazer"?

One theory, asserted in the "Freshman's Handbook" for St. John's College, Cambridge University in England, says *blazer* originated in 1880 as a nickname for the "blazing" scarlet flannel jackets worn by its student rowing team called the Lady Margaret Boating Club.

Another theory, also widely held, says the first blazers were brass buttoned, double-breasted navy blue serge jackets ordered for the crew of HMS *Blazer* by its captain in anticipation of an inspection by Queen Victoria in 1837.

A third theory suggests that it comes from *emblazon*, and refers to the crests that are often sewn onto the breast pockets.

Why is a skin-tight garment called a "leotard"?

Jules Leotard was the inspiration for the song "The Man on the Flying Trapeze." He made his first public appearance in 1859 with the Cirque Napoleon and began a career of trapeze stunts that made him the toast of Europe. Leotard invented a one-piece, skin-tight garment to free his movement and display his physique. The garment made its way into the ballet studios of Paris and was known in English by 1859 as a leotard.

Leotard called his garment a *maillot*, which now means "bathing suit" in French. Born in Toulouse, France, Jules Leotard died from smallpox at the age of 30.

Why is a person neatly dressed said to be all "spruced up"?

If someone is "spruced up," they've gone to some trouble to look smart. *Spruce* is an unexplained alteration of the old French word for Prussia — *Pruce*. During the 1400s, a very stylish sleeveless and expensive form-fitting jacket known as a jerkin, was made of spruce (or pruce) leather and was imported throughout Europe from Prussia. To wear such a garment made such a profound fashion statement that to this day, being "spruced up" means dressed to kill. The spruce tree is a Prussian fir.

Why do the phrases "dressed to the nines" and "putting on the dog" mean very well dressed?

The expression "putting on the dog," meaning showing off, comes from the habit of leisurely wealthy women to carry lapdogs to afternoon social functions. "Dressed to the nines" comes from Shakespeare's time, when the seats furthest from the stage cost one pence, and the closest, nine pence. Sitting in the expensive seats required dressing up to fit in with the well-off. It was called "dressing to the nines."

Why is something conspicuous or weird called "outlandish"?

Outlandish is usually a reference to something bizarre or unconventional, like many teen styles. The word began in Old English as *utlendisc*, literally meaning "out of land" or "unfamiliar" such as the customs, habits, and dress of a foreigner. Its current meaning of grossly eccentric is from 1596.

Old English was the language spoken in Britain before the Norman Conquest.

Exotic has the same meaning as outlandish but has a Greek derivative, *exoticos* meaning "from outside" or "belonging to another country." Its reference to sexy dancers and strip-teasers (exotic dancers) surfaced in America in 1954.

Why are foot and leg coverings called "stockings"?

In the mid-sixteenth century, men wore one solid under garment (hose) that extended from the waist and covered the legs. Around 1520 it became fashionable to cut the garment at the knees so that it became two items. At the time, a form of corporal punishment was the humiliation of being locked in public stockades. These stockades or "stocks" were made of timber with holes through which the confined legs of the convict protruded from just above the ankle; the same length of leg covered by the new garment. This is how they became humorously referred to as stockings.

Why are ankle and foot coverings called "socks"?

The word *sox* or *socks*, is not an abbreviation of *stockings*. *Sock* was spelled *socc* in Old English and is derived from the Latin word *soccus* meaning a light shoe or slipper. The word began in ancient Greece as *sykchos*, a light shoe worn on the stage by comic actors. From this, the short woven foot covering became *socks*. Even shorter socks were the style in 1943 when they became known as "bobby sox." To bob something is to shorten it.

Why is a type of woman's underwear called a "G-string"?

Although our prehistoric ancestors wore leather loincloths that have been excavated from more than 7,000 years ago, underwear as we know it didn't become "normal" until the thirteenth century when it was tied at the waist and knees. The ancient Greeks didn't wear underwear, though their slaves sported a kind of loincloth. The *G* in G-string stands for "groin" and was first used to describe the loincloths worn by North American Natives. As women's wear, G-strings first appeared in the 1930s when they were the exclusive attire of strippers.

Quickies
Did you know...
• that shoe laces were invented to replace buckles in 1790?

Who started the "hippie" craze?

"Hippie" was first used to describe young, wannabe hipsters in the late 1930s. In the mid-1960s, it became associated with a bohemian community living in the Haight-Ashbury district of San Francisco. Haight-Ashbury's hippies believed in universal peace, free love, drugs (especially LSD), and rock 'n roll music. Many sought to go back to the land to enjoy simple lives and renounce materialism. Both men and women wore their hair long and wore bright, inexpensive, or handmade clothing.

Who invented the miniskirt?

Fashion designer Andre Courreges is credited with designing the first miniskirt, which was modelled at a Paris fashion show in 1964. A year later, Mary Quant, who ran a fashion boutique off Carnaby Street in London, began making mini dresses and miniskirts that were six to seven inches above the knee. They caught on and the hemlines continue to rise for the rest of the decade.

Courreges also introduced some small white boots at the show in 1964. These caught on as well, helping to create the go-go dancer look.

medicine
and health

Why is a hospital's emergency selection process called "triage"?

Triage is from the French *trier*, meaning "to compare and select," and was used in reference to sorting livestock for culling or slaughter. Triage entered medicine during the First World War, when battlefield physicians were overwhelmed with the wounded and dying. The least likely to live were treated last. In modern hospitals the order of triage is reversed, with priority given to the most seriously in need.

What is the origin of the red-and-white barber pole?

The Roman word for beard was *barba*, which gave us the term *barber*. Early barbers cut hair and trimmed beards, but they also pulled teeth and practised medicinal bloodletting. This last procedure required the patient to expose his veins by squeezing a pole painted red to hide the bloodstains. When not in use the red pole was displayed outside wrapped in the white gauze used as bandages, and it eventually became the official trademark of the barber.

Why do doctors on television use the word *stat* in an emergency?

It was the Romans who gave the practice of medicine its prestige, and consequently, other than the Church, no other profession is still as influenced by Latin. When a doctor says, "Stat!" he is abbreviating *statim*, meaning "immediately." The use of the word stands out from "Quickly!" or "Hurry!" and conveys urgency; and yes, it's still used by real doctors outside of television.

Why do we get sweaty palms when we're nervous?

If your palms sweat when you're nervous, you can blame evolution. The inside of your hands has more sweat glands than any other part of your body. This is because tens of thousands of years ago, when our primal ancestors were threatened by savage carnivores, the quickest exit was the nearest tree. Stress caused their palms to sweat, and the moisture gave them a better grip on the branches and vines they were climbing.

Why do we say that someone in good physical condition is as "fit as a fiddle"?

If you are "fit as a fiddle," you are in great shape. When the early North American settlers gathered for a barn dance, it was often an all-night session of dancing and romancing for the hard-working and socially starved farmers. The local band of amateurs was led by the fiddler who needed great endurance and stamina to play until the cows came home. This gave us the expression "fit as a fiddler," which evolved into "fit as a fiddle."

Why do "guts" and "pluck" mean courage?

Having "guts" or "pluck" means having courage or backbone, while having neither means lily-livered cowardice, and they are all references to intestinal fortitude. Guts, of course, are internal organs while pluck is collectively the heart, liver, and lungs. Lily-livered comes from the belief that fear drains blood from the liver, making it white. It was once believed that these internal organs, specifically the heart, were the source of a person's character.

In the eighteenth century, the "pluck" contained the heart, liver, lights, melt, and skirt (lights were lungs, melt was the collected blood, and the skirt was the diaphragm).

What is the difference between *nauseous* and *nauseated*?

Today, the words *nauseous* and *nauseated* are often used to mean the same thing, and *nauseous* seems to be more popular with the public at large. But that was not the case when I was growing up. In fact, I rarely heard *nauseous* used, because it was just a weird way of saying *nauseating*. The change has created a rift in linguistic circles, as purists are offended by the poor grammar, but others believe that language should just evolve in response to common usage.

> **Quickies**
> *Did you know...*
> • that Noxzema was invented in 1899 by George Bunting and was named for its ability to cure eczema — "No eczema"?
> • that Ex-lax is an abbreviation of "Excellent Laxative"?

Why does nobody talk about the disease called "consumption" anymore?

There are many names for diseases that we rarely hear anymore. For some of them that's because the diseases are rare today thanks to vaccines. For others, however, it simply signals a better understanding of the disease. One of these diseases is consumption, which continues to ravage the world, but is now better known as tuberculosis. Other names that have fallen by the wayside include apoplexy, the paralysis caused by a stroke; corruption, which we call infection, and grippe, now called influenza.

What diseases were part of the Columbian Exchange?

Columbian Exchange was the name given to the transfer of animals, plants, artifacts, ideas, et cetera, between the Old World and the New World after Christopher Columbus's voyage of 1492. Among the worst things the Europeans carried to the Americas were diseases to which the Native populations had never before been exposed and against which they had no immunity. Smallpox was probably the most lethal. In return, the Natives passed on to the white men a disease that eventually reached epidemic proportions in Europe — syphilis.

Who was Typhoid Mary?

Mary Mallon (1869–1938) was an Irish immigrant who worked as a cook in the New York area from 1900 to 1907. She was the first known "healthy carrier" of typhoid fever in the United States, that is, a person who carries typhoid without suffering from the symptoms. Mallon infected 47 people in homes and institutions where she worked as a cook. Three of them died. Even after health officials identified her as the source of the infections, Mallon refused to believe she was a carrier and even worked under a false name so she could continue cooking. She was finally sent into forced quarantine at a hospital on North Brother Island, where she died at the age of 69 from pneumonia, not typhoid.

Why was the influenza pandemic of 1918–1919 called the "Spanish flu"?

The First World War was raging when the influenza epidemic hit Europe in 1918. Governments of belligerent nations wouldn't allow newspapers to report on the silent killer that was ravaging their populations. In neutral Spain, however, the government saw no need to censor the press. Because Spanish newspapers reported on the epidemic, the Royal College of Physicians in London found it convenient to label the disease the Spanish flu. The pandemic actually began in

China and was carried along trade and military routes to the rest of Asia and to Europe. Infected soldiers returning from France unwittingly took the disease to North America.

What causes influenza?

Flu is caused by a virus. Over a period of time, virus strains can mutate, changing their chemical makeup. This can alter their behaviour and make their effect on the human body unpredictable.

How did the Spanish flu pandemic differ from other influenza epidemics?

In the early twentieth century, nobody knew anything about viruses, but people were familiar with the symptoms of the flu: fever, sore throat, cough, headache, muscular pain, and general weakness. Most victims were bedridden for a few days and then recovered. Usually, only the elderly and very young children were at risk of dying from the common flu. The Spanish flu was a particularly vicious strain of the virus that struck hardest at healthy adults in their late twenties and early thirties. In a three-generational family, children and grandparents stood a better chance of survival than young parents. Doctors often didn't know what they were dealing with and blamed deaths on cholera and pneumonia. Many victims often did develop pneumonia in the later stages of the disease. Estimates of the global death toll range from 22 million to 100 million. In Canada about 50,000 people perished (out of a population of around 8 million), while it is estimated that as many as 675,000 died in the United States and about 28 percent of the American population of just over 103 million was affected by the virus.

What did people do to fight the Spanish flu?

Doctors who believed that the sickness was caused by bacteria developed a vaccine that had to be painfully injected into deep muscle tissue. The treatment wasn't effective. Other remedies and treatments included powdered aspirin, onion and mustard poultices, goose grease and garlic, skunk oil, camphor, salt herring, sulphur (placed in shoes), coffee mixed with mustard, cinnamon, tobacco smoke, and alcohol.

Where is an Englishman going when he's going to "spend a penny"?

Why, he's going to the "loo" of course! A sanitary engineer named George Jennings debuted a flushing lavatory called a "Monkey Closet" at London's famous Crystal Palace Exhibition in 1851, and over 800,000 visitors "spent a penny" to use it. For more than a century afterwards, that was the price the British paid to use public restrooms. In 1971, a currency called New Pence was introduced. The penny soon disappeared, and the price to use a British pay toilet increased.

What are the origins of the word *melancholy*?

In ancient Greece, Hippocrates thought melancholy originated from an excess of black bile from the liver. He accused "melancholy" of causing dejection, seizures, lung diseases, dysentery, ulcers, rashes, and even hemorrhoids. In the fifteenth century it became fashionable to be melancholy, and melancholic characters, the most notable being William Shakespeare's Hamlet, became fixtures in plays. Today, you're more likely to hear that someone is depressed or down in the dumps, than that they are melancholy.

Who was the first person to undergo electroshock therapy?

Electric shock has been a tool in a doctor's medical bag since ancient times when electric eels were used with the aim of providing relief for headache sufferers and the mentally ill. The first machines were developed in the 1930s, inspired by the use of electricity to incapacitate pigs in a slaughterhouse in Rome. Bitter debate swirls around the practice. Some say the electroshock confuses patients, erases memory, and even causes death. Others argue it is the best treatment for severe depression and mania when drugs don't work, and much safer than it used to be.

Why do we say someone is "in the doldrums" when they're feeling depressed?

The word *doldrums* originated in the early 1800s to describe a mood where the mind is dull, *dol* from old English, and the body, lethargic. The ending, *drum* may find its origins in the word *tantrum*, a fit of bad temper, which was first noted as a colloquialism, about 100 years earlier.

The belt of calm ocean north of the equator that sailors call the Doldrums do not appear to have had that name until the few decades after the mood was identified.

Where do we get the term "agoraphobia" for the fear of open spaces?

Agoraphobia is a complex condition, which is often defined as an abnormal fear of open or public spaces. More recently the psychiatric community has realized that it may be the public nature of open places, not their openness, which triggers anxious responses. The name derives from the Greek word *agora*, which translates into "where the people gather" or marketplace. For this reason, agoraphobics are often also claustrophobic, or fearful of being confined.

Agoraphobia can be very disabling, as sufferers may go so far as to imprison themselves in their own houses, or even in a few rooms within the house, in order to avoid panic attacks.

Why is an unstable person called a "crackpot"?

A crackpot is an irrational person. Crackpots have always been with us, but the word only came into use in the late 1800s. The term plays on the obsolete use of the word *pot* to describe a skull. It suggests that the person in question has a cracked skull, which is causing him or her to behave in a mad, foolish, or eccentric manner.

What's involved in a sneeze?

If you sneeze hard enough you can fracture a rib or rupture a blood vessel in your brain and die! When something foreign enters the inside of your nose and it starts to tickle, it sends a message to the brain. This is then relayed through a very complex system of nerves and is received by the muscles of your diaphragm, vocal chords, abdomen, throat, chest, and eyelids. You always close your eyes when you sneeze! The particles are then expunged from the nose at speeds up to 100 miles per hour. Sneezing seems simple, but like most of the body's defensive reactions, it is very complicated.

Quickies
Did you know...
- that the Japanese say that sneezing twice in a row means that someone is talking about you?
- that during the great plague, sneezing was a sign of infection which meant almost certain death? People began saying "God bless you" as a prayer for the doomed infected sneezer. Today we still say "bless you" as a holdover from those terrible times.

Who was the first person to document the effects of an epidemic?

Plagues have long figured largely in myths, legends, and Biblical stories — in the latter often as the wrath of God. The first ancient writer to leave a factual account of an epidemic, from the symptoms shown by individual sufferers, to the demoralizing effects on the population, was the Athenian historian Thucydides. He chronicled the strange plague that devastated Athens in 430 BC while the city was under siege by the Spartans.

What was the Black Death?

From 1348 to 1666 "Black Death" was the name given to bubonic plague, so called because the first symptoms were swelling of the lymph glands — which were then called buboes — in the groin and armpits. The cause of the disease was a bacterium called *Pasteurella pestis*, which was carried by rats and other rodents. It was spread to humans by fleas. The disease was then passed from person to person by droplets of moisture. A sneeze, a cough, or a kiss was all it took. It has been estimated that over 25 million people, about a third of the population of Europe, died.

Why didn't people carry out large-scale rat extermination campaigns to fight the Black Death?

At the time people knew nothing about germs and bacteria. They thought diseases were caused by "evil vapours" that came from the ground, or "ill humours" in the body, caused by an imbalance of fluids; hence the practice of doctors "bleeding" patients to try to get the blood back to a "correct" level. Many people believed the Black Death was sent by an angry God to punish the world for its sinful ways. Sanitation and hygiene were extremely primitive. All houses had rats. Everybody had fleas. Nobody made the connection between the vermin and the disease.

Ten Prescriptions to Prevent or Cure Bubonic Plague

- Wear human feces in a bag around the neck.
- Bathe in and drink human urine.
- Take long, deep breaths of the air in a public privy.
- Apply dried toads or lizards to the boils to draw out the poison.
- Pierce the testicles with sharp needles.
- Smear fevered foreheads with the blood of freshly killed puppies and pigeons.
- Slice open the boils and insert red-hot pokers.
- Put down bowls of fresh milk to absorb the poisons in the air in rooms where patients have died from the plague. This can also be done with large, peeled onions. Be sure the onions are buried in a deep hole later.
- Self-flagellate to atone for sins.
- Search the community for any persons guilty of licentious and voluptuous behaviour and put them to death.

How did Queen Victoria revolutionize childbirth?

Britain's Queen Victoria (1819–1901) was very familiar with the discomforts of childbirth. During delivery of the first seven of her nine children, Her Majesty suffered a lot of pain. This agony made her very interested in the discovery of chloroform, which became available as an anesthetic early in her reign. Despite protests against the practice from the Church of England and the medical establishment, she allowed her doctor to administer chloroform during the delivery of her eighth child, Prince Leopold, in 1853. The success of that delivery led to anesthetics quickly gaining popularity among England's influential upper classes.

The queen was so impressed with the benefits of chloroform that she knighted one of her physicians, Dr. James Simpson (1811–1870), who was the first to use it as an anesthetic in 1847.

Does sucking out blood really help to treat a snake bite?

Sucking blood out of a snake bite is not a good idea. Apart from the fact that very little venom is likely to be removed, there is also a chance that the person administering the treatment may take some of it into an open sore in their mouth. Also, cutting the wound open to make it easier to suck the blood increases the chance of infection for the victim, because snake saliva is full of toxic bacteria.

general sports

Why does the home team wear white while the visitors wear dark coloured uniforms?

Early television was in black and white and the definitions weren't nearly as precise as they are today. When the Canadian Broadcasting Corporation (CBC) was testing for live hockey broadcasts in 1952, the company found that if both teams wore their traditional colours, it was impossible to tell them apart. The CBC solved the problem by having the home team wear white, while the visitors stayed in their darker uniforms.

How many coloured flags are used in auto racing, and what do they mean?

Seven flags are used as signals to drivers in car races: a green flag starts the race; a yellow flag means "don't pass"; a red flag means "stop for an emergency"; a black flag signals a rule infraction; a white flag indicates that the leaders are starting the last lap; a blue flag with a diagonal stripe tells slower cars to move aside; and finally the checkered flag means the race is over.

What do baseball, bowling, darts, and billiards all have in common?

Unlike most sports, baseball, bowling, darts, and snooker offer top-quality players the opportunity to achieve a perfect game. If a baseball pitcher throws for nine innings without giving up any hits, walks, or errors, he will have pitched a perfect game. Twelve successive strikes, or 300 points, are a perfect score in 10-pin bowling. Several combinations of nine darts can lead to a perfect game in 501. A perfect game in snooker can be achieved with 36 consecutive shots that yield a score of 147.

Why is Canada's national sport called "lacrosse"?

Lacrosse, "the little brother of war" was considered good training for Native American warriors. Teams consisting of hundreds of players often involved entire villages in brutal contests that could last as long as three days. To the French explorers who were the first Europeans to see the game, the stick resembled a bishop's ceremonial staff, called a "crozier", surmounted by a cross, or *la crosse* — and the sport had a new name.

Why did it take 48 years for a particular Canadian woman to win an Olympic race?

The winner of the women's 100-metre race at the 1932 Los Angeles Olympics was a Polish athlete named Stanislawa Walasiewicz. The silver medallist was Canadian Hilde Strike. In 1980, when the Polish gold medallist was tragically killed as an innocent bystander during a bank robbery, the ensuing autopsy discovered that she was a he, and Strike was ultimately declared the winner.

How many teams in the four major North American professional sports leagues have names not ending in the letter "s"?

There are eight major North American sports franchises whose team names do not end in "s", and none of them are in football. They are: in basketball, the Miami Heat, the Utah Jazz, and the Orlando Magic; in baseball, the Boston Red Sox and the Chicago White Sox; and in hockey, the Tampa Bay Lightning, the Minnesota Wild, and the Colorado Avalanche.

Why do North Americans call the international game of football soccer?

Football goes so far back in history that one form or another has been played by every known civilization. In the 1800s, British football split into rugby and soccer, two games with very different rules. *Soccer* started out as *socca*, a slang abbreviation of *association* as in "association football," and just like *rugby* became *rugger* through slang, *socca* became *soccer*.

How did the Anaheim Angels, the Indiana Pacers, and the Los Angeles Lakers get their names?

The Anaheim Angels took their name from Los Angeles, the city where the franchise began. *Los Angeles* is Spanish for "the angels." The Indiana Pacers represent the home of the Indianapolis 500, where the pace car leads the field. Although lakes are scarce near Los Angeles, they have a team known as the Lakers because they brought their name with them when they moved from Minneapolis, the land of ten thousand lakes.

Who originated the "high five" hand salute?

The celebratory gesture of raising hands to slap palms was first referred to in print as a "High 5" in 1980 because it was introduced by the University of Louisville basketball team during their 1979/80 NCAA championship season. Derek Smith claims to have invented the gesture and named it a "High 5" after he and two other Louisville players, Wiley Brown and Daryl Cleveland, created and practiced the hand gesture during the preseason (1979) and then introduced it during regular league play.

Why is a fighter's sweeping blow called a "haymaker"?

A haymaker is a powerful blow from a fist that, if it connects, will flatten a boxer's opponent. Farmers used to cut hay by hand with a scythe which is a long handled instrument with an extended very sharp blade. (It's the instrument carried by the "grim reaper.") To use a scythe properly, the farmer used long sweeping motions leaving a flattened swath of hay in his path. This sweeping motion resembled the trajectory of the fighters arm when delivering a punch or a haymaker from left field and the recipient of that punch was flattened like the hay.

Why is fist fighting called "fisticuffs?

Boxing is often referred to as the art of fisticuffs. The word began as *fisty cuffs*. It was first recorded as *fisticuffs* in the early seventeenth century. *Cuff* is from the Scandinavian word *kuffa*, meaning "to push or shove," while *fist* in Old English was spelled *fyst* and meant "a clenched hand." *Fisticuffs* means "to strike with a clenched hand."

Odds & Oddities
- The odds against winning an Olympic medal: 662,000 to 1.
- The odds against becoming a professional athlete: 22,000 to 1.
- The chances of a fan catching a baseball during a major league game: 563 to 1.
- The odds of bowling a 300 game: 11,500 to 1.
- The odds of drawing a royal flush in poker on the first deal: 649,740 to 1.

Why is the game with rocks on ice called "curling"?

The first reference to the game we call curling was recorded in Scotland in 1541 and has nothing to do with the curling path of some stones. The game was, and in many places still is called, "the roaring game" because of the rumbling sound the rocks make while sliding over pebbled ice. This rumbling sound was called a *curr* in the Scots language and is how the game became known as curling. (In the Scots language, a curr is among other things, the sound a dove makes when cooing — related to purr) The word *curling* surfaced in 1620 as the name of the roaring game which would be brought to Canada by Scottish immigrants in the early nineteenth century.

Why is a curling tournament called a "brier"?

In 1927, the first Canadian men's curling championship was sponsored by the MacDonald Tobacco Company. The tournament trophy was called the MacDonald Brier Tankard after the name of MacDonald's most popular pipe tobacco. Brier is the name of a plant from which the roots are used to make tobacco smoking pipes. That first Dominion Curling Championship led to the establishment of the Canadian Curling Association in 1935.

What are the origins of the names for figure skating jumps?

The unfamiliar names for figure skating jumps are from the athletes who introduced them:

Axel — The only jump initiated while skating forward, it was named after Norwegian Axel Paulsen who introduced the move in 1883.

Salchow — A jump performed with a backward inside edge takeoff. Ulrich Salchow of Sweden was the first Olympic gold medalist in men's figure skating and World Champion 10 times between 1900 and 1911. A triple Sachow is three complete airborne revolutions.

Lutz — Performed from a backward outside edge. Alois Lutz of Vienna introduced this move in the first decade of the twentieth century.

Why is it so difficult for women to join prestigious British golf clubs?

Exclusive men's country clubs were called golf clubs long before the game was invented. According to an old wives' tale, "GOLF" is an acronym derived from the phrase "gentlemen only, ladies forbidden." The fact is, the word *golf* has its origin in Medieval Dutch and Scots. The Dutch word *kolf* or *kolve* meant "club." Scots dialect transformed it into *golve* or *gouf* and by the sixteenth century it had become *golf*.

Why would a golfer pull a "niblick" out of his bag?

Like every language, the language of golf sees words come and go. For instance, 100 years ago, achieving par might've been described this way: The "duffer" stepped up to the tee, took a good swing with his "brassie," and sent the ball halfway down the fairway. A "mashie" was chosen to make an approach to the green, but he flubbed the shot, winding up in a sand trap to the left. His trusty "niblick" helped him chip from the sand to the fringe of the green. There he decided a "Texas wedge" was the best choice, and miracle of miracles, the ball went right into the cup.

Other clubs in his bag would have included his reliable old "baffie," what we would call a 5-wood; his "jigger," a 4-iron; a "spade-mashie," or 6-iron; a "mashie-niblick," his 7-iron; and a "pitching-niblick," which was his 8-iron.

What were the most medals ever won by a Canadian at the Olympics?

At the Torino Winter Olympics in 2006, Cindy Klassen became the first Canadian Olympian to win five medals in a single Olympic Games. In doing so she broke a record shared by swimmers Elaine Tanner and Anne Ottenbrite. A short and long distance speed skater, Klassen won gold in the 1,500 metre, silver in the women's team pursuit, silver in the 1,000 metre, bronze in the 3,000 metre, and bronze in the 5,000 metre.

When a bronze won at Salt Lake City in 2002 is added to the total, she is the biggest overall medal winner in Canadian Olympic history.

How much faster can a man run the 100-metre event since the first Olympics?

An American named Thomas Burke won the first gold medal in the 100-metre race at the first modern Olympics in Athens, Greece in 1896 with a time of exactly 12 seconds. Another American, Justin Gatlin, won with a time of 9.85 seconds in 2004 in Barcelona, Spain. The best time ever recorded in the Olympic 100-metre event was in Seoul Korea in 1988 by Canadian Ben Johnson, who posted a time of 9.79 seconds. He was later disqualified after testing positive for steroid use. Ben Johnson has recently been seen on Canadian television, in advertisements for an energy drink called … "Cheetah."

Though not an Olympic record, in May of 2008, Jamaican sprinter Usain Bolt set a new 100-metre world record — with a time of 9.72 seconds — while competing in the Reebok Grand Prix in New York.

Where is the world's oldest tennis court?

Falkland Palace in Fife, Scotland is the site of the oldest tennis court still in use. The court was built in 1539, and is used to play 'real' tennis, a racquet sport played inside a closed room. Unlike most real tennis courts, the Falkland

Court is not fully enclosed as it does not have a roof. Another real tennis court was built by Henry VIII in Hampton Court Palace, near London, England. The original court, built in 1532, was demolished. The one in use today dates from 1625.

There are approximately 45 real tennis courts still in existence around the world. The Royal Tennis Court at Hampton Court Palace is the hub of real tennis activity.

Who invented the game of squash?

Squash is a racquet sport played off the four walls of a room. It started in 1830 at an exclusive boarding school in England called Harrow, when students noticed that a punctured racquetball offered a greater variety of shots and lots of exercise. Two schools of the game developed, the English one using a softball, and a North America version that used a smaller hardball. Both games called for a 32-foot-deep court, but the English court was wider at 21 feet, than the 18 1/2 foot courts of the North American game.

The game is now played in almost 150 countries. Championships are held for men and women in many age groups, and the development of glass-walled courts has led to regular television coverage.

football facts

Why was the Cleveland football team named the Browns?

Football franchises move around, and it was the Rams who represented Cleveland before moving to L.A. and then to St. Louis. In 1946, when the city was given a franchise in the AAFC, they held a contest to name the new team, and the winner was the Brown Bombers, after the great champion Joe Louis. However, the name was colour sensitive for the time, and so they compromised by naming the team the Browns after coach Paul Brown.

What does carte blanche have to do with the name of the San Diego Chargers?

The naming of the San Diego football team had nothing to do with a military or an electrical charge. The team was named by the original owner, Barron Hilton, who called them the Chargers after a credit card. Hilton also owned the Carte Blanche credit card. Although to us *carte blanche* might be "white card," to the French it means "blank sheet," to be used like a blank cheque ... preferably to include a ticket to watch the San Diego Chargers.

What does a football player's number tell you about his position?

American football introduced numbers in 1915 and names in 1961, but in 1967, numbers began indicating a player's position and eligibility. Quarterbacks and kickers wear 1 to 19, running and defensive backs, 20 to 49, centres and linebackers, 50 to 59, guards, 60 to 69, tackles, 70 to 79, and finally ends and defensive linemen wear between 60 and 89.

Why are the rules so different in American and Canadian football?

In 1874, Montreal's McGill University was invited to play football against Harvard. Harvard was used to playing with a round soccer ball, with different rules than the Canadians, who played rugby using an oblong ball. The game ended in a tie, but the Americans were so impressed with the Canadian game that they adopted the rules. Football as we know it evolved differently on both sides of the border from that game — which ended in a tie.

How does attendance at the top American college football games compare to NFL games?

Literally hundreds of college teams play football in the United States, and a huge number of fans put good money on the table to watch their games. In 2005, the top 32 National College Athletic Association (NCAA) teams averaged over 78,000 fans per game. That's 10,000 fans more than the average attendance at games played by the 32 professional National Football League (NFL) teams. What's more, their stadiums were filled to near bursting, with attendance at over 97 percent of capacity.

Overall, the 118 college teams in the 1A division drew 45,000 a game. The 21 Bowl games drew about 52,000 fans each. Talk about big business!

How did the NFL's Ravens, Bears, and Packers get their names?

The Baltimore Ravens took their name from the classic poem "The Raven" by Baltimore native Edgar Allen Poe. When a football team moved into Wrigley Field in 1921, they took the name Bears to relate themselves to the stadium owner, the Chicago Cubs. The Green Bay Packers are named after the Indian Packing Company, which, in 1919, gave the team $500 for their first uniforms.

baseball

How was the distance between home plate and the pitching mound established in baseball?

Baseball has gone through dozens of changes since 1845 when 25 year old Alexander Cartwright set the ideal distance between bases at 90 feet. Back then, the pitchers threw underhanded from a distance of only 45 feet but because this seemed to give an advantage to the pitcher it was increased to 50 feet in 1881 which opened the argument that then the batter had the advantage. To address this, overhand pitching was introduced in 1884 which totally overwhelmed the batters and so in 1893 a distinguished committee settled on placing the pitching rubber on a mound 60 feet from home plate. But, like most committee decisions, there was a slight misreading between conception and inception and the rubber was mistakenly placed 60 feet and six inches from the batter where it remains to this day.

"The pitcher's plate shall be 10 inches above the level of home plate. The degree of slope from a point six inches in front of the pitcher's plate to a point six feet toward home plate shall be one inch to one foot, and such degrees of slope shall be uniform."

Who invented baseball?

The New World Settlers from Britain brought with them a game called "rounders." It was a common mans variation of cricket and was recorded as being widely played in the mid-eighteenth century. In rounders, a batter tried to hit a pitched ball and then run 'round from one to five bases in an attempt to reach home without being "plugged" or hit by a ball thrown by the fielders. A plugged runner was out. The bases were posts in the ground. There is a reference to the game as "base-ball" in a children's book dated 1744.

In 1907 an American Commission decided that baseball was invented in 1839 by Abner Doubleday in Cooperstown New York but it was Alexander Cartwright who established the modern field and drafted the first rules of the new game which included plugging for an out as was a ball caught on first bounce. The winner of the game was the first team to score 21 runs.

It's interesting to note that the first form of baseball played in Canada was in Beachville, Ontario on June 4, 1838, the year before Doubleday played at Cooperstown and seven years before Cartwright and his New York Knicker-bockers established his new rules.

A game similar to rounders that was played by British Soldiers was called "bat" and is recorded as being played in places as diverse as Red River, Manitoba, and Huntington, Quebec, during the 1830s.

What's in a baseball?

The baseball got its present size and weight as a result of a rule change in 1872, but the ball's rubber core made home runs difficult to hit. A lively bounce came from the introduction of a cork centre in 1910, and homerun hitters began to be commonplace. In 1931, the stitching that held the cover on the ball was raised, allowing pitchers to throw a greater variety of pitches. The last major change occurred in 1974, when the horsehide cover was replaced by cowhide. The weight of a baseball must be between five and five and a quarter ounces and its circumference from nine to nine and a quarter inches.

The formation of the ball begins with a 1/2 ounce, 2.9 inch diameter cork core. A layer of black rubber is then applied followed by a layer of red rubber each weighing 7/8 of an ounce. Afterwards, 121 yards of blue-gray wool followed by 45 yards of white wool yarn are added to the outside. The ball is then wrapped in cowhide covering held together by 216 stitches and some rubber cement. Red stitches are placed on the ball to allow pitchers to throw curve balls. Curve balls curve since the air resistance on the stitches is non-uniform.

Why were spitballs outlawed?

Spitball pitches used to be very common in the early days of baseball, when the lack of raised stitching on the ball made putting a spin on it very difficult. When the ball is moistened by saliva or some other lubricant like petroleum jelly, the pitcher can release it more smoothly. From the batter's point of view, the pitch leaves the pitcher's hand looking like a fastball, when it is, in fact, travelling much slower. In 1920, a series of rule changes designed to help hitters resulted in spitballs being outlawed in major-league baseball.

Some pitchers continued to use the spitball after the rule change. Perhaps the most famous was a Hall of Fame pitcher, Gaylord Perry, who won 314 games. At 43, he was thrown out of the game for wetting the ball.

Today, a pitch called the split fingered fastball is in the arsenal of several leading major-league pitchers. It is legal, but its behaviour is said to closely resemble a spitball.

Who first called the baseball field a "ballpark"?

"Ballpark" was first used to refer to a baseball stadium back in 1899. With the dawn of the space age in the 1960s, "ballpark" was used in an article in the *San Francisco Examiner* to refer to the safe zone for the splashdown of a space capsule. "Ballpark figure" is first recorded in print in the late 1960s, in the *Wall Street Journal* to indicate a sum of money that is roughly correct.

Why do baseball socks just have a strap on the foot?

Stirrup stockings are holdover from baseball's early days when fabric dyes were not colourfast, and spike wounds were commonplace. Spike wounds happened, because runners often used their cleats to intimidate infielders when sliding into bases. In order to reduce the chance that dyes would get into a wound and infect it, stirrup stockings were developed, and a plain white sock, called a sanitary because it prevented infection, was worn underneath.

What did the Florida Marlins do that no other baseball team in history has done?

In April, 1993, the Florida Marlins began to play baseball in the National League's Central Division. In October, 1997, they became the first team to win a World Series from the wild-card position, beating the Cleveland Indians in seven games. They also achieved the feat faster than any other expansion team. During the postseason, the team was dismantled to cut costs. The next year, they set a record for ineptitude posting a record of 54–108, making them the first team to lose over 100 games the year after winning a World Series.

How many pitchers for Canadian baseball teams have thrown a perfect game?

Dennis Martínez is the only pitcher for a Canadian team to throw perfect game. He threw to 27 batters in a game against the Los Angeles Dodgers on July 28, 1991, which the Expos won, 2–0. Dave Stieb was pitching for the Toronto Blue Jays in 1988, when he became one of only two pitchers to give up a hit to the 27th batter after retiring the first 26. He went on to lose the game.

What does a batting coach mean by a "roundhouse swing"?

Roundhouses used to be common in railway yards as places to store, switch, and maintain locomotives. They featured a round turntable used to put locomotives on new tracks. The turntable's motion gave rise to the expression "roundhouse swing" used in boxing to describe a punch that starts at the side of the body and is delivered in a wide arc. Roundhouse swing is also often used to describe an inefficient power swing in baseball.

Baseball also has a "roundhouse curve," which was the bread and butter pitch of early Hall of Famer Christy Matheson.

When was softball invented?

Softball was invented by George Hancock. In November of 1887, George was among a group of young Harvard and Yale alumni who were fooling around inside the Farragut Boat Club Gymnasium in Chicago awaiting the outcome of a Harvard–Yale football game. When word came that Yale had won, an enthusiastic supporter picked up a discarded boxing glove and tossed it at the Harvard group who then tried to send it back by hitting the glove in the air with a stick. Hancock took the boxing glove and tied it into a ball with the laces, then chalked off an indoor baseball diamond consisting of a home plate, three bases, and a pitcher's box. The group divided into two teams and softball had begun!

It was moved outside in the spring and was played on fields that were too small for baseball. The game, at that time, was alternately referred to as "indoor-outdoor," "kitten ball," or "mush ball." Eventually the rules and equipment evolved into the softball we know today, which is played by millions of people in over 100 countries.

Why does "balk" mean to stop short?

Those who know baseball understand that when a pitcher makes a deceptive move by interrupting what appears to be an intention to throw to a batter, it's called a balk, an infraction of the rules, and base runners all advance. A balk is much more than a baseball term. A horse can balk, or stop short when spooked by an obstacle or a person might balk at continuing with a commitment when a problem becomes clear. *Balk* is from the ancient Anglo Saxon word *balca*, meaning "ridge" and was commonly used as a reference to the mounds of dirt between plowed furrows. This concept of being a ridge or obstacle, allowed the word to evolve into a description of a wooden beam, especially one used to bar a door before the common use of locks and keys. It became an obstruction to thieves. In baseball, when the pitcher toes the rubber, it limits his options to move and it was originally a small wooden plank or beam on the mound or ridge which is how the word *balk* entered the game in 1845.

hockey

What is the origin of the word *puck*?

The origin of the word *puck* is the Celtic game of hurley, where it means "striking the ball with the stick." A "puck-in" after a foul is the act of sending the ball back into play from the sidelines. Since a ball is unmanageable on ice, Nova Scotians and Quebeckers started using a flat wooden puck instead. Their solution was replaced in 1886 in Ontario by a field hockey rubber ball with the top and bottom cut off. Today, a hockey puck is a vulcanized hard-rubber disc, one inch thick, three inches in diameter, and weighing between 5.5 and six ounces.

In Ireland, to "puck" someone means to strike him. A puck bird is a robin-sized bird that dives down on goats and strikes them on the back with its beak.

When was the first curved stick used in hockey?

Three NHL Hall of Famers are credited with bringing curved sticks into professional hockey. Andy Bathgate, a star right-winger for the New York Rangers, began curving the blade of his stick in the late 1950s. Chicago Blackhawk greats Stan Mikita and Bobby Hull popularized the idea in the early 1960s. Soon many players were curving sticks to add speed and unpredictable movement to their shots. Gradually the curves became more and more extreme, prompting the league to set a limit of one and a half inches in 1968. The following year, the maximum curvature was reduced to one inch, and a year later it became half an inch, which is still the rule today.

Why is Toronto's hockey team called the Maple Leafs?

In 1927, after having just been fired by the Rangers, Conn Smythe took the winnings from a horse race and bought the Toronto St. Pats hockey team, re-naming them the Maple Leafs. Impressed with how brilliantly Canadians had fought in the First World War, Smythe named his new team after the soldiers' maple leaf insignia. Smythe is the man who said of hockey, "If you can't beat them in the alley, you can't beat them on the ice."

Why is the Montreal hockey club called the "Habs," and what does their C.H. logo stand for?

The Montreal Canadiens began as an all-French-Canadian hockey team that would be an honest representation of the Province of Quebec. Their nickname, the Habs, is an abbreviation of *les habitants*, meaning "those who live here." The C.H. logo on their sweaters stands for "Club de Hockey Canadien." The Canadiens won their first Stanley Cup in 1916, the year before the NHL was formed.

What is the legend of the New Jersey Devil?

The New Jersey Devils began their NHL life as the Kansas City Scouts. Their tenure there lasted only till 1978, when the NHL approved the team's move to Denver as the Colorado Rockies. In 1982 the Rockies relocated once again, this time to New Jersey. After a fan vote, the new team was christened the New Jersey Devils.

Most tellers of the legend of the Jersey Devil trace the tale back to Deborah Leeds, a New Jersey woman who was about to give birth to her thirteenth child. The story goes that Mrs. Leeds invoked the Devil during a very difficult and painful labour, and when the baby was born, it grew into a full-grown devil and escaped from the house. People in the 1700s still believed in witchcraft, and many felt a deformed child was a child of the Devil or that the deformity was a sign that the child had been cursed by God. It may be that Mrs. Leeds gave birth to a child with a birth defect and, given the superstitions of the period, the legend of the Jersey Devil was born.

How did the Boston hockey team get the name "Bruins"?

In the 1920s, Charles Adams held a city-wide contest to name his new Boston hockey team. Because the colours of his Brookside Department Stores were brown and yellow, he insisted that the team wear those same colours. He also wanted the team to be named after an animal known for its strength, agility, ferocity, and cunning. The public contest came up with the Bruins, meaning a large, ferocious bear.

Why is Calgary's hockey team called the Flames?

The Flames have not always been a Calgary hockey team. They started out in Atlanta during the second wave of NHL expansion in 1972, where the name "Flames" was chosen to remember the torching of the city in 1864 by Union troops led by General William Tecumseh Sherman, during their long march through the South near the end of the Civil War. When the team moved to Calgary in 1980, the name was kept in honour of Calgary's ties to oil.

Why is street hockey called "shinny"?

Although shins take a beating during a game of shinny, the name comes from the Celtic game of shinty. A pick-up game of hockey, either on the street or on ice, shinny has no formal rules, and the goals are marked by whatever is handy. The puck can be anything from a ball to a tin can. There's no hoisting, bodychecking, or lifting the puck because no one wears pads. "Shinny" is a uniquely Canadian expression.

The first professional shin pads were hand-stitched leather-covered strips of bamboo, wrapped around the lower leg outside knee-high stockings.

For many Canadian kids during the 1930s and 1940s, copies of the Eaton's catalogue shoved into their socks were their first shin pads.

Why is three of anything called a "hat trick"?

While in Canada it refers to three goals by a single player in a hockey game, a "hat trick" means any accomplishment of three and comes from the English game of cricket. When a bowler retired three consecutive batsmen with three consecutive balls, he was rewarded with a hat. It became hockey jargon during a time when most spectators wore hats, which they tossed onto the rink as a celebration of three goals by one player. During the 1930s and 1940s a local Toronto haberdasher gave any Maple Leaf hockey player a custom-made hat if he scored three consecutive goals.

How did the Detroit Red Wings and the New York Rangers get their names?

In 1932 James Norris purchased the Detroit Falcons hockey team and renamed them the Red Wings. Norris had played for a Montreal team named the Winged Wheelers, which inspired the name and the winged wheel logo on the NHL's motor city franchise. After Madison Square Garden president "Tex" Rickard bought the New York team in 1926, people began calling them after their owner — Tex's Rangers.

alcoholic beverages

Does Canadian beer taste better than American beer because it has more alcohol?

Canadian beer might feel better than American beer but its fuller taste comes from its ingredients. Canadian beer is brewed with 50 percent more malt barley than its watery American cousin, which relies more on corn. Regular Canadian beer has an alcohol-by-volume content of five percent, while American beer is 4.5 percent. A standard European beer is fuller still, with 5.2 percent alcohol content. Canadian light beer is four percent, while American light is 3.8 percent.

Why is a pint of American beer smaller than a Canadian one?

Since the adoption of the metric system, pints have become rare in Canada. Liquids are usually measured in litres, but the American pint is smaller than the one in Canada because in 1824, when the British introduced the imperial gallon to the world (including Canada), American pride refused to go along with the change. Instead, they kept the outdated original and smaller English gallon from colonial times.

Where did the expression "mind your Ps and Qs" come from?

"Mind your Ps and Qs" means "watch the details," and there are two popular explanations. The first is that because a lower case p and q are mirror images of each other, printing presses had to pay close attention to which one they used. The other, and more likely, explanation is that English pubs marked Ps and Qs on a blackboard to record each customer's consumption of pints and quarts. "Mind your Ps and Qs" meant "keep an eye on your tab."

Why is a glass of tapped beer called a draft?

The many interpretations of the word *draft* (*draught*) are all derived from the word's thirteenth century meaning of "to draw or drag." This gave us draught horses bred for heavy pulling. It also explains the words use as in a "military draft" because this is a group drawn for service from the greater population. It soon became a word to describe a current of air drawn through an opening such as a chimney or window (or a mouth), which led to its use to describe inhaling or drinking. Draft became a reference to beer drawn through the tap of a keg rather than a sealed bottle because like the military draft it's drawn (or drafted) from the greater mass. The word *draft* for a pint of keg beer was reinforced by the act of pouring it into your mouth.

Quickies
Did you know...
- that many types of mouthwash have a greater alcohol content than wine?
- that 20 million people could be fed on the grain used for making alcoholic beverages?
- that one out of every 13 North Americans drinks alcohol every day?

Why is someone who doesn't drink alcohol called a "teetotaller"?

An 1846 tombstone in Preston, England, has the inscription, "Beneath this stone are deposited the remains of Richard Turner, author of the word 'TeeTotal.'" Turner emphasized the "T" to stress the first letter in total. Another group filled out pledges with a letter after their signature to reflect their positions: "M" for moderation, "A" for abstinence, and "T" for total abstinence.

Why is a reformed alcoholic, said to be "on the wagon"?

"On the wagon" originates from two phrases that offer more context, "on the water cart" and "on the water wagon." These phrases refer to horse-drawn vehicles that used to spray water on the roads to keep the dust down. They became associated with drinkers giving up alcohol during the early years of the temperance movement in the late nineteenth century. Men who swore off alcohol said they would climb on the water wagon for a drink, rather than break their vow.

Where do we get the expression "toast of the town"?

By the eighteenth century, wealthy young men had turned feasting into an art, and at the core of the elaborate ritual was the drinking of wine. It was the custom to offer a toast to someone present with every new glass during dinner. When they tired of toasting themselves they would lift a glass in celebration of someone they might not even know, particularly a beautiful woman — who, if frequently admired this way, became known as the toast of the town.

What is the origin of the toast, "Here's mud in your eye"?

During the First World War, soldiers on both sides lived in trenches full of unbelievable amounts of mud. They spent a lot of time pressing their faces into that mud while ducking to avoid being shot. "Here's mud in your eye" is a wishful expression that came out of those circumstances and it simply meant "better to have mud in your face than being shot." If you had mud in your eye, you'd survived!

Where does the expression "bumper crop" come from?

A "bumper crop" is a result of extraordinary abundance. You can have a bumper business, bumper crowds, or bumper crops. This ancient use of bumper comes from a drinking goblet called a "bumper," which was filled to the brim when used for toasts. While quaffing a bumper of ale, drinkers touched (or bumped) these goblets against one another during a festive or celebratory occasion such as an excellent harvest, business growth, or full houses at theatrical performances.

games
and gambling

Why is being called a "lucky stiff" an insult?

If someone wins a lot of money in the lottery and is called a "lucky stiff," it means we think of him as a hard-working, average person who got lucky, but the original meaning of stiff described a failure — someone with as much chance of earning that much money on his or her own as a dead person, also called a stiff. A lucky stiff then means that a person (the lottery winner, in this case) is unworthy and undeserving of monetary gain.

What card game do we get the expression "left in the lurch" from?

To be left in the lurch means to have been put in an embarrassing or difficult position; it is most commonly used when either a bride or groom fails to show up for a wedding. *Lurch* was originally spelled *lurche* and was the name of a card game now known as cribbage. The first player to score 61 won the round, and if this was accomplished before an opponent scored 30, the loser was said to have been "lurched," or left so far behind they had no chance of winning.

Why is challenging the odds called playing "fast and loose"?

"Fast and loose" was a medieval street game played by tricksters in much the same way as a shell game is played today. A coiled belt was laid out on a table with what appeared to be a knotted loop in the centre. Then a mark was invited to stab a knife in the loop, sticking it "fast" to the table. When the huckster easily lifted the belt the sucker lost his money for falling for the illusion that he had made the belt fast instead of leaving it loose.

Why do we say we've "drawn a blank" when things don't click?

Whether it's our mental prowess or our business ventures, when favorable circumstances don't line up we often say we've "drawn a blank." The expression was born after Queen Elizabeth I introduced a national lottery to raise revenue for the Crown in 1567. At the time a lottery required two pots. The names of those participating where written on tickets which were placed in pot one. An equal number of tickets with prizes written on them as well as enough left blank to balance the number with the ticket buyers were placed in pot number two. At the same time that an individual name was drawn from pot one, another to decide the prize was drawn from pot two. Winners won silverware and tapestries; losers drew a blank.

How did the card game "bridge" get its name?

Bridge evolved from a legion of trick taking card games, the most enduring being whist, which got its name from an old English word for "shush," because it's played in silence. Whist has many variations, including a game called Russian whist. Like bridge, this game allows the dealer to choose the trump suit or pass the choice to his partner. Also, during play, the partner's cards are placed face up on the table, and the dealer plays both hands. An alternate name for Russian whist is Biritch. Biritch, it seems, was gradually Anglicized to become bridge.

What is a "tell" in poker?

"Tells" are nervous habits that players repeat under pressure. Experienced poker players watch their opponents constantly for tells, because identifying them can make the difference between winning and losing a big jackpot. A sigh, brushing back the hair, or a grimace can be tells, if they always happen when the player has a good hand, or when he or she is bluffing. Good players learn to disguise their tells or use them to their advantage when bluffing.

Why do we use the expression "close but no cigar"?

"Close but no cigar" is an expression we should be hearing less of as time goes on, as smokers are driven further to the fringes of society. The phrase appears to have originated at the end of the nineteenth century, when it was customary to give out cigars as prizes at carnivals. It's since been used to describe a "nice try" in sports, business, and life in general.

How did the squares on the original Monopoly board get their names?

The first version of Charles Darrow's game of Monopoly was published by Parker Brothers in 1935. Most of the squares on the original Monopoly board got their names from streets, areas, and services in Atlantic City, New Jersey. A few including the "B&O Railroad" and the "Waterworks" came from elsewhere. One of the yellow squares, "Marvin Gardens," is a misspelling of a housing development south of Atlantic City, properly spelled *Marven* with an *e* Gardens.

A second version of the game, introduced in England in 1936 by Waddington Games uses London place names to populate its board.

How old is the game of checkers?

The game we call checkers is played between two contestants, each using 12 small round black or red discs as playing pieces on a flat surface containing 32 squares. The game comes in dozens of other forms, including several computer formats. It is known as "draughts" in most of Europe, where its most common form reached an apex of popularity during the time of Shakespeare. We know from 2000 BC tomb inscriptions that the game was played by the Egyptians as a spiritual way of predicting the outcome of war. As recreation, it was modified and played in ancient India and then by the Greeks and Romans and is a forerunner of chess. The word *checkers* is from the French word *echec* for a playing piece or man. The extended Old French word *eschkier* meant "chessboard."

There is a remote academic belief that the game was created by a magician (Shamoon) to keep King Ramses II (1279–1213 BC) distracted from the consequences of his many war crimes.

police
and thieves

What does "terminate with extreme prejudice" mean?

Kill or *assassinate* are words that can be overused in spy novels. Consequently, authors have found other ways of expressing these absolute endings. One phrase that grabbed the attention of the public at large is "terminate with extreme prejudice." It really made the big time in the 1979 film *Apocalypse Now* in which it described Martin Sheen's mission. Subsequently, "extreme prejudice" was used as the title of a Nick Nolte film about a Texas Ranger, made in 1987. Both screenplays were written by John Milius.

Why is a rough interrogation called "the third degree"?

The third degree is a very difficult and sometimes brutal questioning, especially by police. In fact, without its sinister connotation, the expression comes from the Masonic Lodge and its three degrees of membership, each requiring an increasingly difficult examination. The first is Entered Apprentice, the second is Fellowcraft, and the third degree, the one most difficult to pass, is Master Mason.

Why is a worthless bully called a "thug"?

In India, the British encountered a sinister sect that worshipped the Hindu goddess of death. Known as *thags* in Hindi, they robbed their victims then strangled them with a silk scarf. Indian authorities wouldn't suppress them, and so in the 1830s, the British wiped them out by hanging 400 and imprisoning thousands. The American press picked up the story, and thags became thugs, a generic term for "hoods."

Why do we say "by hook or by crook" when determined to accomplish something by any means?

"By hook or by crook" means by fair means or foul. Today a crook is a thief who uses deception, and to hook something means to steal it. That particular definition comes from the thirteenth century, when hooks used for shepherding were also used by peasants to bend branches when stealing firewood or fruit from the royal forest, and since their deceit was called "crooked" after the shape of their hooks, these thieves became known as crooks.

What is the difference between a mass murderer and a serial killer?

A mass murderer commits multiple murders in a single outburst of violence in a relatively short period of time. Marc Lépine, who slaughtered 14 women at the École Polytechnique of the Université de Montréal on December 6, 1989, was a mass murderer. A serial killer commits multiple murders over a prolonged period of time. John Wayne Gacy, who murdered 33 boys and young men in Chicago between 1972 and 1978, was a serial killer.

What notorious American bandit was divorced while in prison?

In 1929, not-yet-legendary desperado John Dillinger was serving time in prison on a robbery charge, when his wife Beryl divorced him. Dillinger was paroled in 1933 and embarked on a spectacular but short career as a bank robber before being killed by police in 1934.

Who was the "Kissing Bandit"?

Edna "The Kissing Bandit" Murray was a much married and divorced woman who had a penchant for outlaw-types. She had already been married and divorced twice when she married Fred "Diamond Joe" Sullivan before he was executed for murder in 1924. Then she married hold-up man Jack Murray, and got her nickname for allegedly kissing one of Murray's robbery victims. During a colourful career Edna had an affair with notorious gangster Volney Davis, served a term in prison, and had three escapes — as well as two more marriages and another divorce before her death in 1966.

Why is an unidentified person referred to as "John Doe"?

"John Doe" is the name used to describe someone within legal circumstances when the true name is either unknown or indiscreet to reveal. The practice dates back to British courts in the early nineteenth century, when John and Jane Doe were used as names for unknown or unclear defendants in real estate eviction disputes. "Doe" was an extremely rare name, and there is nothing to suggest that any real John Doe ever existed.

Five Other Infamous American Criminals who were Divorced

- Big Jim Colosimo, Chicago gangster. He divorced his wife Victoria, who happened to be a cousin of gangster Johnny Torrio, Big Jim's right hand man. Colosimo was subsequently killed on Torrio's orders, but it was "just business."
- George "Bugs" Moran, Chicago gangster. Moran narrowly escaped being a victim of the St. Valentine's Day Massacre in 1929. When he continued to be involved in bootlegging and gang wars, his wife Lucille decided she'd had enough and filed for divorce.
- Joe Saltis, Chicago gangster. Saltis tried to protect his multi-million-dollar bootlegging profits from the federal government by putting the money in his wife's name. Then, during an argument, Joe took a shot at Mrs. Saltis, and missed. She divorced him and took the money.
- Charles Arthur "Pretty Boy" Floyd, bank robber. The Oklahoma bandit's wife Ruby divorced him while he was serving a prison term for robbery. They got back together briefly while Floyd was making a name for himself as a Depression Era Public Enemy, but they did not remarry. Floyd was killed by police in 1934.
- Ivan "Buck" Barrow, bank robber. Brother of the notorious Clyde Barrow, of Bonnie and Clyde fame, Buck had been married and divorced twice by the time he married Blanche Caldwell, who was also a divorcee. Bonnie Parker, by the way, was separated from her husband Roy Thornton, but not divorced. Buck was killed in a shootout with police in 1933. Bonnie and Clyde were killed in a police ambush in 1934. Blanche served a term in prison.

Who cleans a crime site after the removal of a body?

Perhaps the most emotionally taxing job at the crime scene is that of the trauma cleanup crews, sometimes called "death cleaners." When someone dies, bodily fluids escape, and depending on the circumstances, other human remains may be left behind. After the body is taken to the morgue, private companies are called to clean up the mess. These specialists are often former medical staff and often know something about construction as well. They enter the premises in haz-mat biohazard suits and collect the remains and anything touched by the victim, which can include walls, carpets, furniture, and more.

Why are British police officers known as "bobbies"?

In 1828 Sir Robert Peel, then home secretary (and later prime minister), reorganized the London police force into a modern law enforcement agency. Officers in the new department were known at first as "peelers," after their Irish counterparts in a similar reorganization when Peel was secretary for Ireland some years earlier. Bobby is the shortened, familiar form of the proper name Robert. *Peeler* was gradually replaced in the public vernacular by *bobby*, and members of the London force are still known as bobbies today.

What does a "rubber bullet" do when it hits somebody?

"Rubber bullets," or baton rounds, were designed in Britain for riot control in Northern Ireland. First used in 1970, they were designed to incapacitate like a truncheon or Billy club hit. They were not designed to kill or seriously injure, but deaths and serious injuries have resulted. In 1973, Britain replaced them with PVC "plastic bullets," which have also been criticized for being too dangerous.

How do lie detectors work?

Lie detectors do not detect lies; they detect symptoms of lies. Their other name, polygraph, came about because their many (poly) sensors record their findings on graph paper. Lie detectors monitor breathing, pulse, blood pressure, and perspiration. John Larson, a medical student at the University of California, built the first one, which received widespread use, in 1921.

Why is a lie or a deception called a "falsehood"?

A falsehood is a lie or a distortion of the truth and derives from a time before men wore hats. They used hoods to cover their heads from the elements, and these hoods were designed with fur or something else to indicate an individual's rank within the community. If a con man wished to deceive you, he put on a hood designed to be worn by a person of substance such as a doctor or a lawyer. This tactic enabled him to gain enough trust to set up an illegal scam. The con man did this by wearing a "false hood."

Why do we sometimes say "fork it over" in place of "hand it over"?

The expression "fork it over" has a connotation of urgency to it and is often used dramatically during a criminal holdup. In fact, the expression does have origins in a long-forgotten underworld. Of course, the phrase can also be employed with humour when asking for a financial payment for goods or services rendered or for the repayment of a loan. The "fork" in question is a reference to "fingers," which were the original dinner forks, especially for thieves and other lowlifes.

Why are private detectives called "gumshoes"?

Around the beginning of the twentieth century a popular casual shoe was manufactured with a sole made of gum rubber. They were very quiet and were favoured by thieves who used them during burglaries and other crimes and consequently became required footwear for the detectives hunting them down. The term *gumshoe* stuck with private detectives as it aptly described the stealthy and secretive nature of their work.

Why are informers called "whistle-blowers"?

A "whistle-blower" is an insider who secretly reveals nefarious or scandalous wrongdoing by an organization or a government. The reference is, of course, to a referee or umpire who calls a foul during a sporting event. It was introduced to our vernacular in 1953 by the American writer Raymond Chandler (1888–1959) in his Philip Marlowe detective novel *The Long Goodbye*.

The most famous whistle-blower of the twentieth century was Deep Throat, who revealed the criminal inner workings of the administration of President Richard Nixon (1913–1994) during the Watergate break-in affair. In 2005 the identity of Deep Throat was finally made public. He was W. Mark Felt (1913–), the former assistant director of the Federal Bureau of Investigation during Nixon's presidency.

Why do we threaten to read the "riot act" to discipline children?

In law, a riot is "a violent disturbance of the public peace by 12 or more persons assembled for a common purpose" and may be committed in private as well as public places. The Riot Act, which carried real weight and is the one we still refer to in the expression, became law in England in 1714. It authorized the death penalty for those who failed to disperse after the act had been formally read to those assembled. Thankfully, there have been modern revisions to that act, though the consequences to those who disobey the order to disband can still be severe. Children beware!

murder
most foul

Who was the most notorious mass murderer ever convicted?

A man named Pedro Alonso Lopez claimed to have murdered more than 300 girls (he showed Ecuadorian police the bodies of 53 of them) in Colombia, Ecuador, and Peru between his release from prison in 1978 and his recapture in 1980. Dubbed the "Monster of the Andes," he received a life sentence in Ecuador. By various accounts, he is thought to have died, been released at the border to Colombia, or escaped around 1998.

As bad a Pedro was, a sixteenth-century Hungarian noblewoman in Transylvania named Erzebet Bathory, "The Blood Countess," may have been worse. In 1611, she went to prison for torturing and murdering 80 girls, but a book she kept listed the names of more than 600.

Ten Serial Killer Movies
- *Se7en* (1995, starring Brad Pitt and Morgan Freeman)
- *Helter Skelter* (1976 starring Steve Railsback)
- *Monster* (2004 starring Charlize Theron and Christina Ricci)
- *Silence of the Lambs* (1991 starring Jodie Foster and Anthony Hopkins)
- *Psycho* (1960 starring Anthony Perkins and Janet Leigh)
- *No Country for Old Men* (2007 starring Tommy Lee Jones and Javier Bardem)
- *Dirty Harry* (1971 starring Clint Eastwood)
- *Natural Born Killers* (1994 starring Juliet Lewis and Woody Harrelson)
- *M* (1931 starring Peter Lorre)
- *Night of the Hunter* (1955 starring Robert Mitchum)

Why is poison so rarely used as a murder weapon today?

Poisoning has been around as long as kings, queens, and rivals in love have been plotting against each other. In the nineteenth century, the practice enjoyed a surge in popularity as motive and opportunity collided when insurance policies appeared and household poisons for use in the garden or for controlling vermin became widely available. That prompted new laws designed to make poison more difficult to get, and better science to detect it so police could make arrests. Poisoning is not often chosen as a means of murder today because common poisons are easily detected during an autopsy. However, some poisoners are more inventive, using stimulants and muscle relaxants, or chemicals like ricin and polonium, to ensure that detection remains a challenge.

Where were fingerprints first used to identify a murderer?

The first person convicted of a crime by fingerprint evidence was Francesca Rojas, an Argentine woman who murdered her two children in 1892. She left a thumbprint in blood on a door that matched perfectly with the one taken from her by a police researcher, Juan Vucetich. When confronted with the evidence, Rojas confessed and received a life sentence.

Who invented criminal profiling?

London police doctors Thomas Bond and George Phillips are credited with developing a psychological profile of a serial killer, based on a determination that the person responsible for the Jack the Ripper murders had to have had medical training. In another step forward, a psychoanalyst named Walter Langer developed a profile of Adolf Hitler in 1943. His profile rightly pointed out that Hitler would commit suicide if he was defeated. A further milestone in profiling was achieved by James Brussels, who correctly predicted the personality of "The Mad Bomber of New York" in 1947.

A profiler must:

• study the criminal's actions;

• look for patterns;

• analyze behaviour for insights into the criminal's character; and

• provide a description of the suspect.

order in
the court

Why do we call a predictable trial a "kangaroo court"?

The expression "kangaroo court" came out of Texas in the 1850s. It meant that the accused's guilt was predetermined and that the trial was a mere formality before punishment. Kangaroo was a Texas reference to Australia, a former British penal colony where everyone had been guilty of something, and so if a convict were accused of a new crime, there would be no doubt of his guilt.

Why is a change described as "a whole new ball of wax"?

Seventeenth-century English law used a unique way to settle the contested division of an estate. The executor divided the estate into the number of heirs, and then wrote down each parcel of land in the estate on an individual scroll. To keep it secret, each scroll was then covered by wax and made into a ball, which was then placed into a hat. Beginning with the eldest, the heirs then drew the balls at random, with the estate settled by the contents of each ball of wax.

How did the legal process called "discovery" originate?

Legal "discovery" is rooted in an uncommon sense of the word, meaning "reveal," which dates from the eighteenth century. It calls upon both sides of a civil or criminal case to share (reveal) information that they plan to use as evidence during the trial. Because trials can result in a huge amount of information being gathered by both sides, examination for discovery can be very complex and time-consuming.

12 Courtroom Movies
- *12 Angry Men* (1957 starring Henry Fonda and Jack Klugman)
- *To Kill a Mockingbird* (1962 starring Gregory Peck)
- *Witness for the Prosecution* (1957 starring Tyrone Power and Marlene Dietrich)
- *The Verdict* (1982 starring Paul Newman)
- *Inherit the Wind* (1960 starring Spencer Tracy and Fredric March)
- *A Few Good Men* (1992 starring Jack Nicholson and Tom Cruise)
- *Anatomy of a Murder* (1959 starring James Stewart)
- *Primal Fear* (1996 starring Richard Gere)
- *The Accused* (1988 starring Jodie Foster)
- *Adam's Rib* (1949 starring Spencer Tracy and Katherine Hepburn)
- *Judgment at Nuremberg* (1961 starring Spencer Tracy and Burt Lancaster)
- *Philadelphia* (1993 starring Tom Hanks and Denzel Washington)

Who started the jury system of justice?

The gathering of laymen under the guidance of a judge to establish the truth during legal proceedings is considered to be one of England's greatest achievements. Yet, even though it is the foundation of our current legal procedure, it wasn't simply an English innovation. The raiding, conquering and native peoples of Britain, including the Germanic tribes, the Anglo Saxons, Vikings, Celts, and Romans all used some form of communal gathering to conduct a trial. However, the 12-man foundation of the current system, most agree, was founded in the Frankish inquest and brought to England by the Norman Kings and established specifically by Henry II who set the number of jurors at 12 during the twelfth century. The Normans realized that they needed a jury of native-born Englishmen to appear to administer fair justice within the conquered land. The number 12 was set to have a formidable local opinion of the trial's outcome. The verdict had to be unanimous to be legal and in the beginning, dealt mostly with land claim disputes.

Most scholars discount the idea that the number 12 was chosen from the scriptures, but consider the influence of the church during that time and the fact that there were 12 apostles and 12 tribes of Israel before dismissing this romantic notion.

What are the major differences between civil trials and criminal trials?

Civil trials, or lawsuits, are a method of solving private disputes between two groups of one or more people or organizations. Criminal trials are always between the government and the accused. Civil trials are easier to win than criminal trials, because the case does not have to be proven "beyond reasonable doubt." Instead, the judge or jury at the civil trial need only consider the "preponderance of evidence." In practice this can mean failure to defend a lawsuit may result in the judgment going against you, even if you are in the right.

How did the terms of divorce evolve?

Divorce to the Athenians and Romans was allowed whenever a man's like turned to dislike. In the seventh century it was recorded that Anglo-Saxon men could divorce a wife who was barren, rude, oversexed, silly, habitually drunk, overweight, or quarrelsome. Throughout history, in societies where men were paid dowries, divorce favoured the husband; however, in matrilineal societies where the woman was esteemed, mutual consent was required. The word *alimony* means "nourishment."

What is the difference between fault and no-fault divorce?

At one time the spouse seeking a divorce had to prove that the other spouse had been "at fault"; that he or she had committed adultery or in some way violated the rules of marriage. Legislators believed that many individuals gave false testimony in court concerning their spouses' behaviour because there was no other way out of marriages that had gone bad. No-fault divorce allows couples to break up without one having to accuse the other of misconduct, and without even having to go to court. They can request a divorce simply because they are no longer in love.

When was the first no-fault divorce law enacted?

In 1918, in Russia, the newly established Bolshevik government, in setting up an officially atheist state, stripped all religious institutions of power. Previously the churches, mosques, and synagogues had controlled everything to do with marriage and divorce. Under their authority, divorce was rare and when it was granted, it was strictly on a "fault" basis. Under the new Marxist regime a person seeking a divorce simply had to file a document with the Russian Registry Office. It was not necessary for either spouse to be guilty of any misbehaviour.

When did the United States and Canada get no-fault divorce?

In 1969 the state of California passed the Family Law Act, pioneering no-fault divorce in the USA. By 1985 every other American state had adopted some form of no-fault divorce. In Canada, the Divorce Act of 1968 stated that any married couple who had been separated for a year could be divorced without either party raising accusations of misbehaviour.

What does it mean to give someone power of attorney?

If you give somebody "power of attorney," that doesn't mean they suddenly become a lawyer; it simply means they can legally sign papers and make decisions for you in the area in which you've given them that power. In many, perhaps most, cases, lawyers are given power of attorney — but it doesn't have to be that way.

The British have several additional terms for people who practice law. Lawyer is a general term describing all of them. Solicitors do most of the office work, draft documents, talk to clients, and may only appear as advocates in the lower courts. Barristers do most of the trial work, especially in the higher courts, where they are the only ones who may act as advocates. Attorney has pretty much the same meaning in Britain as in America — one who acts on behalf of another.

What is the difference between a divorce and a separation?

A separation is a trial "parting of the ways." The husband and wife live apart but are still legally married. Sometimes this is a "trial" period to give the couple time and breathing room to see if they can sort out their problems. More often it is a practical measure to keep the husband and wife apart while the process for the more permanent divorce takes place.

> **Quickies**
> **Did you know...**
> • that the oldest couple on record to get divorced were Simon and Ida Stern of Milwaukee, Wisconsin? When they became divorced in February 1984, she was 91 and he was 97.

What is the difference between a divorce and an annulment?

A divorce is the termination according to law of a legal marriage. An annulment is the cancellation of a marriage which, for any one of a variety of reasons, wasn't legal to begin with. Sometimes the lines between "divorce" and "annulment" can be rather blurred. For example, in the Middle Ages a wife could seek an annulment if the man to whom she was legally married proved to be impotent. In more recent times, Lee Bouvier Radziwiłł, Jacqueline Kennedy Onassis's sister, who has been married three times, secured two annulments from the Roman Catholic Church. The first was from husband number one, Michael Canfield, while the second was from husband number two, Polish prince Stanisław Radziwiłł. With the second husband, Lee had two children. Normally, at the time, an annulment could be obtained if the marriage hadn't been consummated. That was clearly not the case here. As an added twist, Stanisław was granted an annulment from his previous wife so he could marry Lee.

How could the court prove if a husband was impotent?

According to one church legal expert, "The man and woman are to be placed together in one bed and wise women are to be summoned around the bed for many nights. And if the man's member is always found useless and as if dead, the couple are well able to be separated." There is a recorded case from 1433 in York, England, in which — as the "wise women" looked on — the unhappy wife did everything possible to arouse her even more unhappy husband, but: "the said penis was scarcely three inches long … remaining without any increase or decrease."

14 Reasons to Annul a Marriage in the Middle Ages

- One or both of the parties were already married to someone else.
- Bride and groom were too closely related by blood, marriage, or some other relationship (i.e., godchild and godparent).
- Either the bride or the groom was too young to be legally married.
- Either the bride or the groom was a heretic.
- The bride wasn't a virgin.
- The marriage wasn't consummated.
- One of the parties didn't consent to the marriage.
- One of the parties was an imposter.
- The dowry wasn't paid.
- The parents of either the bride or groom hadn't consented.
- The clergyman who conducted the marriage was an imposter.
- The wife proved to be infertile.
- The husband proved to be impotent.
- Either the bride or groom had previously consented to marry someone else.

How did the terms of divorce evolve?

Divorce to the Athenians and Romans was allowed whenever a man's like turned to dislike. In the seventh century it was recorded that Anglo-Saxon men could divorce a wife that was barren, rude, oversexed, silly, habitually drunk, overweight, or quarrelsome. Throughout history, in societies where men were paid dowries, divorce favoured the husband; however, in matrilineal societies where the woman was esteemed, mutual consent was required. The word alimony means nourishment.

How could you get a divorce in England in the first half of the nineteenth century?

Until the passing of the Matrimonial Causes Act of 1857, which established divorce courts, the only way an English couple could get a legal divorce was through an act of Parliament. This was not a realistic option for most people. Therefore, many unhappy couples simply parted ways without a formal divorce, and sometimes married other people illegally. This could result in charges of bigamy, with resulting fines and jail sentences.

How did the Matrimonial Clauses Act of 1937 improve the 1857 law?

The Matrimonial Clauses Act passed by Britain's Parliament in 1937 recognized desertion, cruelty, and "incurable un-soundness of mind" as legitimate causes of divorce. Either the husband or the wife could seek a divorce based these causes, as well as the traditional reason of adultery. Moreover, a wife could divorce her husband if he were guilty of rape, sodomy or bestiality. The waiting time for "desertion" was placed at three years, and this was later reduced to two years.

> **Quickies**
> *Did you know...*
> • that in the Middle Ages, when divorce was next to impossible for common people, a husband had an alternative way to relieve himself from the nagging of a wife who was known as a "scold"? He could have her tied to the village ducking stool, and dunked in a river or pool until she almost drowned.

What was considered "desertion" in early-nineteenth-century North America?

In nineteenth-century Canada and the United States there were vast frontier territories in which a man could lose himself, cutting off all family ties. Many husbands who had lost interest in their marriages simply moved on. A wife could divorce a husband who had gone away and not returned for a specified length of time. A husband could divorce a wife if he, as head of the household, decided to move the family to a frontier region, and she refused to go. This was considered "desertion" on the wife's part.

> **Five Steps to Obtain a Legal Divorce in England Before 1857:**
> • Hire an attorney to take legal action against the spouse.
> • Prepare evidence, instruct counsel, prove the case in court.
> • Employ a proctor.
> • Institute a suit in the Ecclesiastical Courts for a divorce a mensa et thoro.
> • Obtain a private act of Parliament to dissolve the marriage.
> All this would have cost about 1,000 pounds, at a time when a working man earned less than 100 pounds a year.

Where did a beauty parlour become a factor in a divorce case?

In London, Ontario, about the turn of

the twentieth century, the wife of a local businessman opened her own beauty parlour. Many people in the community took a dim view of a woman who was married to a successful man operating a business of her own. They asked the husband if he was trying to "corral all the money in London", and withdrew their patronage from his business. The divorce that soon followed was officially due to adultery, but the wife's operation of the beauty parlour placed a strain on the marriage, and was a factor in the divorce trial.

Who gets the better settlement following a split-up?

The survey showed that in 30 percent of the cases the husband and wife shared the assets equally. In 60 percent of the cases the wife walked away with a greater share of the assets than the husband. In the remaining 10 percent of the cases the husband achieved a better settlement than the wife.

Who is more likely to file for divorce, the husband or the wife?

The survey carried out in 2004 indicated that 93 percent of the divorce cases were the result of the wife wanting to end the marriage. Only a small number of the husbands involved contested the divorce.

Quickies
Did you know...
• that in Malaysia, which is ruled by Islamic law, it is now legal for a husband to divorce his wife by mobile phone text message, as long as the message is clear and unambiguous?

What is alimony?

Alimony is allowance for support that a person pays to his or her former spouse. It is usually part of a divorce settlement. Alimony is generally awarded in cases where a spouse is unable to support him- or herself. At one time alimony was paid only by ex-husbands to ex-wives, but now, if the wife is wealthier, it may be she who must pay alimony. A court can order alimony to be paid temporarily while a divorce is in the process of being settled. Alimony is not automatic. It must be applied for. The need for alimony must be proven in court, as well as the ability of the former spouse to pay. Alimony payments stop with the death of the person who has to pay them. They cannot be taken from the deceased's estate. Today almost 90% of divorce cases are alimony-free.

How old is alimony?

Alimony dates back to ancient times. The Code of Hammurabi stated that if a couple divorced, the wife had custody of the children, and the husband was obliged to pay for their sustenance until they were grown. If there were no children, the husband had to return the dowry. However, if the wife had violated the rules of marriage; i.e., committed adultery, the husband could keep the children, was free of financial obligations, and could even sell his wife into slavery. Alimony laws existed in the Roman Empire and in the Byzantine Empire. Alimony as we know it today grew from old English Common Law.

What is child support?

Child support and alimony are not the same. Child support is an ongoing financial obligation that must be met by both parents when minors are involved. The parent who is not actually residing in the same home as the children is nonetheless required to contribute to their support. If an ex-spouse fails to make alimony payments, the other spouse must go through the collection procedures that are available to all creditors; i.e., a collection agency. If a parent fails to make child support payments, the other parent can take legal action that could (in some places) lead to a jail term.

How did divorcing couples divide their property under the old common law?

Before the twentieth century, formal divorce among ordinary people was rare. However, when couples did break up, the ideal arrangement was for them to divide everything evenly, either by deciding who should take which piece of property, or by selling off the property and dividing the money. Sometimes there were special considerations. If the couple owned livestock, the husband got the pigs and the wife got the sheep. This was because the husband had greater freedom of movement, and would be able to herd the pigs, which foraged in the woods. The sheep tended to graze in fields near the house, which is where the wife would most likely be, especially if there were children.

Quickies
Did you know...
- that at one time a woman could seek financial support from a man if she could prove he had promised to marry her, and then reneged on the promise? This is no longer possible today.

What is palimony?

The term *palimony* is a combination of *pal* and *alimony*. It is not a legal term, and is not even officially Standard English. (The legal term is "non-marital relationship contract.") Palimony became part of the jargon in 1977 when divorce attorney Marvin Mitchelson used it in a lawsuit that actress Michelle Triola had brought against her former live-in lover, actor Lee Marvin.

What was the story behind the Triola/Marvin case?

Lee Marvin, a very successful Hollywood actor, and Michelle Triola, a wannabe, had lived together for six years but had never been legally married. When they split up, Triola (who was calling herself Michelle Marvin) attempted to sue Lee Marvin for half of the $3.6 million he had earned during the time they'd been together. Marvin Mitchelson said his client had been Lee Marvin's wife in all but name, and therefore was entitled to the money. The case was widely covered by the media. Triola said, "I gave Lee the best years of my life." Marvin responded, "Yeah? Well, I also gave her the best years of her life." Initially a judge denied Triola the full 50 percent of Marvin's earnings, but ordered the star to pay her $104,000 for rehabilitation purposes. Later the California Court of Appeal ruled that there had been no contract of any sort between Marvin and Triola, and he was not obliged to pay her anything. At the time of the trial, many other male celebrities in non-marital relationships worried about being "Marvinized."

How does palimony differ from alimony?

A palimony lawsuit is more like a lawsuit for breach of contract than a divorce suit. Unlike marriage, which is regulated by law, there are no set laws for unmarried co-habitation. Each palimony case must be decided upon individually, and they are generally difficult for the plaintiff to win, unless there is a signed contract. Unlike alimony, which involves ongoing payments of money, a palimony settlement is a lump sum.

Famous Palimony Cases
- In 1982 entertainer Liberace was sued for $113 million by former lover Scott Thorson. The court awarded Thorson $95,000.
- In 1989 Marc Christian successfully sued the estate of his former lover, the late Rock Hudson, for $14.5 million on the grounds that Hudson had concealed having AIDS.
- In 1991 author Judy Nelson sued her former lover, tennis star Martina Navratilova, for $15 million. They settled out of court.
- In 1996 pianist Van Cliburn was sued by former lover Thomas Zaremba. The case was dismissed.
- In 2004 comedian Bill Maher was sued for $9 million by ex-girlfriend Nancy "Coco" Johnson. The case was dismissed.

What was the largest divorce settlement to be made public in Canada?

In the year 2000 mining magnate Charles (Chuck) Fipke had to pay $120 million to his wife of 34 years, Marlene. Fipke struck it rich when he discovered diamonds in Canada's Far North. Marlene had been with him from the beginning, prospecting all over the world.

12 Factors for Deciding How Much a Spouse Will have to Pay:
- The length of the marriage.
- The financial needs of each spouse and the ability to pay.
- The physical and emotional health and age of each spouse.
- The standard of living established during the marriage, and each spouse's ability to maintain a standard of living reasonably close to that standard.
- Each spouse's ability to hold a job or in some manner earn a living.
- The length of time it has been since the party seeking alimony has held a job.
- The child care responsibilities of the spouse seeking alimony.
- Each party's financial and other contributions to the marriage.
- Other income available to either spouse.
- The possible tax-related effects of any alimony awarded.
- The division of marital property.
- Any other considerations the court feels relevant.

What was the world's largest divorce settlement?

In the year 2000 Australian-American media tycoon Rupert Murdoch had to pay $1.7 billion to Anna (nee Torv), to whom he'd been married for 32 years. Anna had once been a journalism student working for one of Murdoch's papers, the Sydney Daily Telegraph, and was author of two novels.

Who gets the cat (or any other pet) in a divorce settlement?

As far as the courts are concerned, family pets are personal property and therefore must be dealt with through the process of equitable distribution rather than through orders for custody and visitation rights. However, court officials also take into consideration the fact that the affection people feel for pets is real and palpable. They generally feel that decisions on who gets possession of the pet should be based on what is in the best interests of the pet.

How did "condonation" affect divorce?

If a person learned that his or her spouse had been unfaithful, the person was expected to cease cohabiting with the offending spouse immediately. To remain under the same roof was seen as "condonation" of the immoral behaviour. This would seriously hamper an attempt to divorce the spouse on the grounds of adultery. The idea of condonation could make things especially difficult for a wife whose husband was guilty of adultery. In many instances the wife was financially dependent on the husband, and had nowhere to go if she left his house.

What are "connivance," "provocation," and "collusion"?

Connivance means setting up a situation so that another person commits, or appears to commit, a wrongdoing; i.e., one spouse arranges for the other to be in the same house as a third party, and then accuses them of having an affair. Provocation is inciting another person to do a certain act; i.e., one spouse purposely behaves in such a manner that the other spouse moves out, allowing the first spouse to plead abandonment. In a jurisdiction that does not allow no-fault divorce, or the separation time is longer than a couple wants to wait, they might pretend that one of them is at fault in order to obtain a speedier divorce. This cooperative effort to deceive the judge is called collusion.

The Largest Celebrity Divorce Settlements
- Basketball star Michael Jordan to wife of 17 years Juanita Vanoy — $150 million+
- Singer Neil Diamond to wife of 25 years Marcia Murphy — $150 million
- Director Steven Spielberg to wife of four years Amy Irving — $100 million
- Actor Harrison Ford to wife of 17 years Melisisa Matheson — $85 million
- Actor Kevin Costner to wife of six years Cindy Silva — $80 million
- Director James Cameron to wife of 18 months Linda Hamilton — $50 million
- Pop star Sir Paul McCartney to wife of 4 years Heather Mills — $48.6 million
- Actor Michael Douglas to wife of 23 years Diandra Luker — $45 million
- Singer Lionel Richie to wife of 12 years Diane Alexander — $20 million
- Pop star Mick Jagger to wife of nine years Jerry Hall — $15 million+

**food
and dining**

Why is a select roast of beef called a "sirloin"?

Legend has it that in 1617, during dinner and after a few goblets of wine, King James I of England suddenly stood and drew his sword and, laying it across the entrée, declared: "Gentlemen, as fond as I am of all of you, yet I have a still greater favourite — the loin of a good beef. Therefore, good beef roast, I knight thee Sir Loin and proclaim that a double loin be known as a baron."

Where did croissants, or crescent rolls, originate?

In 1683, during a time when all the nations of Europe were at war with each other, the Turkish army laid siege to the city of Vienna. The following year Poland joined Vienna against the Turks, who were ultimately forced to lift the siege in 1689. As a celebration of victory, a Viennese baker introduced crescent-shaped rolls, or "croissants," copying the shape of the crescent Islamic symbol on the Turkish flag.

Why is a certain kind of bread roll called a "bagel"?

Many North Americans associate bagels with breakfast, but few people realize they were originally made to pay homage to a Polish king who saved Vienna, Austria, from a Turkish invasion in 1683. A local Jewish baker thanked the king by creating a special hard roll in the shape of a stirrup to commemorate the Polish cavalry. One word used to describe a stirrup in Austria is beugel.

In Yiddish, *bagel* means a "ring," often a bracelet. Sprinkled with onions, a bagel is called a *bialy*, for the Polish city Bialystock.

How did pumpernickel bread get its name?

During the winter of 1812, while Napoleon's army was retreating from Russia, the only available food was stale, dark bread. Although his men were dying from hunger, Napoleon ensured that his great white horse, Nicholl, always had enough to eat, which caused the soldiers to grumble that although they were starving there was always enough *pain pour Nicholl*, or "bread for Nicholl." When anglicized, *pain pour Nicholl* became the word *pumpernickel*.

Quickies
Did you know...
- that both Adolph Hitler and Charles Manson were vegetarians?
- that a teaspoon of dry sugar will stop the hiccups?
- that it requires two tons of water to grow enough wheat for a single loaf of bread?
- that the average North American is about 10 lbs overweight? If they lost this weight the savings in energy used to transport them would be approximately one million gallons of gasoline a year.
- that North Americans spend over $400.00 per family each year on pizza?
- that Americans and Canadians throw out about 10 percent of the food they buy?

How long can you keep a fruitcake?

The polarizing fruitcake — loved by some and reviled by others — has some serious staying power! According to *The Joy of Cooking*, a fruitcake soaked in alcohol, buried in powdered sugar, and stored in an airtight tin can last up to 25 years.

Why when humiliated are we forced to "eat humble pie"?

"Humble pie" is an Americanization of the original English expression "umble pie," a staple in the diet of very poor people during the eleventh century. After bringing down a deer, only the men could eat the choice meat from the kill; women and children were fed the innards, or the *umbles*, which they seasoned and baked into a pie. To be forced to eat umble pie was to be placed among the lowest in the social order.

Why are potatoes called both "spuds" and "taters"?

Back in the fifteenth century a "spud" was a short-handled spade that had a general use but was best known for digging up potatoes. People who sold potatoes were called "spuddies." In Britain, "taters" means cold, and — as is suggested in the rhyme "potatoes in the mould equals cold" — potatoes when grown in the mould, which is topsoil, are colder than if they'd grown deeper in the ground; therefore, cold spuds are taters.

What is the difference between maize and corn?

There is no difference between maize and corn in North America. However, there could be a lot of difference between the two in Europe. *Maize* is a Spanish word that probably came from a word that Tahino Indians used to describe their staple crop to Columbus. In Europe, corn is synonymous with grain, and it is used to describe the seed of any grain-producing plant. The fact that corn was more narrowly defined in North America may trace back to early Protestant settlers who were forbidden from eating any food that was not mentioned in the Bible.

> **Quickies**
> *Did you know...*
> • that aside from their own species, humans consume milk from a wide variety of domestic animals? The vast majority is from cows but goats, sheep, and buffalo combine to supply about 55 percent. Other sources include camels, llamas, reindeer, yaks, and horses.
> • cows average a milk production of 38 quarts per day?
> • goats produce between six and 10 quarts per day?
> • ewes (sheep) deliver about one quart per day?
> • buffalo produce about five quarts per day?
> • camels average around nine quarts per day?
> • lactating human women produce about three cups of milk per day?

Where did the coffee habit come from?

Muslims were the first to develop coffee. As early as 1524 they were using it as a replacement for the wine they were forbidden to drink. According to legend, an astute Arab herder noticed that his goats became skittish after chewing on the berries of a certain bush, so he sampled a few himself and found them to be invigorating. The region of Abyssinia where this took place is named Kaffa, which gave us the name for the drink we call coffee.

Why is a wiener on a bun called a "hot dog"?

The evolution of the sausage began in Babylon, and modern incarnations include the Viennese wiener and the frankfurter, which was shaped in the form of a Frankfurt German butcher's pet dachshund. The Dachshund Sausage Dog became very popular in America, where the bun was added in 1904. In 1906, cartoonist Ted Dorgan couldn't spell dachshund, so he simply named his drawing of a dog on a bun covered in mustard a hot dog, and it's been called that ever since.

Why is lemon served with fish?

Although lemon enhances the taste of fish, that isn't the original reason the two were served together. Six hundred years ago, lemon was introduced with fish as a safety precaution. People believed that if someone swallowed a bone, a mouthful of lemon juice would dissolve it. We now know that this isn't the case, but we also understand why they believed it. Sucking on a lemon causes the throat muscles to contort, helping to dislodge any stuck bone.

Where are the breeding waters of the species of fish known as "sardines"?

The name "sardines" is used in reference to over 20 species of fish, and so they breed everywhere. A can of sardines is filled with one of dozens of species of immature ocean fish that happen to get caught in a trawler's net, including pilchard and herring. The same is true of freshwater smelts, which are scooped up by the thousands along inland waterways after hatching in the spring and then fried as a delicacy in butter.

Why is a group of 13 called "a baker's dozen"?

In 1266, the English passed a law regulating the weight and price of beer and bread sold in the marketplace. Bakers depended on middlemen to sell their excess, especially during a good harvest year, but the new law forbade them to offer a discount or a wholesale price. They found a way to skirt the law by adding one extra loaf to each dozen. This thirteenth loaf provided the profit for the middlemen. The practice of adding the thirteenth loaf is older than the phrase; "a baker's dozen" only dates from 1599.

Why did diners name the best bargain of the day a "blue plate special"?

The first fast food restaurants were mobile wagons, and they appeared during the late 1800s. They were called diners because they resembled railroad dining cars. These special cars introduced the blue plate special during the Great Depression of the 1930s after a manufacturer invented a dish with separate, sunken compartments for potatoes, meat, and greens. Disposable and available only in blue, these delicious, quick meals were promoted as the blue plate special.

What is North America's favourite snack food?

North Americans devour 1.2 billion pounds of potato chips each year, making chips our favourite snack food. In 1852 at a resort in Saratoga, New York, Cornelius Vanderbilt sent his French fries back to the kitchen, complaining that they were too thick. Chef George Blum retaliated by cutting new potatoes ridiculously thin, frying them, and sending them back to Vanderbilt — who loved them. Today, a pound of potato chips costs 500 times more than a pound of potatoes.

Ninety-three percent of Americans snack: 50 percent do so two or three times a day, 40 percent four times a day, and three percent five or more times a day. Almost 90 percent of North American households buy potato chips about every three weeks; 76 percent buy tortilla chips once a month. 86 percent of American teenagers eat candy at least once a week.

Why is there a chocolate bar named Sweet Marie?

The Sweet Marie chocolate bar was inspired by a love affair. In 1893, after an evening stroll through the streets of London, Ontario, with his girlfriend Marie, author Cy Warman was so smitten that he sat down in a park and wrote a poem called "Sweet Marie." When musician Raymond Moore read the poem he put it to music, and the song became a hit that inspired a chocolate company to create the Sweet Marie chocolate bar. Cy married his sweet Marie, and together they raised four children in London.

How were "licorice allsorts" invented?

Licorice has been popular in Britain since the Middle Ages when the Crusaders returned with the plant it is made from. Many different candies have evolved that contain licorice, including varieties that surround or layer the licorice with coconut paste. In 1899 a sales representative named Charlie Thompson for the Bassett Company accidentally dropped a tray holding samples of licorice candies in front of a customer. As Thompson picked them up off the floor, the customer asked if he could order them all as a mixture, and "licorice allsorts" were born.

Why is an easy task called a "piece of cake"?

Nothing could be more immediately rewarding than a piece of cake, and to indicate delight, we sometimes say a chore was a "piece of cake." The expression first appears in English literature in a 1936 Ogden Nash (1902–1971) poem called "Primrose Path." During the Second World War, the phrase was adopted by British pilots to describe a target that was easy and fun to attack or destroy, and from there the expression graduated into everyday English.

Why do we say that someone we consider stupid "doesn't know which side his bread is buttered on"?

To not know which side your bread is buttered on comes from a Yiddish folk tale describing the stupidity of the men of Chelm in Poland. The story goes that one day, when someone dropped a piece of bread, the wisest men in town gathered to ponder why it landed butter side up. After weeks of deliberation they concluded that the bread had been buttered on the wrong side.

What is the origin of the expression "done like dinner"?

"Done like dinner" is a Canadian invention that means something like your goose is cooked. It stands proudly alongside a host of other excellent Canadian words and expressions like *canucklehead, grocery police, pogey* (as in UI), *Newfie screech, snowbirds, toonie,* "have the biscuit," and "Take off, eh!"

Why do we call that delicious crustacean a "lobster"?

The average lobster weighs about two pounds, and even though Shediac, New Brunswick, promotes itself as the Lobster Capital of the World, the largest lobster caught was in Nova Scotia and weighed 44.4 pounds. Before the twentieth century, eating lobster was a mark of poverty because to many people they resemble an insect, which is why their Latin name is *locusta*, meaning "locust," which became *lobster*.

When did lobster become popular?

Lobsters have always been popular in Europe, especially in coastal regions, but not so in North America. Early pilgrims found lobsters were so plentiful — covering the beaches at low tide up to two feet deep — that they ground them up and spread them on corn fields as fertilizer. In Massachusetts, servants sometimes protested against having to eat them too frequently.

Why do we say we will take someone's opinion with a "grain of salt"?

This is an expression that goes back to ancient times and probably originated from the observation that salt can spice up a meal that is otherwise indigestible by mind or body. Another theory suggests that it comes from the Roman General Pompey's belief that adding a bit of salt to a poison antidote will help it counter poison more effectively.

We take salt for granted today but it used to be very difficult for many people to come by, and was therefore considered valuable and special.

Why is a small restaurant called a "bistro"?

Legend has it that when the Russian Cossacks occupied Paris in 1815, they were notoriously rude and demanded quick service from local restaurants and bars by shouting what the French understood to be "Bistro!" which sounds very much like a Russian word for "quickly." The word *bistro* has no French root, and so the legend is plausible. Regardless, whether French or otherwise, a bistro promises intimate and rapid service.

Which restaurant meals do North Americans like best?

North Americans eat about half of their meals away from home. Fifty-five percent of the average diet is fast food or junk food, but at a sit-down restaurant, fried chicken is the most popular meal, followed by roast beef, spaghetti, turkey, ham, and fried shrimp. On the other hand, Kentucky Fried Chicken sells approximately 11 pieces of chicken annually for every man, woman, and child in both Canada and the United States.

Why is an important person called the "big cheese"?

The "big cheese" is the person with the authority and responsibility for everything within an organization. In this case, *cheese* is an Anglicization of *chiz*, the Urdu word for "thing." In colonial India, the natives picked up the pre-existing English idiom "the real thing" and made it "the real chiz," which in turn was carried home by the British where to homeland ears *chiz* sounded like *cheese*. In the United States, the "real cheese" was converted to the "big cheese" to describe the most important person in a group.

What is "Yorkshire pudding"?

The eating customs of the poor from all over the world were intended to fill stomachs with little cost. Yorkshire pudding is one of England's answers to this culinary problem. Although we think of pudding as a dessert, Yorkshire pudding is quite different. It can be eaten as a dessert with the addition of toppings, but it is a savoury dish that really shines when it is eaten with meat. The recipe is similar to pancakes, but the batter is cooked in an oven. Traditionally, the batter would be showered with the drippings of a leg of mutton. Today it is more often cooked with the fat from roast beef. Cooked properly, it rises in airy majesty out of its pan and spills over the sides.

A popular variation on Yorkshire pudding is toad in the hole, which is made by roasting sausages in the Yorkshire pudding batter.

Known as "drippings pudding" since the Middle Ages, Yorkshire pudding got its current name from Hannah Glasse, an eighteenth-century cook from northern England who included the formula in a popular book of recipes.

Why do we look wistfully back upon our "salad days"?

Salad days are the "green" days of our youth. William Shakespeare refers to "salad days" negatively when he has Cleopatra mention them in his play *Antony and Cleopatra*, where she claims that her youthful naïveté led to her love affair with Julius Caesar. Since then the phrase has come to mean "youthful good times that are fondly remembered." Curiously, the word *salad* comes from a Latin word meaning "salted vegetables."

Why is a dried grape called a "raisin"?

A raisin is, of course, a dried grape, and like two-thirds of the English language, the word *raisin* comes from Old French, where it means "grape," shrivelled or otherwise. The word *grape* also comes from Old French and means "bunch of grapes." Sultanas and Thompson seedless grapes are the two varieties commonly enlisted to make raisins. Sultanas are used to create golden raisins, while Thompsons fashion dark ones, or they are lightened with sulfur dioxide to turn them golden.

A raisin is a "worried" grape.

Why is a leisurely outdoor lunch called a picnic?

The word *picnic* began as a reference to a fashionable, potluck social gathering held either in or outdoors in England during the eighteenth century. The word *picnic* is from the French *piquenique* which is derived from *piquer* meaning "to peck or pick." The evolution into the common language as *picnic* took place as ordinary people accepted its meaning as "something simple."

Who was the originator of the Graham Cracker?

In the nineteenth century, a New England minister, Sylvester Graham, created the Graham Cracker to fight alcoholism and promiscuity which he believed were caused by eating red meat. A diet of his crackers made with unsifted flour, along with fruits and vegetables was intended to make a person healthier. Now they're popular simply because they taste good and for this reason make up 15 percent of the cracker market. Graham's was the first of a series of dietary health products that would become the breakfast cereal industry. His cracker encouraged Dr. John Harvey Kellogg who followed with Corn Flakes and Charles W. Post who developed Grape Nut Flakes.

Who was the first to preserve food through canning?

Before canning, food on board long ocean voyages and military campaigns was terrible. Scurvy and hunger as well as related diseases brought down more men than combat. In 1795 the French government offered 12,000 francs to anyone who could find an effective means to preserve food for long periods of time. The challenge was taken up by a Parisian chef named Nicholas Appert who figured that if wine could be bottled and preserved, then why not food? It took 15 years of trying before successfully sealing partially cooked food in bottles, then immersing the corked bottles into boiling water before concluding with the theory that properly prepared food sealed in airtight containers wouldn't spoil. He sent samples to Napoleon's army and navy where the supply of 18 different foods, including fresh vegetables and poultry with gravy stayed fresh for more than four months. The Emperor Napoleon personally presented the 12,000-franc reward to Appert.

When the British learned that through preserved food, the French could extend their military campaigns King George III gave Peter Durand a patent in 1810 for his idea of extending the process by using unbreakable sealed tin cans coated in iron instead of glass to preserve food.

Why are members of the Queens Guard called "Beefeaters"?

There are 12 colourfully dressed guards of the Tower of London. Officially known as Yeoman Warders, they were established in 1485 as Henry VIII's body guards. Their chief duty since has been to safeguard the Crown jewels and to look after any Tower prisoners. Today they act as tour guides.

The remaining 73 Beefeaters are officially titled Yeomen of the Guard. As the oldest existing military corps in Britain, they are the Royal Family's principle ceremonial body guard. These guards are called beefeaters because up until the nineteenth century, they were paid with chunks of beef. The nickname was given to the guards by the mass of the envious lower classes that seldom had the luxury of eating beef. Some believe that beefeater is from buffetier which is what the French kings called the guards who protected their royal food, but this is unlikely.

What is "corned" beef?

The delicious delicatessen corned beef sandwich has nothing to do with corn as we know it. Corn originally meant a small seed of wheat or of any other grasses used for food such as oats or rye but was extended as a description of any seed-sized item such as sand or, in this case, a grain of salt. So, corned beef isn't cured with corn at all but with "corns," or rather, grains of salt.

Why is a delicious morsel of food or gossip called a "tidbit"?

Whether food or information, a tidbit is any morsel that is small and tasty. It combines *tid*, a folk word from *betide* or *tidings* which means "chancing across good fortune" and *bit* which is a pronunciation of *bite* or "a small amount."

Quickies
Did you know...
- that biscuit literally means twice baked?
- that pretzels were shaped by a medieval Italian monk to represent arms folded in prayer?
- that hardtack is a sea biscuit, baked with only flour and water for preservation on long ocean voyages?
- that zwieback is German for twice baked?

**pop
culture**

Who first said "heavens to murgatroid"?

Bert Lahr, who played the cowardly lion in the 1939 film *The Wizard of Oz*, starring Judy Garland, used the phrase "heavens to murgatroid" in a 1944 film called *Meet the People*. Later, his voice was imitated by Daws Butler, who provided the voice for Snagglepuss, a Hanna-Barbera character who often used the phrase, and was seen frequently in Yogi Bear cartoons.

Who coined the expression "garbage in, garbage out"?

"Garbage in, garbage out" became famous when used by the brilliant lawyer Johnnie Cochrane (1937–2005) during the O.J. Simpson trial. Its source is the computerese-abbreviated GIGO, which surfaced during the early 1960s. The acronym means that computers can only give you what has been put into them. Unfortunately, in spite of this shortcoming, some people insist on believing computers can't be wrong, so we get the expression "garbage in, Gospel out."

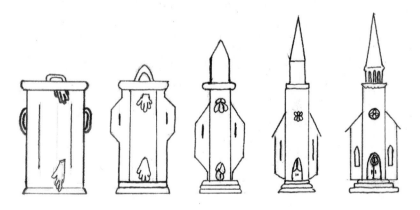

Why is Batman's hometown called Gotham City?

"Gotham City" is a nickname for New York and was introduced by Washington Irving in 1807 as the home of fast-talking know-it-alls. Irving took the name from a legend about King John, who wanted to build a regal estate near the actual Gotham in England but was discouraged when the citizens, not wanting to pay the added taxes, enacted a plan of feigning madness (like real New Yorkers), which caused the king to change his mind in a "Gotham minute."

Is *truthiness* a word?

It is now! Comedian Stephen Colbert's continual use of the word *truthiness* on his "Colbert Report" television show caused the word to be declared the 2005 Word of the Year by the American Dialect Society. Colbert uses an extreme right wing persona in a very clever comedic sense. He is referring to the American "Truth Squad" during the early 1950s when *truthiness* became a political "act or quality of preferring concepts or facts one wishes to be true, rather than those known to be true."

"What probably distorts everything in life is that one is convinced that one is speaking the truth because one says what one thinks" — Sacha Guitry, 1947

Why is a citrus soft drink called 7-Up?

In 1929, Charles L. Grigg of St Louis began selling a lemon-lime soft drink under the slogan "Takes the Ouch out of Grouch," and it became a sensation. One of the soft drinks key ingredients was lithium, a powerful anti-depressant, which was removed in the 1940s. The "7" in the name means seven ounces, while the "Up" is a reference to the carbonated bubbles rising to the surface.

How did the Barbie doll get its name?

Barbie was designed by Ruth Handler and named after her daughter. However, she didn't realize that the original moulds came from an existing German doll named Lili, a popular cartoon prostitute of the time. At first stores refused to stock the anatomically correct doll, until it was neutralized in 1959. By the way, Barbie's measurements if she were life-sized are 39-23-33 ... still pretty sexy.

Why did Charles Schulz name his Charlie Brown comic strip "Peanuts"?

Charlie Brown first appeared as a character in a syndicated cartoon in September of 1950, which was named "Li'l Folks." The most popular children's television show at the time was *Howdy Doody*, and the syndicator insisted that the strip be renamed for the kids in Doody's cordoned-off area for his live children's audience, which was called the "peanut gallery." And so the most popular comic strip in history became known as "Peanuts."

What is the origin of the name of the popular ice cream Haagen-Daazs?

In the 1960s, Reuben Mattas, a Polish-born American from the Bronx, was struggling to sell his quality ice cream when he took note of the popularity of all things Danish modern. He decided to tap into the fad by putting a map of Denmark on his cartons and calling it Haagen-Daazs. Of course, there's no such Danish word as Haagen-Daazs, but this inspiration of marketing genius became a billion-dollar idea.

How did the Singing Chipmunks get their names, and who are the namesakes of Rocky and Bullwinkle?

The Singing Chipmunks were inspired by a near accident when their creator,

Ross Bagdasarian, had to swerve sharply to miss hitting a chipmunk while driving on a country road. He named the trio Alvin, Simon, and Theodore after three record company executives. As for Rocky and Bullwinkle, their creator, Jay Ward, named them after fighter Rocky Graziano and used car salesman Clarence Bullwinkle.

What is the origin of the Frisbee?

In 1870, Frisbee's New England bakery sold pies in round tins, which students at nearby Yale took to tossing as a pastime. In the 1940s, the Wham-O toy company was trying to capitalize on the new UFO mania by selling a plastic flying saucer. When Wham-O noticed Yale students tossing the metal pie plates, they trademarked the name Frisbee and mass-produced the discs in plastic — and a craze was born.

How did the Ferris wheel get its name?

The first Ferris wheel was built by and named after George Washington Gale Ferris (1859–1896) and was constructed as an attraction for the 1893 World's Columbian Exposition in Chicago. Ferris had set out to build a structure that would rival the Eiffel Tower built four years earlier for the Paris Exposition. The two towers that supported the wheel were 140 feet high, the wheel itself was 250 feet across, and the top of the structure was 264 feet above the ground. It held more than 2,000 passengers, cost $380,000 to build, and earned more than $725,000 during the fair.

Unlike the Eiffel Tower, which was going to be dismantled before it found use as a communications tower, the first Ferris wheel was destroyed when the Chicago fair ended.

How did the soft drink Dr. Pepper get its name?

In Virginia in the 1880s, Wade Morrison, a pharmacist's assistant, wanted to marry his boss's daughter. But her father considered Morrison too old for her and asked him to move on. After Morrison had settled down and opened his own drugstore in Waco, Texas, one of his employees came up with a new soft drink idea, which Morrison developed and named after the man who gave him his start in the drug business: his old girlfriend's father, Dr. Kenneth Pepper.

How did the drink Gatorade get its name?

In 1963, Dr. Robert Cade was studying the effects of heat exhaustion on football players at the University of Florida. After analyzing the body liquids lost during sweating, Cade quickly came up with a formula for a drink to replace them. Within two years, Gatorade was a $50-million business. The doctor named his new health drink after the football team he used in his study, the Florida Gators.

Why were teenage girls once called "bobbysoxers"?

Frank Sinatra (1915–1998) was the first pop singer to experience primal teenage female screaming and tearful shrieking during a musical performance. These legions of young women and girls were called bobbysoxers because they were the first generation to wear short or cutoff stockings, leaving their nubile bare legs to disappear beneath a shorter rather than longer skirt. "Bobby socks" or "bobbed socks" first appeared in the 1930s and were so called because they had been cut short. *Bobbed* meant "cut short" like the tail of a "bobtailed nag" or a woman's "bobbed hair."

Teenager was a new word during the time of the bobbysoxers.

Nubile had always meant "marriageable" until 1973 when it came to mean "sexually attractive."

Why is the children's play kit known as LEGO?

LEGO is a trademark name for a child's plastic construction set derived from a 1934 invention by a humble and struggling Danish carpenter named Ole Kirk Christiansen (1891–1958). The company name LEGO comes from the Danish words *leg godt*, meaning "play well." There is a myth that Christiansen didn't realize that *lego* in Latin means "I assemble." In fact, the word in Latin means "I read" and has nothing to do with the legend or the truth of the play kit or the company's name. The motto on the wall of Christiansen's carpentry workshop was "Only the Best Is Good Enough."

Who invented Smarties?

Smarties are a British invention. In 1937, Rowntree of the United Kingdom introduced a line of chocolate beans that, a year later, were given the name Smarties. Packaged in cylindrical tubes, the original eight colours were red, yellow, orange, green, mauve, pink, light brown (coffee centre), and brown (chocolate centre). In 1989 the brown was replaced by blue.

Rowntree merged with the British candy-maker Mackintosh in 1969, and in 1988 the Swiss food-and-beverage conglomerate Nestlé took over Rowntree Mackintosh.

Nearly 16,000 Smarties are eaten every minute in the United Kingdom. Each day about 570,000 tubes of Smarties are made at Nestlé's York factory and shipped to the Middle East, Far East, and South America.

Smarties are also manufactured in Canada by Nestlé, but are not available in the United States because another candy product has trademarked that name.

How did Pepsi-Cola get its name?

During the 1890s, Caleb Bradham (1867–1934), a pharmacist in New Bern, North Carolina, invented a drink for sale to his customers. At first it was only available at his store, so people called it Brad's Drink. Bradham preferred to call it

Pepsi-Cola because he claimed it aided digestion by relieving dyspepsia, a gastric problem, and it tasted a lot like a more established product named Coca-Cola. In 1902, Bradham patented the drink, and his company was successful until 1923 when the high price of sugar forced him into bankruptcy. The company started up again shortly afterwards under new owners. However, Bradham never got back into the business. He died in 1934, owning less capital than he had when he started Pepsi.

Some people argue that pepsin, an enzyme good for treating stomach upset, not dyspepsia, was the source of Pepsi's name, but others say pepsin wasn't part of the original recipe.

Cola comes from the West African Mandingo word *kolo*, a type of tree that grows the leaves that provide a key ingredient for Pepsi-Cola and Coca-Cola.

How did Clark Kent get his name?

When conceived in 1934, Superman was endowed with the strength of ten men, but he couldn't fly. After being turned down by 15 syndicators, the Man of Steel took to the air and acquired the needed strength to become a super legend. Some say Superman's success is within the storyline of his secret identity, whose name was derived from two popular actors of the time: "Clark" Gable and "Kent" Taylor.

Where did the yellow smiley face come from?

The yellow smiley face, with its dotted black eyes, first appeared with a slightly crooked smile as a promotion for the deejays of radio station WMCA in New York in 1962. However, in 1963, commercial artist Harvey Ball introduced the version that's still with us when he curved the smile as a promotion for a major insurance company. Unable to copyright his smiley face, Ball received 45 dollars for its creation.

Why does Tonto call the Lone Ranger "Kemo Sabe"?

In 1933, during the Great Depression, radio station WXYZ in Detroit introduced *The Lone Ranger*. His faithful Native companion, Tonto, was supposed to have been from the Potawatomi tribe, but linguistic scholars were stumped by his reference to the Lone Ranger as "Kemo Sabe." Co-creator Jim Jewell eventually confessed that he had made up the expression from the name of his father-in-law's summer camp, Ke-Mo-Sah-Bee.

Why is hair trimmed straight across the forehead called "bangs"?

Since the beginning of the nineteenth century, a bobtail has described a horse with a very shortly cut tail, while a long but neatly trimmed tail has been called a bangtail. The "bang" refers to the quickness of the cut. The Americans abbreviated *bangtail* to *bangs* in 1878 when hair cut straight across the human forehead became popular. Like the ponytail, the word *bangs* is borrowed from the business end of a horse.

Who was Mortimer Mouse and whatever happened to him?

Mortimer was Walt Disney's original name for a cartoon mouse in the historic 1928 cartoon "Plane Crazy." When Walt came home and told his wife about the little mouse, she didn't like the name "Mortimer" and suggested that "Mickey" was more pleasant-sounding. Walt thought about it for a while and then grudgingly gave in, and that's how Mickey, and not Mortimer, went on to become the foundation of an entertainment empire.

How did the cartoon character Bugs Bunny get his name?

In 1940, Warner Bros. asked its illustrators for sketches of a "tall, lanky, mean rabbit" for a cartoon titled "Hare-um Scare-um." Someone in the office labelled the submission from cartoonist "Bugs" Hardaway as "Bugs' Bunny" and sent it on. Although his drawings weren't used, the words that labelled them were given to the rabbit star of the 1940 cartoon "A Wild Hare," which introduced "Bugs Bunny."

What does IKEA mean?

Born in 1926 in the Swedish village of Agunnaryd, Ingvar Kamprad got his start by riding his bicycle from farm to farm selling wooden matches. Once everyone had a supply of matches, Ingvar wisely decided to diversify his offerings and soon was pedaling around the countryside delivering Christmas tree ornaments, ballpoint pens, and, though it must have been a bit awkward, fresh fish. By age 17, Ingvar had formed his own company and named it IKEA, an acronym made up of his own initials, the name of his family's farm (Elmtaryd), and the village of his birth.

Delivering his products (which now included picture frames, watches, and jewellery) by bicycle was no longer practical, so Ingvar transformed IKEA into a mail-order operation; by 1948 he was also selling furniture produced by local artisans. So successful was his low-priced but sturdy furniture that by 1951 he had dropped all his other products and decided to concentrate on inexpensive but stylish home furnishings.

Quickies
Did you know...
- that the S.O.S. in the cleaning Pads means Save Our Saucepans?
- that S.O.S. was first commercially used to promote mass produced paper bags by a machine invented in 1883 in Fremont Ohio by Charles Stilwell? S.O.S. meant "Self-opening Sack.
- that aluminum foil was developed and introduced by the Reynolds Tobacco Company to protect cigarettes from moisture?

Where did the name Wendy originate?

The name Wendy was invented by J.M. Barrie for a character in his 1904 play *Peter Pan*. The poet W.E. Henley, a close friend of Barrie's, had a four-year-old daughter, Margaret, and because her father always referred to Barrie as "friend," she would try to imitate him by saying "fwend" or "fwendy-wendy." Sadly, Margaret died at the age of six, but her expression lives on in *Peter Pan* and all the Wendys that have followed.

Why is a beautiful blonde called a "bombshell"?

The expression "blonde bombshell," often used to describe a dynamic and sexy woman with blonde hair, came from a 1933 movie starring Jean Harlow. Hollywood first titled the film *Bombshell*, but because it sounded like a war film, the British changed the title to *Blonde Bombshell*. It originally referred only to the platinum-haired Miss Harlow, but has come to mean any gorgeous woman of the blonde persuasion.

How old are baby boomers?

The baby-boom generation is different in some countries because it is defined as those children born to families of servicemen returning home after the Second World War and for the 18 years following. It was decided that in North America this term included people born between 1946 and 1964. In 2006 there were about 76 million baby boomers in the United States and about 9.8 million in Canada. In that year the boomers began turning 60, with the youngest, of course, being 42.

North America's first baby boomer, Kathleen Casey Wilkens, was born in Philadelphia one second after midnight on January 1, 1946.

Was cocaine ever an active ingredient in Coca-Cola?

When Coca-Cola was introduced in 1886 it was sold as a cure for sore throats, nervousness, headache, colds, neuralgia, and sleeplessness, and like other patent medicines of the time, its formula did include a secret amount of cocaine as well as an extract of cola leaves and kola nuts. As knowledge about the dangers of cocaine became known in the new century, the drug was reduced and eventually eliminated in 1929.

Why, during a time of million-dollar prizes, do we still say, "That's the $64 question"?

Quickies
Did you know...
- that after spending $120 for supplies and advertising in their first year, Coca-Cola sold only 25 bottles?
- that Coke® went public in 1919, and one share from that time is currently worth close to $100,000?

In 1941, Bob Hawk emceed a radio quiz called *Take It or Leave It*. Chosen from a live studio audience, the contestants went through seven levels of difficulty, starting at $2 and culminating with a chance at $64. The show's success inspired a dozen imitators, but the original gave us the expression that stuck: "That's the $64 question."

What is the true inspiration for paranormal movies about men in black?

Since the start of the UFO phenomenon in 1947, many who experienced sightings have reported visits from men in black. After approaching Washington claiming that he had proof that flying saucers exist, Albert Bender was visited by three men dressed in black, after whose visit he became gravely ill and refused to elaborate. These men in black, who inspired the popular movies, have only been seen in America.

time
and measure

Why is the letter *K* used to signify a thousand?

If someone tells you they made 40K, they mean 40,000 dollars. The *K* is a symbol for *kilo*, an abbreviation of the ancient Greek word for thousand which is *khilioi*. *K* represents 1,000 in the metric system while *M* represents the same number in Roman numerals.

Quickies
Did you know...
- that there is no system for subtracting Roman numerals?
- that Europeans put a stroke through the number "7" so it won't be confused with the number "1"?

Why is gunpowder weighed in "grains"?

Measurement began with natural units like the width of a thumb, which equalled an inch, or a human foot which, not surprisingly, equalled a foot, and a yard which was the length of the King's arm from the nose to the tip of the middle finger. The basis of Anglo-Saxon weights and measures was the barleycorn. Three barleycorns in a line were another way to measure an inch, and the weight of one barleycorn equalled a "grain."

Why is something obscene said to be "gross"?

Gross began as a prejudicial reference to those who are overweight, during the 1950s. *Gross* is from the Latin *grossus*, meaning thick or large, which in the fourteenth century gave us the word *grocer* for a wholesale merchant who bought and sold in large quantities. To an accountant, *gross* means "without deductions." To "gross out" in the broad sense, as in being disgusted by anything crude or excessive, took hold during the 1960s.

What does it mean to be "on the dot"?

To be "on the dot" means to be on time. It simply means that the minute and second hands are precisely over the dots on the clock face indicating the exact time of the appointment. During a day there are 86, 400 opportunities to be on the dot because that's how many seconds there are in 24 hours.

What is the origin of quarter hour clock chimes?

Clock towers and chimes were once the principle way for people to follow time. Before wrist watches or modern electronic devices, the bell tower kept the community on schedule. Strokes counted out the appropriate number at the top of the hour, while each quarter hour had its own distinct melody. Although there are still many such clocks, the tradition is best known and kept alive by Big Ben at the British Houses of Parliament. The melody of the quarter hour chimes, known as the Westminster Quarters, was written in 1794 by William Crotch. His inspiration was the four variations on the fifth and sixth bars of a section from within Handel's *Messiah* specifically known as "I Know That My Redeemer Liveth." The traditional words added to these chimes are (1) "Oh Lord our God (2) Be thou our guide (3) That by thy help (4) No foot may slide."

Is it the tower or the clock on the British Houses of Parliament that is called Big Ben?

"Big Ben" is neither the tower nor the clock of England's Houses of Parliament. Rather, it's the largest of the bells in the tower clock, which was installed in 1858. London newspapers of the time named it "Ben" after Sir Benjamin Hall, the commissioner of works who was responsible for adding the huge 13.5-ton bell to the tower.

What is the origin of the saying, "There's a time for everything"?

"There's a reason for everything," or better still, "There's an appropriate time for everything", is one of the Bible's greatest simplifications of human life's mystery (Ecclesiastes III). The Biblical passage was set to music in 1952 by Pete Seeger and titled "Turn! Turn! Turn!" It became an anthem within the social turmoil of the 1960s after an arrangement by Roger McGuinn was sung by Judy Collins on a 1963 album and then became The Byrds' first hit in 1965.

> 3:1 To everything there is a season, and a time for every purpose under the heaven:
> 3:2 A time to be born, and a time to die; a time to plant, and a time to pluck up that which is planted;
> 3:3 A time to kill, and a time to heal; a time to break down, and a time to build up;
> 3:4 A time to weep, and a time to laugh; a time to mourn, and a time to dance;
> 3:5 A time to cast away stones, and a time to gather stones together; a time to embrace, and a time to refrain from embracing;
> 3:6 A time to seek, and a time to lose; a time to keep, and a time to cast away;
> 3:7 A time to rend, and a time to sew; a time to keep silence, and a time to speak;
> 3:8 A time to love, and a time to hate; a time for war, and a time for peace.

**america
the beautiful**

Why is the American presidential home called the "White House"?

From 1800, when John Adams became the first president to inhabit it, until 1814, when the British burned it because the Americans had torched Toronto, the presidential building was a grey Virginia freestone. It was painted white to cover up the fire damage done by the British. It wasn't officially called the White House until Teddy Roosevelt began printing its image on the executive mansion stationery in 1901.

How did the American flag come to be known as "Old Glory"?

This famous name was coined by Captain William Driver, a shipmaster of Salem, Massachusetts, in 1831. As he was leaving on one of his many voyages aboard the brig *Charles Doggett* — one that would climax with the rescue of the mutineers of the *Bounty* — some friends presented him with a beautiful flag of 24 stars. As the banner opened to the ocean breeze for the first time, he exclaimed, "Old Glory!"

Why was Abraham Lincoln often called "Honest Abe"?

Probably the most nicknamed president in history, Abraham Lincoln was called "Honest Abe" because he did lots of things to prove he was honest. As a boy he once walked several miles to return a few pennies to someone he overcharged. As a lawyer he often worked for free or very little, and tried to encourage clients to settle out of court, even though he would get no pay. Other Lincoln nicknames included the "Rail Splitter" because he was very good at chopping wood, and the "Great Emancipator," for his role in abolishing slavery in the United States.

How long did the first American astronaut spend in space?

Alan Shepard was the first American astronaut to go into space, using a spacecraft he dubbed *Freedom 7*. The seven was a tribute to him and the other six astronauts selected for Project Mercury, the first American manned space program. On May 5, 1961, his spacecraft reached an altitude of 116.2 miles, and travelled almost 311 miles. He spent a total of 15 minutes and 22 seconds in space.

He went into space again in 1971, with *Apollo 14*, where he spent an additional 216 hours and 42 minutes in space. He also spent some of that time — nine hours and 17 minutes — on the moon's surface.

Yuri Gargarin was the first Soviet cosmonaut. He upstaged Shepard by becoming the first man in space with a flight on April 12, 1961, that included the first complete orbit around the earth. He died while piloting a fighter jet in 1968.

Why did Cape Canaveral become Cape Kennedy and then Cape Canaveral again?

Cape Canaveral, Florida, was named by the Spanish and began to appear on maps around 1564. After the 1963 assassination of President John F. Kennedy (1917–1963) and because he had been such a driving force behind the space program, Jacqueline Kennedy (1929–1994), his widow, asked President Lyndon Johnson (1908–1973) to rename the space facility located there after her late husband. Instead Johnson renamed not just the facility but the entire cape. The move was so strongly opposed by local residents that in 1973 the name Cape Canaveral was restored.

The space facility is still named the Kennedy Space Center. *Cañaveral* means "canebreak" in Spanish, and Cape Canaveral is usually interpreted as "Cape of Canes."

Why are the people of Oklahoma called "Sooners"?

In the 1800s, when the American West was first opened, the early pioneers were offered free land east of the Rockies, but to ensure fairness, they could only stake out 40 acres after a race to the region on a specific date and time. Those heading for Oklahoma who jumped the gun and settled on the best land before the official start of the race were cheating and were called "Sooners" because they arrived "sooner" than those who obeyed the law.

Quickies
Did you know...
- that Ellis Island is named after tavern owner Sam Ellis?
- that between 1892 and 1954, more than 16 million people passed through Ellis Island, hoping to become Americans?
- in 1892 Annie Moore, a 15-year-old Irish girl, was the first person to be processed at Ellis Island?
- that the last person processed through Ellis Island was a Norwegian named Arne Peterssen in 1954?
- that the Bronx borough of New York took its name from the areas first settler, James Bronk?

Why is Missouri called the "Show me" state?

The license plate slogan "show me" implies that the proud people from Missouri need to be convinced before blindly following or believing new ideas. Legend traces its origin to Willard Duncan Vandiver who represented the state in the U.S. Congress from 1897 to 1903. He was more than likely repeating a local homily "I am from Missouri. You have got to show me" when he used it in a Philadelphia during an 1899 naval banquet in Philadelphia.

Why is Boulder City the only city in Nevada where gambling is illegal?

Boulder City was created specifically to house workers from the Hoover Dam building project. Because of the danger and precision of their labour, the government didn't want these men, who earned 50 cents an hour, to be distracted by the consequences of gambling. In 1931, the state of Nevada legalized gambling everywhere except for Boulder City. To this day, Boulder City is gambling free.

The Hoover Dam is 726 feet tall and 660 feet thick at its base. Enough rock was excavated in its construction to build the Great Wall of China.

Why do American broadcasting stations use the call letters *K* and *W*?

During the 1920s, while radio was in its infancy, the FCC assigned the letter *K* to all stations west of the Mississippi and the letter *W* to all those east of the river. Exceptions were made for stations with established call signs, like KDKA in Pittsburgh, and those affiliated with a network. The other three letters are the broadcaster's choice.

What American state has the lowest divorce rate?

Massachusetts, with a rate of 5.7 divorces per 1,000 married couples, has the lowest divorce rate in the United States. Other New England states such as Connecticut and Rhode Island also have relatively low divorce rates.

Why are divorce rates low in New England?

Though it's a matter of much debate, some people believe New England's low divorce rate is due to the large percentage of Catholics and Lutherans in the population. Those congregations have lower divorce rates than other Christian groups. Other people say it has nothing to do with religion, but is due to education. Massachusetts has the nation's highest rate of high school and college completion, which means fewer kids are dropping out of school and marrying young. They also say residents in the New England states tend to live in more stable communities and find more social and family support than in other regions of the country, and therefore enjoy a more nurturing environment for marriage.

What American state has the highest divorce rate?

Nevada consistently places number one as the state with the highest divorce rate, but that is because so many people from outside the state go there for quick divorces. Only about ten percent of the people who get divorced in Nevada each year are actually residents of the state. The state with the highest divorce rate is actually Arkansas, with a rate of 12.7 divorces per 1,000 married couples. Mississippi with a rate of 11.1 and Kentucky with a rate of 10.8 are second and third.

Why are there higher divorce rates in some southern states?

Again, this is a matter of considerable debate. Some people will point out that the states with the highest divorce rates are in what is traditionally called the Bible Belt. Conservative Christian churches discourage young people from having sex before marriage. This, some argue, leads couples into very young marriages. In Oklahoma, another Bible Belt state with a high divorce rate, the average age of people who get married is two-and-a-half years younger than the national average. The churches also encourage young people to marry rather than live together. Other people argue that the higher divorce rates in these states result from lower levels of education and a lower socioeconomic status.

How do divorce laws differ from state to state?

There are more than 35 different legal grounds for divorce in the United States, but not one of them is valid in all 50 states. A person can seek a divorce in Kentucky and Illinois because his or her spouse has a loathsome disease. Joining a religious sect that does not believe in divorce is grounds for divorce in Kentucky and New Hampshire. If one spouse attempts to murder the other, that is grounds for divorce only in Tennessee and Illinois. Divorce can be granted for intolerable severity only in Vermont. In Virginia a person who has been divorced because of adultery cannot remarry without the consent of the court. In 20 states adultery is actually on the books as a crime and the guilty parties can be fined.

What Christian religions in the United States have the highest rates of divorce?

Non-denominational Christians; that is, fundamentalists who do not belong to any of the mainstream churches, have the highest rate of divorce at 34 percent. They are followed by:
Baptists — 29 percent

Mainline Protestants — 25 percent
Mormons — 24 percent
Roman Catholics — 21 percent
Lutherans — 21 percent

What is the divorce rate in the United States for non-Christians?

The divorce rate of American Muslims has been increasing sharply and is now at about 31 percent, but there are concerns within the Muslim community that it could go as high as 50 percent. The divorce rate in the Jewish community is about 30 percent. Among atheists and agnostics the divorce rate is about 21 percent.

How does the American divorce rate break down along racial lines?

White Americans have the highest rate of divorce at 27 percent. They are followed by:
Black Americans — 22 percent
Hispanic Americans — 20 percent
Asian Americans — 8 percent

Why did Reno, Nevada, become the "divorce capital" of the United States?

In the latter part of the nineteenth century, when the rigid ideals of the Victorian Age were taking hold everywhere else, Nevada held onto the rather loose marriage and divorce laws it had legislated during its wild days as a frontier territory. In 1898 New York lawyers discovered that divorces were much more easily obtained in Nevada than in other states. In Nevada, a married person had to be a resident of the state for only six months to be eligible for divorce. In

> **On My Way to Reno**
>
> Billy Murray, an early American singing star, recorded "On My Way to Reno" in 1910. The lyrics were:
>
> My wife and I don't get along
> We simply fight and fight
> I married her to win a bet
> It really serves me right.
> The love she once declared was mine
> Has simply turned to hate
> So I've made up my mind
> To visit old Nevada State.

1913 a morality group in the state had the residency requirement changed to one year — the same as the other states — but Nevada businessmen soon had it changed back to six months. In 1927 this was lowered to three months, and in 1931 to six weeks. By 1940 Reno was the number one divorce spot in the United States. Reno divorce attorneys did a booming business, as did Reno hotels, restaurants, and casinos.

Why is Reno's Virginia Street Bridge famous?

The Virginia Street Bridge, built in 1905, is the oldest functioning bridge in Nevada. According to legend, during Reno's heyday as America's divorce capital, newly divorced people would stand on the Virginia Street Bridge and throw their wedding rings into the Truckee River.

> **Ten Celebrities Who Got Quickie Divorces in Nevada**
>
> - Eddie Fisher — singer
> - Jack Dempsey — boxer
> - Mary Pickford — actress
> - Cornelius Vanderbilt — railway tycoon
> - Estelle Taylor — actress
> - Earl Russel — musician
> - Rita Hayworth — actress
> - Clark Gable — actor
> - Ava Gardner — actress
> - Marquise de la Falaise — filmmaker

oh canada!

What colour is the Canadian flag — white or red?

The Canadian flag is red. On February 15, 1965, when Canada's new flag became official and flew over the country for the first time, the ceremonious proclamation read: "A red flag of proportions two by length and one by width containing in its centre a white square the width of the flag with a single red maple leaf therein."

What flag did Canada use before the red and white Maple Leaf was adopted in 1965?

Before the Maple Leaf, Canada flew a flag based on a design used by the British Merchant Marine since 1707. The flag was red, with a small version of the British Union Jack in the upper left-hand corner. It distinguished itself from the British design by a composite shield which bore Canada's coat of arms. Called Canada's "Red Ensign," the flag was never officially recognized by the Canadian government, and was not flown on federal buildings including the Houses of Parliament until 1948. The Union Jack was used instead.

What tax did the GST replace?

In Canada in 1989, the seven percent Goods and Services Tax (GST) replaced the Manufacturer's Sales Tax (MST), a hidden tax of 13.5 percent charged on manufactured goods that many people didn't even know about. Manufacturers wanted the new tax because they felt the MST made them less competitive against international competitors. Canadians taxpayers didn't want it. Three things upset people about the tax: one, the tax applied to lots of services, like dental appointments, that hadn't been taxed before; two, suspicion abounded that savings from the removal of the MST weren't passed on; and three, it was visible and in your face every time you bought something.

Voters were so enraged by the new tax that when the 1993 election rolled around they threw out the Conservative government of Brian Mulroney, which had brought in the tax, and elected the Liberals, who promised to remove it.

Liberals further fuelled the controversy by failing to deliver on their promise.

In 2006, a new Conservative government was elected. A major plank in its platform was a promise to reduce the GST from seven percent to five percent. The Conservatives kept their promise, and the GST currently stands at five percent.

Why are natives of Nova Scotia called "Bluenosers"?

The famous schooner on the Canadian dime took its name from the natives of the province of Nova Scotia, who are called Bluenosers. The reason for this is that at one time, the province's chief export was a type of potato that featured a protruding blue end, which resembled a nose. As for the proud schooner Bluenose, she earned her way onto the dime by outracing the American schooner Elsie to become the fastest fishing boat on earth.

What are "mummers"?

Mummers put on disguises and go merrymaking through Newfoundland neighbourhoods during the 12 days following Christmas. Wearing costumes that make them appear to be members of the opposite sex and travelling in small groups, mummers begin their visit to a house with a loud knock on the door, which is followed by the cry, "Mummers allowed!" should nobody answer. Once inside, they are noisy, insistent, and uninhibited, and speak while inhaling. The surprised host is expected to offer refreshments and try to guess the identities of the mummers.

The tradition originated in the United Kingdom during the Middle Ages and takes many forms around the world. In Newfoundland, another highlight of the mumming festival is a parade in St. John's.

Is it proper to call Canada's northern Natives Eskimo or Inuit?

Legend has it that the word *Eskimo* was picked up from the Abenaki by European explorers as meaning "eaters of raw meat," but the word was originally *ayashkinew* and referred to the way they tied their snowshoes. It isn't a derogatory word, though erroneously believing this and responding to demands from Eskimo political associations, Canada replaced *Eskimo* with *Inuit*, meaning "human being," in the 1970s. Outside of Canada, Arctic Natives are still called Eskimo.

The Eskimo are the native inhabitants of the seacoasts of the Arctic and sub-Arctic regions of North America and the northeastern tip of Siberia. Their habitation area extends over four countries.

The term *Eskimo* is still used in Alaska, whether or not they are Eskimo culturally or linguistically. For example, while the Yupik people prefer to be called Yup'ik, they don't generally object to being called Eskimo, but they don't consider themselves Inuit.

The Inuit Circumpolar Conference meeting in Barrow, Alaska, in 1977 officially adopted *Inuit* as a designation for all Eskimo peoples, regardless of their local usages.

What Canadian provinces share the longest bridge over ice covered water in the world?

New Brunswick and Prince Edward Island share the Confederation Bridge, which is just over eight miles long, and takes about 10 minutes to cross by car. Ice and salt water were the main challenges faced by the bridge builders. Ice had the potential to destroy the concrete piers that support the bridge. The engineers neutralized this threat by making the piers very heavy, spacing them far apart and placing shields at their bases that force the ice flows to ride up and around them. Salt water corrosion and abrasion from the ice was reduced by developing new types of concrete.

Wind challenged the usability of the bridge. Whistling down the Northumberland Strait, it posed a real threat to large trucks. After extensive wind tunnel testing, barriers more than three feet high were installed on both sides of the road to act as windbreaks.

Where did the most deadly avalanche in Canadian history occur?

Rogers Pass, in British Columbia's Selkirk Mountains, is a well-travelled route through the mountains that is also very prone to avalanches. On the night of March 4, 1910, workmen were busy clearing away the snow and debris from an avalanche that had buried a section of the Canadian Pacific Railway line earlier in the day. That avalanche had come down Cheeps Mountain on the west side of the pass. At about 11:30 p.m. another avalanche came crashing down into the pass, this time from Avalanche Mountain on the east side of the pass. The work crew was caught completely by surprise, and 62 men were killed. Between 1885 and 1911, avalanches in Rogers Pass claimed 250 human lives. The Connaught Tunnel, completed in 1916, allows trains to bypass this deadly corridor.

Where was Canada's first grist mill built?

North America's first grist mill was built by Jean de Biencourt, Seigneur de Poutrincourt, on the Allains River, near Port Royal in the Acadian region of Nova Scotia. He ordered the water-powered mill built because he had witnessed the deaths of six men who were grinding grain by hand. Grist mills and sawmills were among the first industries in new settlements, because they took a great load off the pioneers.

Where was Canada's first newspaper published?

Halifax, Nova Scotia, is generally recognized as the home of Canada's first newspaper. The *Halifax Gazette* made its debut on March 23, 1752. It was published by John Bushnell, at a print shop that had been opened by Bushnell's business partner, Bartholomew Green Jr., who died a few months earlier. Recently, some people have argued that another newspaper, the *Québec Gazette*, which was not published until 1764, should be Canada's first newspaper, because Nova Scotia was not officially part of Canada in 1752.

Where is Canada's only desert?

Canada does have a desert, a true desert, and it's found in the southern part of the fruit basket of British Columbia, the Okanagan Valley. It is not a large desert, it's just 15 miles long, but it is part of a much larger desert complex called the Sonora Desert, which begins in Mexico. There are jackrabbits, horned toads, and rattlesnakes in Canada's desert, as well as cactus, sagebrush, and bush grass, and the Calliope hummingbird, Canada's smallest bird.

When was Canada's first census and who was counted?

Canada's first census was commissioned by the intendant of New France, Jean Talon in 1666. It did not include aboriginals or French soldiers and calculated the population to be 3,215. The first census following Confederation was held in 1871. It found that 3,689,257 people lived in the four founding provinces of Canada; Ontario, Québec, New Brunswick, and Nova Scotia. Today, censuses are held every five years.

The 1871 census asked 211 questions. On marital status, it offered three choices, married, widowed, or other (no mention of single, separated, or divorced). It also asked whether any members of the household were blind, deaf, or simple-minded — questions that were discontinued in 1921.

What was the divorce law in Canada after Confederation?

Section 91 of the British North America Act of 1867 (the Act that made Canada a self-governing nation) placed marriage and divorce under the authority of the Parliament of Canada. Section 92 of the same Act placed the solemnization (wedding ceremony) of marriage in the jurisdiction of the provinces.

Was divorce common in Canada in the nineteenth and early twentieth century?

Between 1867 and 1900, all of Canada had an average of nine divorces a year. In 1900 there were 11. The number slowly began to climb until 1918 when it passed the 100 mark for the first time, with 114 divorces across the country. Even though the population of Canada was growing through birth and immigration, antiquated laws made it very difficult to get a divorce.

Why were inadequate divorce laws not changed?

In the view of many people, any attempt to change the divorce laws amounted to an attack on the institution of marriage. An attack on marriage was seen as an attack on the accepted concept of family and on the distribution of power between the sexes — which of course was heavily in the favour of men. Also, a large number of the legislators in Parliament were Roman Catholic, especially MPs from Quebec, and they were solidly against divorce.

Quickies
Did you know...
• that in late-nineteenth-century Canada it was considered part of a "healthy attitude" to refuse to accept divorced persons into social circles? Divorced people were treated like pariahs. Canadians looked at the United States, where divorce laws were being dramatically reformed, as a frightening example of immorality run rampant.

How did the divorce rate change in the twentieth century?

Slight changes in the laws made it possible for people to apply for civil divorce. More and more people were turning to the courts, instead of Parliament, to get a divorce. For example, of the 51 divorces granted in all of Canada in 1910, 20 were parliamentary. In 1940, of the 2,369 divorces granted in all of Canada, only 62 were parliamentary.

How did divorce in Quebec differ from the rest of Canada?

The civil code of the province of Quebec — strongly influenced by the Roman Catholic Church which was almost invincible in Quebec — absolutely forbade divorce. Quebec couples whose marriages had gone sour had the right, under federal law, to seek a parliamentary divorce, but few did so. Ironically, for those Quebec residents who used the federal law to override the civil code so they could get a divorce, that same civil code provided the wife with a much fairer share of the property than was available to divorced wives in the other provinces. For this reason, in Quebec it was much more likely to be a wife than a husband who initiated a divorce. Of the 117 divorces that took place in Quebec from the beginning of 1900 to the end of 1909, only 10 were initiated by husbands.

When were Canada's divorce laws modernized?

In 1968 Parliament passed the Divorce Act. This Act made it easier for couples to obtain a divorce through the courts, and extended the grounds on which a court could grant a divorce. It covered certain areas that had been neglected by the old law, such as the payment of support by one of the divorced spouses. It partially removed the old concept of "fault" as a requirement of divorce. The Divorce Act was the first law of its kind to be in effect in every province and territory of the nation. This eliminated problems in Quebec and Newfoundland, which previously had no effective laws regulating divorce.

How did the Divorce Act affect the divorce rate in Canada?

In the years immediately following the passing of the Divorce Act, the divorce rate in Canada more than doubled. In 1967, the last year before the Divorce Act became law, there were 11,165 petitions for divorce in Canada. By the early 1970s the number had shot up to 35,000 a year.

Quickies
Did you know...
• that in early-twentieth-century Canada, failure of a husband and wife to exchange Christmas presents was offered as proof that they had withdrawn from a full marital relationship to one in which housekeeping was exchanged for support?

What is Canada's most famous divorce case?

Most Canadians would probably say the most well-known Canadian divorce was that of Prime Minister Pierre Elliott Trudeau and his wife, Margaret. Trudeau and Margaret Sinclair were married on March 4, 1971. She was 22 years old and 30 years his junior. They had three children, the youngest of whom, Michel, was killed in a skiing tragedy in 1998. The publicity and pressure of being Canada's "First Lady" was too much for Margaret, especially when certain aspects of her behaviour in public raised eyebrows across the nation. She allegedly had an affair with an American senator, rumour had her involved with Rolling Stones guitarist Ronnie Wood, and there was an embarrassing photograph of her dancing at Studio 54 in New York. She and Trudeau separated in 1977, and the divorce was finalized in 1984. Trudeau thus became Canada's first divorced prime minister. Trudeau didn't marry again. Margaret did marry a second time, but that marriage, too, ended in divorce.

Why are the Gulf Islands of St. Pierre and Miquelon owned by France and not Canada?

The St. Lawrence Gulf Islands of St. Pierre and Miquelon are governed by France because they were a sweetening of the deal offered by Britain as an incentive for signing the 1763 Treaty of Paris ending the Seven Years' War. France tossed in Grenada and the Grenadines but kept fishing rights off Newfoundland while demanding the return of Guadalupe and Martinique in the Caribbean. There were other negotiated deals, but when the dust had settled, Britain took possession of Canada, which the French had described as "a few acres of snow."

What does the French and Québécois symbol *fleur-de-lis* represent?

The English translation of *fleur-de-lis* is "flower of the lily." The Québécois and French symbol is a stylized depiction of a lily or a lotus flower and was adopted and used by French royalty to signify perfection, light, and life.

Legend has it that an angel presented Clovis I (circa 466–511 AD), the Merovingian king of the Franks, with a golden lily as a symbol of his purification when he converted to Christianity. Another legend claims that Clovis adopted the symbol after water lilies showed him shallow water where he was able to cross a river with his army and win a major battle.

Number of Divorces in Canada by Province and Territory for the Years 1906 and 2003. (In 1906 Newfoundland and Labrador was not a province; 1906 figures for what are now Yukon, Nunavut, and the Northwest Territories not available.)

Place	1906	2003
Newfoundland and Labrador	n/a	662
Prince Edward Island	0	281
Nova Scotia	5	1,907
New Brunswick	1	1,450
Quebec	3	16,738
Ontario	10	27,513
Manitoba	0	2,352
Saskatchewan	0	1,992
Alberta	1	7,960
British Columbia	17	9,820
Yukon	n/a	87
Northwest Territories	n/a	62
Nunavut	n/a	4

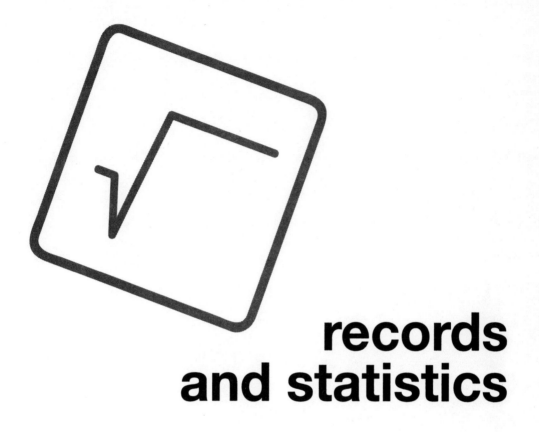

**records
and statistics**

Who is the most married-and-divorced person in the world (on record)?

Mrs. Beverly Nina Avery, a barmaid from Los Angeles, California, had her sixteenth divorce in October, 1957. Mrs. Avery claimed that five of her husbands were wife-beaters who broke her nose.

Who was the most frequently married but never-divorced person in the history of monogamous cultures?

If Theresa Vaughn of Sheffield, England, doesn't hold the record, she must at the very least make the short list. On December 19, 1922, Mrs. Vaughn was taken before a police court in Sheffield on a charge of bigamy. The 24-year-old Theresa confessed to having married 61 men over a period of five years without ever obtaining a divorce from any of them.

What are the statistics for remarriage?

Statistics from the United States Census Bureau show that 12 percent of men and 13 percent of women had married twice. Three percent married three or more times. For people 25 years of age and older, 52 percent of men and 44 percent of women remarried. Canadian statistics show that 75 percent of men and 65 percent of women remarry. Most people wait about three-and-a-half years between their first and second marriages. It has been estimated that 25 to 35 percent of divorced people who don't remarry, enter into a relationship in which they cohabit with a partner.

What is the likelihood that children of divorced parents will also get divorced?

The children of marriages that end in divorce are more likely to become divorced than children of parents who stay together. The rate is 23 percent higher for males and 50 percent higher for females.

Ten of the Shortest Celebrity Marriages
- Rudolph Valentino (actor) and Jean Acker (actress), for six hours in November 1919.
- Jean Arthur (actress) and Julian Anker (photographer), for one day in 1928.
- Zsa Zsa Gabor (actress) and Felipe De Alba (attorney), for one day in 1982.
- Robin Givens (actress) and Svetozar Marinkovic (tennis instructor), for one day in 1997.
- Britney Spears (pop star) and Jason Allen Alexander (Spears' childhood friend), for 55 hours in January 2004.
- Dennis Hopper (actor) and Michelle Phillips (singer, actress), for eight days in the autumn of 1970.
- Cher (pop star) and Greg Allman (pop star), for nine days in July, 1975.
- Carmen Electra (actress) and Dennis Rodman (basketball player), for nine days in November, 1998.
- Catherine Oxenberg (actress) and Robert Evans (producer), for 12 days in July 1998.
- Drew Barrymore (actress) and Jeremy Thomas (bartender), for 29 days in the spring of 1994.

Where was the first same-sex divorce?

On June 18, 2004, two women whose names were not made public were married in Toronto a week after the Ontario Court of Appeal legalized gay marriage. They filed for divorce five days later (making it also the quickest same-sex divorce). They had been living together for several years, and the relationship had become strained. They'd thought that by getting married they might solve some problems.

What was the world's shortest known marriage?

According to a British Broadcasting Company news report, on July 28, 2003, an unidentified Saudi Arabian man divorced his new wife minutes after the wedding ceremony. The bride's brother had just taken a photograph of the newlyweds, and the bridegroom became angry. He tried to strike the brother, but was prevented from doing so. Instead, he told his wife he was divorcing her. Under Islamic law the husband need only repudiate his wife to divorce her. However, this must be followed up with official documentation.

What countries have the highest divorce rates?

Information from some countries can be incomplete, and the numbers are always in a state of change. However, according to data collected by the United Nations, the countries that currently have the highest rates of divorce, based on divorces per 1,000 inhabitants per year, are:

- Maldives   10.97
- Belarus   4.63
- United States   4.34
- Cuba   3.72
- Estonia   3.65
- Panama   3.61
- Puerto Rico   3.61
- Ukraine   3.56
- Russia   3.42
- Antigua and Barbuda   3.40

What countries have the lowest divorce rates?

Once again, based on available information, the countries with the lowest number of divorces per 1,000 inhabitants per year are:

- Belize   0.17
- Libya   0.32
- Mongolia   0.35
- Tajikistan   0.36
- Bosnia and Herzegovina   0.39
- Georgia   0.42
- St. Vincent and the Grenadines   0.43
- Vietnam   0.50
- Armenia   0.62
- Mexico   0.62

How do the odds of getting divorced in Canada compare with those of the United States?

Numbers change from year to year, region to region, and age group to age group. Generally speaking, the divorce rate in Canada is slightly lower in Canada than it is in the United States. Canadian figures show that in the first year of marriage, there is less than one divorce for every 1,000 marriages. After one year of marriage there are 5.1 divorces for every 1,000 marriages. After two years of marriage, there are 17 divorces for every 1,000 marriages. After three years the number jumps to 23.6 per 1,000, and after four years it rises to 25.5 for every 1,000 marriages. After that the chances of divorce decline with each year of marriage, making year four the most dangerous one for Canadian marriages. In the United States the figures are presented a little differently. After five years approximately 10 percent of marriages are expected to end in divorce, with the second year being the one with the highest rate of divorce. By the end of the tenth year of marriage approximately 20 percent of marriages end in divorce. After that the divorce rate goes down with each year of marriage.

What are the main causes of divorce?

According to an Internet survey taken in 2006, 22.8 percent of respondents blamed extramarital affairs, 21.6 percent communications problems, 18.2 percent basic incompatibility, and 16.8 percent emotional or physical abuse.

How did these figures compare with those of previous years?

Causes of divorce for the years 2003 and 2004 were as follows:

Extramarital affairs: 2003 — 29 percent; 2004 — 27 percent
Family strains; 2003 — 11 percent; 2004 — 18 percent
Emotional/physical abuse: 2003 — 10 percent; 2004 — 17 percent
Mid-life crisis: 2003 — not available; 2004 — 13 percent

Addictions (e.g., alcohol, drugs, gambling): 2003 — 5 percent; 2004 — 6 percent
Workaholism: 2003 — 5 percent; 2004 — 6 percent

How did men and women differ in the surveys?

Men were more likely than women to blame basic incompatibility as the cause of their divorce. Of the marriages that broke up because of extramarital affairs, 75 percent were due to the husband being involved with another woman, and 25 percent because the wife was involved with another man. Of the marriages that failed because of family strain, 78 percent placed the blame on the wife's family, and 22 percent on the husband's. In emotional/physical abuse cases, 60 percent had the wife as the abused and 40 percent the husband. For divorces caused by workaholism, in 70 percent of the cases the workaholic was the husband.

Who is more likely to be happy to be single again?

About 85 percent of divorced women say they are very happy with their single status. Only 58 percent of divorced men report the same level of satisfaction.

Quickies
Did you know...
- that divorced men are four times more likely to have a fatal accident than married men?
- that divorced women are twice as likely to have a fatal accident as married women?
- that divorced women are 60 percent more likely to be victims of violent crime than married women?
- that divorced women are 400 percent more likely to commit violent crime than married women?
- that divorced men are 300 percent more likely to commit violent crime than married men?
- that divorced men are four times more likely to commit suicide than married men?
- that divorced women are three times more likely to commit suicide than married women?
- that married men have a six percent lower chance of dying from a heart attack than divorced men?
- that married women have a 37 percent less chance of dying from a heart attack than divorced women?

How does level of education affect divorce rates?

Both men and women who are well educated are less likely to marry while very young. That in itself makes the divorce rate among well educated people lower than it is among people who are not well educated. Even among those who marry at a more mature age, the well educated are less likely to get divorced than the poorly educated.

cities
and towns

What do a "one-horse" and a "jerkwater" town have in common?

In the early days of the railroad, huge tanks were built along the routes where the steam engines could stop and refill by pulling, or jerking, a spout into place, allowing the water to flow from the tank to the engine. The tiny community that grew up around the tank was called a "jerkwater" town. A "one-horse" town was so small that one horse could do all the work and transportation for the entire community which made it about the size of a jerkwater town.

How many cities are there with a population of a million or more?

The United Nations Population Division has projected that the world's population will become seven billion by 2013 and increase to 9.1 billion in 2050. Since most people continue to move to cities, the million-population club of urban centres grows ever more quickly. Rome, Italy, was the first city to reach a million in 133 BC, though after the fall of the Western Roman Empire, that city's population declined so precipitously that it wasn't until about 1930 that it again reached a million. London, England, achieved the one million mark in 1810, and New York City attained it in 1875. In 2005 there were 336 cities in the world with populations exceeding one million.

What is the population of the world's largest cities?

Population of the world's cities is measured in two ways. One is by population within metropolitan boundaries. By that measure, Mumbai (formerly Bombay), India, is the world's largest city with almost 12 million people. Measuring by urban agglomeration, which means the city plus surrounding communities, Tokyo, Japan, leads with a staggering 35 million people, 16 million more than Mexico City, the second-largest.

Measured as an agglomeration, Tokyo has a population of five million more inhabitants than all of Canada. Toronto, Canada's largest city, ranks about fiftieth in the world as an agglomeration of around 4.5 million people.

What is the difference between "uptown" and "downtown"?

When New York City was only a town, its growth was restricted by the shape of Manhattan Island. The word *uptown* first appeared in about 1830 and was used to describe the residential area growing up the Island away from the southern business centre. Within a few years, *downtown* appeared to describe the opposite of *uptown*, or the main commercial district. Today, the suburbs are uptown, while downtown remains the heart of the business district.

What is the full name of the California city known as L.A.?

If any community name ever begged for an abbreviation it would be the California city of Los Angeles. The original Spanish name is *El Pueblo de Nuestra Senora La Reina de Los Angeles*. The English translation is, "The Town of Our Lady the Queen of the Angels" — L.A. is a lot simpler to write on an envelope.

How did the city of Toronto get its name?

There are those who say that "Toronto" was a First Nations chief, while others insist the name refers to a Native tribe. Still others contend the name was derived from the Huron word *toronton*, meaning "meeting place." Research into early French explorers' maps from the 1670s, however, has uncovered the truth. These maps show present-day Lake Simcoe, 75 miles north of Toronto, as Lac Taronto. In Mohawk, *taronto* means "fish trap." The French later applied the name to a trading post at the mouth of the Humber River, inside the boundaries of present-day Toronto.

Besides the trading post, the French also had Fort Rouillé built inside the area of today's Toronto. By the time the British captured the fort in 1760, it was generally known as Fort Toronto. In 1793 Lieutenant-Governor John Graves Simcoe changed Toronto's name to York because he didn't like aboriginal names. The name was changed back to Toronto in 1834.

The Simcoe counties of Tay and Tiny were named after Lady Simcoe's pet dogs.

Why is the city of Toronto nicknamed "Hogtown"?

Toronto became known as "Hogtown" in the 1890s when meat packing was one of the city's principal industries. Animals of all kinds, including the squealing hogs, were off-loaded at the railway yard to be processed and shipped back out as hams.

Why is an area of Toronto known as "Cabbagetown"?

The central, upper-class urban area of Toronto, known as "Cabbagetown" took its name from the front gardens of the poor Irish immigrants who settled there and grew potatoes and cabbages to survive.

**new york,
new york**

Why did the centre of the song-publishing industry become known as "Tin Pan Alley"?

Tin Pan Alley is an actual place in New York City. It's the nickname for the side streets off Times Square, where for generations music publishers have auditioned new songs. The name came from the late 1800s, when the awful sound of cheap tinny pianos coming through the open office windows of hundreds of publishers was likened to the beating of tin pans.

When was the first Macy's Thanksgiving Day Parade?

The Macy's Thanksgiving Day Parade first made its way through the streets of New York in 1925. Since then, it has become the most famous of all the holiday parades, even figuring prominently in the film *Miracle on 34th Street*. The parade is best known for its giant balloons, many of which take the form of popular cartoon characters.

What was the origin of a New York "ticker tape parade"?

Before the electronic age, ticker tape was a thin paper ribbon of information fed mechanically to the brokers on Wall Street. At day's end, floors were ankle deep with ticker tape. On October 28, 1886, the elaborate dedication of the Statue of Liberty was visible from the brokers' windows, causing such excitement that they began tossing ticker tape out the windows. That's how the ticker tape parade became a New York tradition.

How were the NBA's New York Nets named?

A charter member of the American Basketball Association in 1967, this team was first known as the Americans. When they moved to Commack, New York, a year later they chose the name Nets because nets were an important part of the game, and the name rhymed with other pro teams from New York: the Mets and the Jets.

Why do we say, "If you believe that, I've got a bridge I'd like to sell you"?

After the Brooklyn Bridge was built in 1883, a young con man named George Parker approached the gullible as its owner, and after explaining the fortune to be made through toll booths, he would sell the bridge for as much as 50,000 dollars. Parker went to jail for life, but not before selling the Statue of Liberty, Grant's Tomb, and Madison Square Garden — and leaving us the expression, "I've got a bridge I'd like to sell you."

What does the Statue of Liberty have to do with the word *gadget*?

The word *gadget* first appeared in 1886, the year the French gave America the Statue of Liberty. That same year, a man named Gaget, one of the partners in the French company that had built the Liberty, conceived the idea of creating miniature statues to sell to Americans in Paris as souvenirs. The Americans mispronounced *Gaget* and called their miniature Libertys "gadgets," and a new word for something small was born.

What is the full text of the Statue of Liberty poem?

The Statue of Liberty, formally called Liberty Enlightening the World, was a gift from the French to the people of the United States. It has stood since 1886 in New York City Harbor on Liberty Island. The famous poem engraved on a plaque at the base of the statue is a sonnet entitled "The New Colossus." It was written by Emma Lazarus (1849–1887) in 1883 to assist in raising money for the statue's pedestal. In 1903 the sonnet was engraved on a bronze plaque and put in place on a wall in the museum located in the statue's base. The poem was never engraved on the statue itself as frequently portrayed in editorial cartoons. Today the poem sings as a beacon not only to new immigrants but to all who seek to understand the human need for freedom and the original idea of the United States of America.

Emma Lazarus was a child of very successful Jewish immigrants who extended her universal compassion beyond her own cultural heritage. The full text of "The New Colossus" is as follows:

> Not like the brazen giant of Greek fame,
> With conquering limbs astride from land to land;
> Here at our sea-washed, sunset gates shall stand
> A mighty woman with a torch, whose flame
> Is the imprisoned lightning, and her name
> Mother of Exiles. From her beacon-hand
> Glows world-wide welcome; her mild eyes command
> The air-bridged harbor that twin cities frame.
> "Keep ancient lands, your storied pomp!" cries she
> With silent lips. "Give me your tired, your poor,
> Your huddled masses yearning to breathe free,
> The wretched refuse of your teeming shore.
> Send these, the homeless, tempest-tost to me,
> I lift my lamp beside the golden door!"

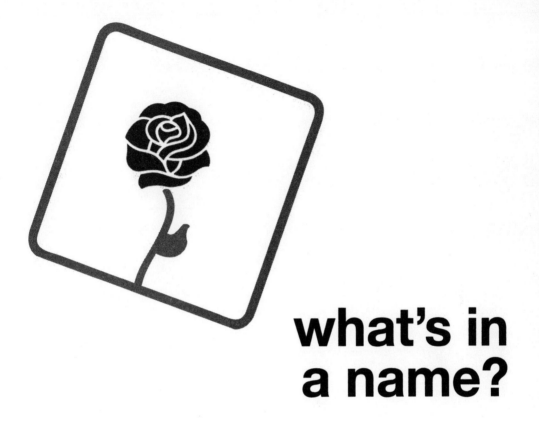

**what's in
a name?**

What do European Jewish names have in common with those of Scotland?

In the sixteenth century, when surnames became necessary so that governments could enforce taxation and conscription, census-taking was introduced. This development meant that everyone needed a last name, something that was against the traditions of both the Gaels of Scotland and the Jews of Poland. Both had survived for centuries with traditional name forms such as "son of ..." (Mac or Mc in Scotland and Ben in Jewish Europe).

After Russia, Prussia, and Austria partitioned Poland in the eighteenth century, Jews, like the Scots, took the names of their hometowns or that of their noble landowners. In Prussia and Austria, the governments went one step farther and decreed that all Jewish surnames would be decided by the state.

In the first few years of the nineteenth century, E.T.A. Hoffmann (1776–1822), a Prussian administration clerk in Warsaw, Poland, amused himself by handing out insulting Jewish surnames according to his own whims, which is why so many Jewish immigrants to North America changed their names as soon as they landed.

Shmiel Gelbfisz arrived in North America from Warsaw at the turn of the twentieth century as Samuel Goldfish. He legally changed his name by keeping "Gold" and adding the last syllable of his friend Archibald Selwyn's last name. Shmiel went on to become the movie mogul Samuel Goldwyn, one of the founders of Metro-Goldwyn-Mayer or MGM.

Besides being responsible for forcing unwanted surnames on Polish Jews, E.T.A. Hoffmann was also a writer of fantasy fiction whose short story "Nutcracker and Mouse King" inspired the ballet *The Nutcracker* by Pyotr Ilyich Tchaikovsky (1840–1893).

Where did our last names come from?

In the Middle Ages, most common people didn't have a last name. Many of our familiar surnames came from the necessity to distinguish between two people with the same first name by adding their occupation, location, or a physical characteristic. William the tanner and William the blacksmith became William Tanner and William Smith. Poor country people who worked the land took the name of their landlord, so a regal surname usually doesn't mean regal ancestry.

Other occupational last names:

Taylor — makes or repairs clothing
Carter — makes or repairs carts
Miller — grinds flour from grain
Wainwright — wagon builder
Bishop — worked with a Bishop

Last names with geographic origins:

Atwood — one who lives near the forest
Eastman — one who is from east of here
Westwood — one who is from the western forest
Dunlop — from the muddy hill
Churchill — lives near a church on a hill

What is the origin of nicknames?

Nicknames are usually pet names of endearment or affection and are derived from a distinct characteristic of or the appearance of the subject. The source is the Old English word *eke*, which means "as well as" or "in addition to." The linguistic transition to *nick*, meaning "devilish," came later. To a stranger a nickname signalled the kind of person they were dealing with by exaggerating either the person's good or bad characteristics.

Why do we say that someone snooping into our lives is "digging up the past"?

When someone is "looking for dirt," or scavenging for scandal in another's earlier life, if they dig long enough they're bound to find something. Of course if you're scrounging through an attic trunk or old scrapbooks, you too are "digging up the past." The expression logically comes from the science of archeology, where people make a profession of "digging up dirt" to understand the present by looking into the past.

How did England get its name?

The country of England got its name from a Germanic tribe that migrated there in the fifth century AD. These Germans called themselves Anguls or Anglas, which became Angles around the fourteenth century. The Angle invaders called their new home Land of the Angles or Engla Land, which through time became England.

The German invaders called themselves Anguls because they were from a district in Schleswig that was shaped like a fishing hook. *Angul* was derived from the Latin *angulus*, meaning "corner," which originated in an earlier Indo-European word *ank*, or "to bend," which had given the district and the people that name.

The word *angling*, as in "fishing," also comes from the Latin *angulus* and was a reference to a bent fish hook.

What is the reason for the "sex" affix in the English regions of Middlesex, Essex, and Wessex?

It's important to understand that the Saxons, along with the Angles and Jutes, were the Germanic tribes which settled in Britain during the fifth and sixth centuries AD. They became what we call the Anglo-Saxons (as opposed to those Saxons still in Europe) and settled in England and the Scottish Lowlands.

Their Germanic language (Old English) prevailed in that country until the Norman conquest of 1066. The place names ending in *sex* are all left from the time and language of the ancient Saxons. *Essex* means a territory of the east Saxons; *Middlesex*, middle Saxons; *Wessex*, west Saxons. The language of the Germanic invaders, along with Latin and French is still a major component of modern day English.

geography

How were The Virgin Islands named?

The Virgin Islands are divided into two parts, one of which is governed by the United States and the other by Britain. They are an archipelago in the Leeward Islands in the Caribbean Sea. They were named by Christopher Columbus after Saint Ursula and 11,000 nuns who in 238 AD were returning from a pilgrimage to Rome when they were massacred by the Huns in a village on the Rhine.

Why does the word *Lake* precede the name of some bodies of water and follow others?

The French word for lake is *lac* and those lakes discovered and named by the early French settlers and explorers have all been named in their own language with the principal name preceded by *Lac*. When the English followed, they left the lake names as the French had recorded them but anglicized *Lac* to *Lake*. The bodies of water beginning with *Lake* generally follow the old French fur trading routes. (Lake Ontario, Lake Rosseau, Lake Muskoka etc). Those ending in *Lake*, were discovered and named by the English.

Odds & Oddities

Antarctica literally means "opposite to the Arctic." The region was first explored in the early 1800s. It has no permanent settlements. The Antarctic Treaty of 1959 prohibits military operations and provides for the international exchange of scientific research. It isn't sovereign and yet belongs to no other country. Ninety-five percent of the continent is covered by an icecap with an average thickness of one mile. This icecap contains 75 percent of all the fresh water in the world. Although covered with ice, the Antarctic is the driest place on earth with an annual precipitation of about 2 inches. Its absolute humidity is lower than the Gobi Desert. The driest place on Earth is in the Antarctic and it has had no rainfall for two million years. In an unsuccessful effort to claim sovereignty over the Antarctic, Argentina sent a pregnant woman to the region in 1978 and although that child was born there, the subsequent claim of citizenship was ignored by the rest of the world.

How much water is in the Great Lakes?

The Great Lakes consist of Michigan, Superior, Huron, Erie, and Ontario. As the largest deposit of freshwater in the world, they hold about 5,472 cubic miles or 22 percent of the world's fresh surface water. The combined surface of the Lakes is roughly 94,250 square miles, which is about the same size as the entire United Kingdom and larger than the combined surface mass of Rhode Island, New York, New Jersey, New Hampshire, Vermont, Connecticut, and Massachusetts. There is enough water in the Great Lakes to cover the 48 contiguous (mainland) states to a depth of 9.5 feet.

Odds & Oddities

The volume of water in the Amazon River is greater than the combined volume of the next eight largest rivers in the world. It has more than three times the water flowing in all the rivers in the United States. The Amazon is so powerful that the fresh water it pushes out into the Ocean can still be used for drinking 100 miles into the Atlantic.

Is Mount Everest the world's tallest mountain?

Mount Everest may be the world's highest mountain, but it's not the tallest. Hawaii's Mount Mauna Kea is 4,000 feet taller, but its huge base is submerged, which means Everest rises higher above sea level. Actually, satellite measurements indicate that the Himalayan peak K2, at 29,030 feet, is two feet higher than Everest, but snow and erosion make precise measurements difficult to attain.

Which American national park is in the mouth of a volcano?

Yellowstone, in the northwest corner of Wyoming, sits in the caldara or basin of a huge, active volcano that last erupted 640,000 years ago, killing prehistoric camels and other wildlife as far as 100 miles away. Visitors to the park see manifestations of its volcanic nature in the many hot springs, mud pots, and geysers that dot the landscape. Park scientists monitor the volcano with sensors scattered throughout the park.

A recent review by the U.S. Geological Survey of 169 volcanoes in the United States rated the threat presented by Yellowstone to be high on a scale of very low to very high, but consistent with historical levels.

Should the volcano erupt again, scientists believe modern detection equipment will give them weeks, months, or even years of warning. Park newsletters keep visitors informed about current conditions.

Quickies
Did you know...
- that Siberia contains more than 25 percent of the world's forests?
- that Africa is 28 percent wilderness?
- that America is 38 percent wilderness?
- that there is a town in the Sahara Desert (Tidikelt) which did not receive a drop of rain for ten years?
- that Spain literally means "the land of the rabbits"?

What are the seven wonders of the world?

The seven wonders of the ancient world were;
1)   The Egyptian pyramids of Giza
2)   The Hanging Gardens of Babylon (Iraq)
3)   The Greek Temple of Artemis (Turkey)
4)   The statue of Zeus at Olympia (Greece)
5)   The tomb of King Mausolus (Turkey)
6)   The colossus of Rhodes (Greece)
7)   The lighthouse at Alexandria (Egypt)

The seven wonders of the modern world (Colliers Encyclopedia) are;
1)   The Pyramids
2)   The Hagia Sophia (Istanbul)
3)   The Leaning Tower of Pisa
4)   The Taj Mahal
5)   The Washington Monument
6)   The Eiffel Tower
7)   The Empire State Building

work
and career

How do the left and right sides of the brain influence a person's choice of career?

Most people tend to emphasize characteristics of the left side of the brain, which controls verbal and analytical skills such as speech, language, and grammar. Lawyers, accountants, politicians, business executives, salespeople, and teachers depend on these skills. On the other hand, the right brain is visual; it jumps easily to conclusions and it gets the big picture. Artists tend to exploit their right brains, while architects, engineers, and doctors effectively utilize both the left and right sides of their brains.

The fact that creative writers use language (governed by the left brain) for their artistic expression doesn't contradict that they are more influenced by the artistic right side. The American writer Mark Twain once sent a manuscript to his publisher with the following message: "Gentlemen: ....???""333......., ,,,,,"(((((()))))!!!..;;;;:!" please scatter these through the attached according to your taste."

Why is a notice of dismissal called a "pink slip"?

When someone is fired or receives their "walking papers," it's often referred to as getting the pink slip.

The expression comes from the nineteenth-century American University custom of notifying their students of exam failures on pink paper. Since then, regardless of the paper colour, notices of "not making the grade" have been referred to as "pink slips."

When being dismissive, why do we say, "Go fly a kite"?

Flying a kite is a good way to see which way the wind is blowing. In the nineteenth century, when a man was looking for employment or searching for investors, he would send out letters to strangers in much the same way as people send out resumes today. "Go fly a kite" meant "I can't help you, but keep sending out those letters."

Why do we say someone's being "called on the carpet" when they're in trouble?

You're "called on the carpet" when you're going to face serious discipline for a mistake, error in judgment, or lie. The expression originated in the military where only senior officers had carpets, and the only reason a soldier would get to stand on one would be if he was in a lot of trouble. The expression has since moved into the business world, where the thought of it continues to strike fear in the heart of any employee who hopes to stay with their company until retirement.

Why is the person with the least significance called the "low man on the totem pole"?

First Nations tribes told their history through the elaborate carvings of creatures on tall totem poles, but the idea that the bottom image was the least important is wrong. It originated with comedian Fred Allen, who, in 1941, wrote, "If humorist H. Allen Smith were an Indian he'd be low man on the totem pole." Smith later used the phrase as a book title, and the expression caught on.

Why is a work supervisor called a "straw boss"?

A "straw boss" is usually a supervisor or foreman of menial work and the label comes from the farm. The "big boss" was in charge of the entire threshing crew, whose main task was to harvest the wheat from the chaff, which was straw. The "straw boss" was in charge of the secondary crew, whose job it was to gather and bail the discarded by-product. "Straw boss" has come to mean a petty supervisor without any real authority.

What is the difference between a coroner and a medical examiner?

Medical examiners and coroners are found in both Canada and the United States. In the United States, medical examiners are doctors or forensic pathologists; coroners, on the other hand, are elected and do not require any specific training. Four provinces — Alberta, Manitoba, Nova Scotia, and Newfoundland — use medical examiners, who go out to the crime scene to investigate. Ontario's coroners are appointed and must be licensed physicians. The remaining provinces also use appointed coroners. Unlike medical examiners, coroners do not go to the crime scene. They rely on reports from other death investigators.

Is a corporate financial officer a "comptroller" or a "controller"?

A corporation's senior financial officer is an accountant who supervises or monitors a company's financial operations and usually reports to a chief financial officer who in turn answers to the CEO. He/she is called a comptroller because when the word (and function) was created during the sixteenth century, the emerging English language was still heavily influenced by the language of the French conquerors (1066). At the time all written records were kept on scrolls. *Comptroller* emerged in part from the French word *contreroule* meaning "a copy of a scroll." Someone who checked the scrolls was called a "countroller" in the new Middle English but because the French word for "on account" is *compte*, when a title was created for the person who specializes in financial ledgers was required they combined the languages and came up with the word *compteroller* which today has dropped one *e* and evolved into *comptroller* or even *controller* in some cases. Both mean the same thing.

**wicked
weather**

How are hurricanes and tropical storms named?

In 1953, the U.S National Weather service began giving storms names to assist in dealing with insurance claims and other legal problems arising from the impact. It also helped in alerting areas in danger as the storm moved inland. During the Second World War, lonely weathermen serving in the Pacific named storms after their wives and girlfriends and this custom of using female names was continued until 1979 when it became sensitive to women. Men's names were then added to the active list of the 232 now in use. Names from this list are rotated over a six year cycle, unless one is so severe that the name must be retired or placed out of use for at least 10 years. The first female storm name was Alice in 1953. The first masculine storm name was Henri in 1979.

Which was the deadliest hurricane on record?

Hurricane Mitch ranks as the deadliest in the past two centuries. It formed in the Caribbean in October, 1998, and slowly moved through Central America, causing widespread flooding and up to 11,000 deaths before reaching Florida as a tropical storm. In 1900, Galveston, Texas, was struck by a Category 4 hurricane that swept over parts of the city that had been, in an act of hubris, built on a barrier island; it killed 8,000 people. A hurricane in 1780 is considered the most devastating of all, killing an estimated 22,000 people and decimating the Caribbean navies of Britain, France, and several other European countries during the American Revolution.

The deadliest tropical cyclone on record hit India and East Pakistan (now Bangladesh) on November 12, 1970. The Bhola Cyclone packed 115-mile-per-hour winds, caused a huge storm surge, and left an estimated half-a-million people dead in its wake.

What triggers a tsunami?

The phenomenon we now call a tsunami was once incorrectly called a tidal wave. Actually, the tide has absolutely nothing to do with tsunamis, which can also be called seismic sea waves. Tsunamis are usually caused by earthquakes with epicentres at the bottom of the ocean. Less frequently, they can be caused by submarine landslides or submarine volcanic activity. The shock wave generated by a sea-floor quake races through the water at speeds of 80 miles per hour. Tsunamis have been known to travel from one side of the Pacific Ocean to another in a day. In deep water a tsunami passes beneath a ship with barely any notice. But when this mass of energy hits shallow water, it builds up into one of nature's most powerful forces, sending walls of water smashing against coastal areas.

What is the origin of the word *tsunami*?

The word comes from the Japanese for *harbour* (*tsu*) and *wave* (*nami*). It translates literally as "harbour wave," which is an accurate description, since usually the monster smashes into a harbour before people even know it is coming.

What was the largest tsunami ever recorded?

After the Great Krakatoa Volcanic Eruption of 1883, coastal villages were erased by waves that towered over 125 feet above sea level. Nearly 300 villages were destroyed or damaged and at least 36,000 people died. The tsunamis affected the tides in the English Channel on the other side of the world.

There is a story that in 1737 an earthquake that shook Japan caused a tsunami that reached a height of 210 feet, but there is little documentation to support the claim.

Why was the Southeast Asian tsunami of 2004 so devastating?

At about 7:00 a.m. on December 26, 2004, the floor of the Indian Ocean shook with an earthquake so massive that it caused the Earth to wobble in its rotation. Unbelievably powerful shock waves raced through the sea at velocities faster than a jet. Scientists in Australia and Hawaii saw the readings on their instruments and warned of a tsunami developing in the Indian Ocean. Their alert wasn't heeded, however, because the Indian Ocean rarely experiences tsunamis. The coastal areas of Southeast Asia and East Africa were therefore completely unprepared. The earthquake that triggered the tsunami registered 9.0 on the Richter scale and, according to the U.S. Geological Survey, released an amount of energy equivalent to 23,000 Hiroshima-type atomic bombs. More than 200,000 people were reported killed or missing in one of the worst disasters in history.

What was America's deadliest tornado?

The deadliest twister in United States history occurred on March 18, 1925. Dubbed the Great Tri-state Tornado, it touched down in the Ozark Mountains in Missouri and then proceeded to cut a path of destruction through Illinois and Indiana. The twister, with a forward speed that topped 60 miles per hour, continued for three and a half hours, and travelled more than 219 continuous miles. The storm, a mile wide at times, killed more than 700 people and injured thousands more as it made its way through 13 counties and 19 communities — damage was spread over 164 square miles. At that time there were no weather radar or warning systems, so most people didn't even know the tornado was approaching nor had any time to seek shelter.

Quickies
Did you know...
• that tornadoes are also called twisters, ropes, funnel clouds (before they touch the ground), whirlwinds, wedges, windhoses, or cyclones? Smaller cyclonic events include dust devils, gustnados, and willy-willies.

How does the Fujita tornado scale work?

The smallest tornado, category 0, called an F0 on the scale, needs a wind of at least 40 miles per hour; otherwise, it would be considered a dust devil, whirlwind, sand auger, etc. Tornadoes of this intensity are likely to knock down a few trees and do minor property damage. At the other end of the scale, F5 storms can pack winds of 318 miles per hour, stronger than anything else seen at ground level. F5 tornadoes can carry houses and cars for hundreds of feet.

Why do thunderstorms occur mainly in the late afternoon?

As the day unfolds, the sun warms the ground, encouraging evaporation that provides for a storm at the end of the day. If warm low-level winds are also present, the storm may carry on into the evening. The orange hue that often accompanies thunderstorms is caused by the same atmospheric conditions that bring us beautiful sunsets.

What are the different types of lightning?

Lightning can occur between clouds, inside clouds, and from clouds to ground. The most common type is forked lightning, which we call sheet lightning when it is far away and the forks become indistinguishable from each other. Ball lightning is seen as a ball of light that moves slowly and sometimes ends with an explosion. Satellites, space shuttles, and high-flying aircraft have observed two other types of lightning on top of thunderheads: red sprites are weak discharges that shoot up above the cloud, and blue jets are cone-like emissions that travel up from the core of the thunderstorm to altitudes of 25 or 30 miles.

The light we see from lightning occurs after it strikes the ground and is on its way back up into the cloud. The heat generated during the electrical discharge causes it.

How many people die from lightning strikes each year?

In Canada, six to 10 people die every year as a result of being struck by lightning. In recent years, the United States has suffered an average of 67 fatalities annually. Florida is the most lightning-prone area in the United States. Over a 35-year period from 1959 to 1994, when 3,329 Americans died from lightning strikes, the National Weather Service noted 350 deaths in Florida alone, more than 10 percent of the total, and far more than North Carolina, which was second with 160 deaths.

Where is the most dangerous place to be during a thunderstorm?

If you are in a boat on open water, under an isolated tree or a large tree in a forest, or in the middle of a large open area like a golf course or soccer field, you are a prime candidate to be struck by lightning or injured by a falling tree. Should you feel your hair stand on end, get a tingling sensation on your skin, or hear a crackling sound, a lightning strike may be imminent. Your best bet then is to squat and make yourself into a ball in the hopes that the lightning will go around you and not damage internal organs.

Why do we call a severe snowstorm a "blizzard"?

Quickies
Did you know...
- that tall structures are designed to absorb frequent lightning strikes? Toronto's CN Tower gets clobbered a whopping 75 times a year.
- that most people are hit by lightning in the 30 minutes before or the 30 minutes after a thunderstorm?
- that lightning bolts strike the Earth more than three billion times annually? 85 percent of those strikes are on land.
- that lightning starts about 45 percent of Canadian forest fires and burns more than 80 percent of the timber lost?

The word *blizzard* didn't mean a snowstorm until 1870, when a newspaper editor in Estherville, Iowa, needed a word to describe a fierce spring storm. The word *blizzard* had been hanging around with no particular origin for about 50 years and was used to describe a vicious physical attack, either with fists or guns. After its use by the editor, what better word to describe a violent snowstorm than *blizzard*?

royalty

When did the British monarchy first broadcast their annual Christmas message?

In 1932, George V finally accepted an invitation from the BBC that had been sent his way for nine years, and broadcast the first Royal Christmas Message on the radio. The King's message that year was written for him by Rudyard Kipling. Ever since, every Christmas Day the reigning British monarch has delivered a message to the Commonwealth. The tradition moved from radio to television with Elizabeth II's 1957 broadcast. While the messages were originally delivered live at 3 p.m. GMT, since 1960 they have been pre-recorded and aired at times chosen by individual broadcasters.

How can I talk to the Queen of England?

You can't email the Queen, because that kind of contact information is not for the public, but she would be happy to get a letter by regular mail. If you're making a formal request, inviting her to tea for instance, you would open the letter with "Madam" and close it with "I have the honour to be, Madam, your Majesty's humble and obedient servant." If you want to be more relaxed, you can open with "Your Majesty" or "Your Royal Highness" and end with "Yours sincerely," just like a business letter.

Why are royal families said to have "blue blood"?

During the first few centuries following the death of Mohammed, Islam quickly spread across North Africa and East to India. It even gained a foothold in Western Europe, through Spain. The Moslems who invaded Spain were dark skinned Moors. Spain's Christian nobility was fair skinned, and the veins on their pale arms looked blue. "Blue blood," or blue veins, became a way to distinguish children born of the original Spanish aristocrats from those who resulted from marriages between Moors and Spaniards.

In the early 1800s, the term made its way into English, and was applied to nobility in general.

What led to the divorce of Prince Charles and Princess Diana?

The "fairytale marriage" of Charles and Diana was on shaky ground from the start. He was 13 years older than she. They had vastly different interests. Charles was already romantically involved with Camilla Parker Bowles, but his mother the Queen had arranged the marriage to Diana, who "passed inspection" with the Royal Family. Diana accused Charles of continuing his relationship with Camilla after their wedding, and of having an affair with Tiggy Legge-Bourke. She said Charles was dominated by his mother. Charles said Diana was having an affair with her riding instructor. With their marriage in an absolute shambles, the royal couple separated in December 1992 and were divorced in August 1996. One year later Diana was killed in a car accident in Paris.

Quickies
Did you know...
• that before Charles and Diana's divorce was finalized, Queen Elizabeth issued Letters Patent that Diana, as she was no longer the wife of the Prince of Wales, could no longer be styled "Her Royal Highness"? Since she was the mother of the second and third potential heirs to the throne, she could still be styled "Diana, Princess of Wales." Prince William has said that when he is king, he will restore the style of "Her Royal Highness" to his late mother.

Why did Henry VIII of England want to divorce his first wife?

The argument Henry presented to the pope and to the English people was that he had been forced to marry Catherine of Aragon, who was his older brother Arthur's widow. (Catherine swore the marriage to Arthur had never been consummated). Upon Arthur's death if his father, King Henry VII, had sent

Catherine back to her father, King Ferdinand II of Spain, he would also have had to return the rich dowry Ferdinand had provided. Henry declared that the marriage was invalid, because Catherine had been his sister-in-law. Actually, Henry wanted to replace Catherine because after more than 20 years of marriage she had given him one daughter and no sons. Henry desperately wanted a male heir, and he had cast his eye on the lovely Ann Boleyn.

Why did the pope not grant Henry VIII a divorce?

Like popes before him, Pope Clement VII had always been willing to help European monarchs end inconvenient marriages. However, the pope was under pressure from Catherine of Aragon's nephew, who was both Holy Roman Emperor Charles V and King Charles I of Spain. Catherine did not want her marriage dissolved, and Charles backed her up. As the pope saw it, Charles was more powerful than Henry, so he did what Charles told him to do.

What new religion did Henry VIII then help to found?

When Henry couldn't get a divorce from the pope, he broke his kingdom away from the Roman Catholic Church. He founded the Church of England (Anglican Church), with himself as the head, and then had the archbishop of Canterbury formally grant him a divorce.

What Englishman lost his head for opposing Henry's wishes?

Sir Thomas More, a lawyer, writer, statesman, and author of the novel *Utopia*, wouldn't support Henry's divorce and was firmly opposed to the break with the Roman Catholic Church. More considered all Protestants to be heretics. Henry had him charged with treason and beheaded in 1535. Four hundred years later the Catholic Church had Thomas More canonized as a saint.

What British monarch got divorced before he became king?

In 1714 George of Hanover, a German duke, became King George I of England on the death of his distant cousin, Queen Anne. George didn't speak English, didn't particularly like England, and brought some scandalous baggage with him to his new kingdom. He had been involved in extramarital affairs, but in 1694 when he learned that his wife of 12 years, Princess Sophia Dorothea of Celle, was romantically involved with a Swedish officer named Philip von Konigsmark, he was furious. He divorced Sophia Dorothea and had her locked up for the rest of her life in the Castle of Ahlden. She was forbidden to have any contact with their children: George Augustus (later King George II) and Sophia Dorothea (mother of Frederick the Great). Von Konigsmark disappeared, and it was rumoured that George had him killed. The body was supposedly found many years later under the floorboards of George's palace in Hanover. The English people were never very fond of "German George," who spent as much time as he could in Hanover. When George I died there in 1727, his son, who hated his father for his mother's imprisonment (she died in 1726), was content to leave the body in Germany rather than bring it to England to lie among other British monarchs in Westminster Abbey.

Henry VIII's Wives: Divorced, Died, or Executed?

- Catherine of Aragon, mother of Mary I, was divorced.
- Anne Boleyn, mother of Elizabeth I, was beheaded on false charges of adultery and witchcraft.
- Jane Seymour gave Henry his male heir (Edward VI) but died a month later of a fever connected with childbirth.
- Anne of Cleves was a German princess Henry had never met but agreed to marry for political reasons. He divorced her because he considered her ugly.
- Kathyrn Howard was beheaded on factual charges of adultery.
- Katherine Parr, Henry's sixth bride, was still his wife and still alive when he died in 1547.

An English Rhyme to Remember the Fates of Henry VIII's Wives:

> Divorced, beheaded, died.
> Divorced, beheaded, survived.

What led to the divorce trial of Queen Caroline in 1820?

In 1795, George the Prince of Wales, son of King George III, married his cousin, a German princess named Caroline Amelia of Brunswick. Young George already had the reputation of being a womanizer and a lazy, drunken lout who ran up enormous debts his father had to pay off. When he married Caroline, he was already secretly married to a Catholic commoner named

Maria Fitzherbert. At the time it was illegal for a member of the Royal Family to marry a Catholic. It was soon evident that George and Caroline were a very bad match, as well.

How were the royal newlyweds poorly suited for each other?

Prince George was a boor, but he also had educated tastes in art and literature. Caroline cared nothing about such things. Moreover, she never bathed or washed her clothes. It was said she smelled like a barnyard. She was loud and vulgar, and an embarrassment to George. For his part, George insisted on spending most of his time with his drunken friends. He even took them along on the royal honeymoon. Nine months after the wedding, The Princess of Wales gave birth to a baby girl, Princess Charlotte. George took custody of the child and threw Caroline out.

Why didn't Caroline assert her rights?

As a woman, even though officially the Princess of Wales, she had no rights. Caroline took to living a scandalous life of parties and affairs with men of common birth — or so it was rumoured. The House of Lords conducted an investigation into her conduct that George hoped would turn up proof of adultery, so he could divorce her. However, no conclusive proof was found. In 1818 Princess Charlotte died. In 1820 George III died and the prince became King George IV. Caroline tried to attend the coronation to take her place as queen, but guards slammed the door in her face.

What was the "Bill of Pains and Penalties"?

This was the bill placed before Parliament to grant King George a divorce from Caroline. It was an extremely controversial bill, because Caroline was very popular with the English people, and mobs of her supporters roamed the streets shouting "Long live the queen!" In the end the bill was defeated. George would not get his divorce, but he refused to acknowledge Caroline as his queen. A few weeks after George's coronation, Caroline fell ill. She died, certain she had been poisoned. George IV died without an heir nine years later.

What divorce scandal rocked the British monarchy in 1936?

In January, 1936, King George V died, and the very popular Prince of Wales became King Edward VIII. The British public was stunned to learn that the new king was romantically involved with an American woman who was already married to someone else. As if that were not shocking enough, she had already been divorced once. Born Bessie Wallis Warfield, the woman who would become notorious as Mrs. Simpson, even after she was formally named Duchess of Windsor, had been married to an American naval pilot named Earl Winfield Spencer, whom she had divorced. Then she had married Ernest Simpson, whom she was in the process of divorcing when the world learned of her relationship with Edward.

Why did Edward's affair cause such a scandal?

A king of England was supposed to be married to someone who was his social equal. Wallis Simpson, an American of common birth, was considered far beneath Edward's royal station. Moreover, he would be marrying a twice-divorced woman. At that time a divorced woman was looked upon as having a checkered past. To many people, Wallis Simpson was an adventuress who was not as much in love with Edward as she was with the glamour of royalty.

How was the Wallis Simpson crisis resolved?

Edward did not really want to be king, but was prepared to do his duty if he could have Wallis at his side. He believed the British people would accept her as his queen. He had the support of Winston Churchill and a few other prominent men. But his mother and the rest of the Royal Family were against it, as was Parliament. Edward delivered an ultimatum; either he be allowed to marry Wallis, or he would abdicate. In December, 1936, after making a moving speech to the British people by radio, Edward announced that he was giving up his throne for "the woman I love." Edward and Wallis were married in France and granted the titles Duke and Duchess of Windsor. Edward's younger brother became King George VI.

death and
funeral traditions

What is the Grim Reaper?

The Grim Reaper is the embodiment of the human fear of what to most, is the mysterious and dreaded moment of death. This creature is also known as the Angel of Death and has been depicted in many ghastly forms since at least the dawn of ancient religion. The image we are familiar with is the darkly hooded skeletal phantom concealing any facial or gender identity (although the assumption is masculine). The scythe "it" carries was added to the image during the eighth century when that farm instrument was introduced for mowing hay or grain for harvest. It became a morbid metaphor for the "harvest" of millions who died in Europe during the great plagues of the dark ages.

What do "code making" and "code breaking" have in common with places to bury people?

Cryptology and *crypt* share the same Greek root *kryptos* which means "hidden." Cryptologists are the men and women in the back rooms of the spy business. They spend their time creating coding systems that hide the content of messages sent by their side, and decoding messages intercepted from the enemy to reveal their hidden meanings. Crypts conceal the bodies of loved ones in a church or churchyard.

Why is the box used for burial called a coffin?

Coffin came into English during the late Middle Ages from an old French word for *sarcophagus* that was spelled *cofin*. *Sarcophagus* is a Latin word referring to a box made of "flesh eating" limestone. The first coffins were reserved for the very wealthy, whose bodies would go into coffins that were placed in a crypt in the church. The rest of people were buried in the churchyard wrapped in a shroud of cloth.

In the United States, you often hear the word *casket* used instead of *coffin*. *Casket* is an advertising word thought up by the funeral industry.

The term "Coffin nail" as a slang for a cigarette was first used in 1880.

Why is a mortician called an "undertaker"?

The word *undertaker* first appeared in the fifteenth century as a "contractor of any sort." It has nothing to do with taking bodies underground for burial. The familiar definition, as one who relieves the family of the burden of preparing the deceased for burial or cremation, began in the late seventeenth century as funeral-undertaker. Now more commonly known as funeral directors, they still are contracted to oversee or "undertake" the responsibility of disposing of the dead.

What's the difference between an epitaph and a cenotaph?

We gather at the cenotaph on Remembrance Day because a cenotaph is a monument inscribed to honour the dead but which does not contain any remains. An epitaph is inscribed on the tombstone above a grave. Both words and concepts are Greek in origin. Today, the simplest epitaphs are for Catholic clergy: seven crosses for a bishop, five for a priest, and one for parishioners.

Why is a burial ground for the poor called "Potter's Field"?

Judas Iscariot repented after betraying Jesus and returned the 30 pieces of silver to the conspiring priests. He then took his own life. Because they couldn't return blood money to the temple treasury and Judas couldn't be buried in hallowed ground, the priests used the silver to purchase Jerusalem's Potter's Field, where they buried Judas and gave a name to a burial place for all outcasts.

high
flyers:
airplanes and flight

Why do we say he's "flying by the seat of his pants"?

Early aircraft had few instruments and had to be flown by feel. "Flying by the seat of his pants" was an expression that originated during the First World War to describe this piloting technique. It has since come to mean doing something instinctively in many walks of life, without advance planning, and in response to the conditions of the moment.

Why do we call someone shady a "fly-by-night"?

A "fly-by-night" can refer to any person or thing that is untrustworthy. It suggest that after gaining your confidence or money, that individual or operation will secretly and quietly disappear leaving you the stranded victim of a scam. Fly-by-night dates from 1796, as a reference to the sinister habits of a witch. It was exclusively used against women. It took its modern meaning in 1823.

Why do we say that someone doing well is "on the beam"?

Early aviators had a system of radio signals to guide pilots through fog and bad weather. Dots and dashes were beamed out from a landing field and picked up in the pilot's earphones. If he heard dot-dashes, he was too far left, and dash-dots meant he was too far right. But when the signals converged into a continuous buzzing sound, the pilot was "on the beam," or safely on course.

Nine More World's Worst Air Disasters

- August 12, 1985, Tokyo, Japan: Japan Airlines 747 crashes after takeoff, 520 killed.
- November 12, 1996, Delhi, India: Midair collision between Kazakhstan IL-76 cargo plane and a Saudi 747, 349 killed.
- March 3, 1974, Paris, France: Turkish Airlines DC-10 crashes after equipment malfunction, 346 killed.
- June 23, 1985, Irish coast: Air India 747 en route from Toronto to Bombay blows up as a result of Sikh terrorist bomb, 329 killed.
- August 19, 1980, Riyadh, Saudi Arabia: Fire breaks out aboard a Saudi L-1011, 301 killed.
- July 3, 1988, Straits of Hormuz: USS Vincennes mistakenly shoots down an Air Iran Airbus, 290 killed.
- May 25, 1979, Chicago, Illinois: American Airlines DC-10 takes off from O'Hare Airport and an engine falls off, causing the plane to roll and explode, 273 killed.
- December 21, 1988, Lockerbie, Scotland: Pan Am 747 explodes in the air as a result of a Libyan terrorist bomb, 270 killed, including 11 on the ground.
- September 1, 1983, Near Sakhalin Island in the Soviet Union: Korean Airlines 747 shot down by Soviet fighter plane after crossing into Soviet airspace, 269 killed.

Why is the paved runway of an airport called "tarmac"?

The hard pavement surface we now call asphalt was discovered by chance when an Englishman named E. Purnell Hooley accidentally spilled tar onto some crushed stone. Hooley named this new black pavement by taking the last name of Scotsman John MacAdam, who had developed the use of crushed stone for a firm, dry highway, and prefixing it with *tar*. *Tarmacadam* was a mouthful, however, and was soon shortened to *Tarmac*. Hooley patented Tarmac in 1903.

Where was the world's deadliest airplane crash?

If we except the horrific events of September 11, 2001 — which clearly belong in a category all their own — the air disaster that resulted in the single greatest loss of life occurred on March 27, 1977, at the airport at Tenerife in Spain's Canary Islands. Due to foggy weather, confusion over takeoff instructions, and interference in radio transmissions, a KLM Boeing 747 collided on the runway with a Pan Am Boeing 747. The fuel tanks of both aircraft exploded, and 583 people were killed. Miraculously, some people sitting in the front of the Pan Am plane survived.

How hot did the supersonic Concorde get?

When the Concorde cruised beyond the speed of sound, its exterior reached temperatures well beyond the boiling point of water, even though the air at 56,000 feet was thin and temperatures were colder than the coldest places in Antarctica. The high temperatures caused the metal skin to expand, making the plane as much as 12 inches longer than normal.

To keep the skin of the Concorde as cool as possible, special white paint was developed that was twice as reflective as that used on normal jets. To cope with the stresses of expansion, a special aluminum alloy was invented.

Passengers experienced the heat of supersonic flight when they touched the Concorde's cabin walls, which got a little warmer.

Quickies
Did you know...
• that between 1950 and 2006 there were 1,843 fatal commercial air crashes? 53 percent were caused by pilot error, including reaction to weather and mechanically related circumstances. Human error accounted for 7 percent, weather 11 percent, pre-existing mechanical failure 21 percent, sabotage 7 percent and 1 percent are listed as other. These percentages do not include private or military aircraft nor do they include helicopter disasters.

Why is going beyond the known limits called "pushing the envelope"?

"Pushing the envelope" is an aviation expression that refers to how test pilots received instructions to challenge the known limits of flight. These instructions, if not a death sentence, were very often a flirtation with disaster. The gravity of issuing such an order was understood but not spoken. Instead, the impersonal assignment came within an envelope, silently slid or pushed across a desk from one man to another.

Why do paratroopers shout "Geronimo" when they jump from a plane?

During the Second World War, Native American paratroopers began the custom of shouting the name of the great Indian chief Geronimo when jumping from a plane because, according to legend, when cornered at a cliff's edge by U.S. cavalrymen, Geronimo, in defiance, screamed his own name as he leaped to certain death, only to escape both injury and the bluecoats.

Where did sunglasses originate?

Modern sunglasses were a consequence of twentieth-century flight, designed by the American Army Air Corps in 1932 to keep the glare out of a pilot's eyes.

In the thirteenth century, the Chinese invented dark glasses to be worn by judges so that none in the courtroom could read their eyes. The narrowly slit Inuit goggles are prehistoric and are a protection against snow-blindness, not the direct sun.

Why is a risky mission said to be flown "on a wing and a prayer"?

If someone is operating "on a wing and a prayer," whatever they are doing involves serious risk. The expression became popular with fliers on dangerous missions during the Second World War and was derived from the song "Comin' in on a Wing and a Prayer," which tells of landing a damaged aircraft. The tune was written in 1943 by Harold Adamson (1906–1980), who also penned "A Lovely Way to Spend an Evening," "Winter Wonderland," and the theme song for the television sitcom *I Love Lucy*. The lyrics of "Comin' in on a Wing and a Prayer" include the title line, which was taken from an actual cockpit transmission from a damaged bomber attempting to land.

When did the first aviation accident that could be classified an "air disaster" occur?

There had been accidents among the pioneers of aviation, some of them fatal. The first that might be termed a disaster was the fiery crash of the German dirigible *LZ-18* on October 17, 1913. All 28 people aboard died in the crash, or succumbed to severe burns within a few hours.

Why did the *Hindenburg* disaster mark the end of the era of lighter-than-air passenger travel?

The German dirigible *Hindenburg* was the largest and fastest airship in the world. It could carry 97 passengers and 61 crew members across the Atlantic much faster than an ocean liner, and with all the luxurious accommodation offered to first-class passengers on the finest ships. The big airship had made several successful transatlantic crossings and had become the pride of Nazi Germany. Then, on the evening of May 6, 1937, as the *Hindenburg* approached the mooring tower at Lakehurst, New Jersey, the great hydrogen-filled sphere caught fire. Within seconds the entire ship was ablaze and dropping to the ground. Horrified witnesses watched as people jumped or fell from the stricken ship. Thirty-five of those aboard were killed, and many were injured. The cause of the fire was never satisfactorily established. It might have been static electricity or sparks from the engine's exhaust igniting escaping gas. Some people suspected it was the work of an anti-Nazi saboteur.

The *Hindenburg* tragedy wasn't the deadliest dirigible disaster. The 1933 crash of the USS *Akron* killed 73 people. But the *Hindenburg* disaster was broadcast live on radio and was captured by newsreel cameras. Millions of people heard Herbert Morrison's eyewitness broadcast and saw the terrifying event in movie theatres. The wealthy few who could afford to travel by airship were no longer willing to take the risk.

**our fine
feathered friends**

Why is the pursuit of the unattainable called a "wild goose chase"?

First of all, catching a wild goose isn't easy! Shakespeare took this folk expression and introduced it to our language in *Romeo and Juliet* (1592) as meaning "chasing after the impossible." It is derived from a follow-the-leader steeplechase where the leading horseman is either incompetent or incapable of finding the prey (the wild goose). In this exercise, the entire hunting party forms a "V" formation in the same way that geese fly.

Is there a difference in the quality between brown and white chicken eggs?

Chickens need between 24 and 26 hours to produce one egg. After a half-hour rest, they start the process over again. Occasionally they will stop laying and rest from between three to ten days. The colour of the eggs' shells has nothing to do with their quality. Brown eggs come from hens with red feathers and red earlobes, while white eggs come from chickens with white feathers and white earlobes.

Why do we say people showing their age are no "spring chickens"?

To say someone is "no spring chicken" is to suggest he or she is past his or her physical prime. This expression grew from a time in New England before raising chickens had become the cruelly sophisticated industry it is today. Chickens came from free-range family farms with no incubators or warm henhouses, which meant baby chicks couldn't be hatched or raised in the winter. The prime price for chickens sold during the summer was for those born the previous spring. Anything older and less succulent that was pawned off as part of the spring crop was quickly identified by shrewd shoppers as "no spring chicken," or not as young as what was being presented.

Why do we call a deliberately misleading story a "canard"?

A "canard" is a story or a statement that is a hoax or a lie. *Canard* is French for "duck," but in English the word refers to a deliberate falsehood and is based on a French proverb about cheating or swindling. *Vendre un canard à moitié* literally translated means "to half sell a duck." However, the expression probably means "to sell half a duck." Selling a bag containing a half duck as if it were whole at a busy farmers' market would constitute a deliberate "lie" with the intention of cheating the purchaser.

The United States' reason for invading Iraq has been called a canard.

What is a "coot" in "bald as a coot"?

Bald, of course, immediately suggests a hairless person. It also conjures up thoughts of worn tires, eagles, or a sparse patch of grass on a lawn but the word *bald* began in the Celtic language meaning a blaze of white, usually on a horse or other animal's head. A coot is a water bird with a flash of white in the front centre of its forehead, and is the reason for the expression, "bald as a coot." Today, *coot* can also mean an eccentric old man but this use isn't the original reason for the expression.

Where did we get the myth that storks deliver babies?

The suggestion that storks delivered babies came from Scandinavia and was promoted by the writings of Hans Christian Anderson. Storks had a habit of nesting on warm chimneys and would often lift articles from clotheslines then stuff them into these nests, which to children looked like they were stuffing babies down the flue. The stork is also very nurturing and protective of its young, which helped it become symbolic of good parenthood.

What part did Newfoundland play in naming the penguin?

The now extinct great auk of the North Atlantic was a large bird with small wings, making it very similar in appearance to the Antarctic penguin that we know today. Because of these underdeveloped wings, the auk was called a "pin-wing," and so in 1578, when the first description of the bird came out of Newfoundland, it was written as it sounded in the local dialect. *Pin-wing* became *penguin*. The name and the spelling were then given to the auk's southern look-alike. Coincidentally, the auk's Latin name is *pinguinis*.

Why do sailors call seabirds, "Mother Carey's Chickens"?

One of the many superstitions among the crews of the early sailing ships was that the Virgin Mother of Jesus watched over them through the eyes of small seabirds which they called "Mother Carey's Chickens." Mother Carey comes from the Latin *mater cara* which means "dear mother," a name given the Virgin Mary.

The birds are said to warn sailors of approaching storms and it is highly unlucky to kill them.

What do chickens have to do with chicken pox?

Chickens have nothing to do with chicken pox. It was so named to distinguish the weaker form of the highly contagious but usually nonfatal pox from the dreaded and extremely deadly form of smallpox. Because smallpox was named first, doctors needed a timid name for its less lethal cousin. To make it clear, they chose the unscientific but unassuming chicken.

journalism

Why is irresponsible reporting called "yellow journalism"?

"Yellow journalism" means sensational, usually chauvinistic and exploitive reporting and was first used during the 1880s when publishers, especially William Randolph Hearst, used their influence to drum up hatred of Spain which led to the Spanish-American War. The yellow came from the use of that colour within a cartoon strip, "Yellow Kid," which ran in the *New York World*, a paper infamous for its sensationalism. Yellow was the only colour used within the strip and sometimes ran on the front page. The kid's clothes were yellow.

Why is "forty winks" used as a synonym for napping?

In 1571 the Church of England introduced 39 articles which clergymen of the church were required to accept before their ordination. An 1872 publication of the British humour magazine *Punch* suggested that reading these catechisms was tedious and that their meaning could be missed: "If a man, after reading through the thirty-nine articles were to take forty winks ..." From this point on, "forty winks" has meant a brief nap.

Why are both a published periodical and a place to house ammunition called a "magazine"?

The word *magazine* is from the Arabic word *makhzan*, meaning "a place to store arms and ammunition." The word entered English to describe a munitions warehouse or the chamber that holds bullets in a loaded gun. In 1731, the word took on its new meaning with the publication of *The Gentlemen's Magazine*, so called because it held an assortment of articles of different shapes and sizes.

Why is someone who exposes political corruption called a "muckraker"?

When President Teddy Roosevelt called the reporters who exposed political and corporate corruption "muckrakers," the term caught on and is now used to describe tabloid journalism. Muck is manure, and the word was borrowed from John Bunyons's book *Pilgrim's Progress*, wherein a man — even though he had been promised a celestial crown — constantly kept his eyes and his muck rake on the filth of the floor instead of looking only to his halo.

Are the letters in the word *news* an acronym for *north*, *east*, *west*, and *south*?

Some early news sheets were headed with N-E-W-S as points of a compass, but it was simply a clever gimmick. The word *news* predates these publications and emerged with its current meaning within a letter written by King James of Scotland in 1423. In 1616, his descendant, James I of England, wrote another letter, which included the first recorded use of "No news is good news."

What is the meaning of the word *factoid*?

Norman Mailer introduced the word *factoid* in his 1973 book *Marilyn*. He invented it by combining the word *fact* with *-oid*, a scientific suffix that means "resembling but not identical to." In other words, it's something that looks like a fact, but isn't. Factoids are built from rumours and used by irresponsible journalists to create a story when none exists.

kid stuff

Why is a clever child called a "whiz kid"?

Since the early twentieth century, a clever or remarkable person of any age has often been referred to as a *whiz*. The word is a shortened form of *wizard*. "Whiz kid" derives from a 1930s takeoff of the popular radio show *Quiz Kids*. A whiz in this application means anyone who has a remarkable skill.

If you're wondering why going to the bathroom is called "taking a whiz," it's because *whiz* has a cousin with another meaning. A *whizz* is a hissing sound made by an object speeding through the air.

Why is a small child called a "little shaver"?

During the period when settlers spent a lot of time cutting wood, if a son looked or acted like his father he was called a "chip off the old block," meaning that except for size, the two were as clearly related as a chip cut from its original block of wood from the family tree. A "little shaver" is the same, except that a shaving is smaller than a chip. A "sprig," on the other hand, is a child too small yet to even have a branch on the family tree.

Why is a young rascal or rogue called a "scallywag"?

Scallywag is usually a reference to a mischievous, youthful little scamp who seems to cause trouble continually. The original English spelling of *scallywag* was *scalawag* and is a reference to Scalloway, one of the Shetland Islands, where the famous Shetland ponies are bred. The word was created as an insult to the residents of Scalloway whose horses were so much smaller than the standard breeds.

The hostile, damp, and chilly environment of the Shetlands is the major reason ponies bred there are so much smaller than standard horses. Their small stature helps them conserve body heat and huddle out of the wind behind low hills. Shetland ponies became extremely sought after in Britain during the nineteenth century when many thousands were used in coal mining to haul carts in the tunnels after a piece of legislation called the Mines Act banned children from working in the mines in 1847.

Scallywag is also used in the United States to describe Southerners who collaborated with Union Reconstructionists after the Civil War. The word has also been employed to describe unscrupulous politicians and men who won't work.

Why does the childhood word *dibs* mean "It's mine"?

To put "dibs" on something, like a piece of cake (or Dad's car), is to express first claim to a share of that object. The word dates from before 1700 and comes from a very old children's game called dibstone, a forerunner to marbles, which was played with either sheep knuckles or small stones. The object was to capture an opponent's stone by declaring, "I dibs!" meaning, "It's mine!" The plural of the word was *dubs*.

Why is foolish behaviour called "tomfoolery"?

A buffoon was first called a "Tom fool" in 1650 because *Tom* was a nickname for a "common man." Although *fool* once meant "mad" or "insane," by the seventeenth century it was a reference to a jester or a clown. The name *Tom* became influenced by "Tom the cat" in the 1809 popular children's book *The Life and Adventures of a Cat*. Tom the cat was quite silly and was a promiscuous night crawler. This all led to *tomfoolery* becoming a word for crazy behaviour.

Another *Tom* phrase was "Tom o'Bedlam," the nickname given to the insane men who, because of overcrowding and spiralling costs, had been released from London's Bethlehem or "Bedlam" Hospital for the Insane and were given a licence to beg on the streets. (The term is also a dig at the Irish). *Bedlam* is a cockney pronunciation of *Bethlehem*.

Why are institutions of learning called "kindergartens" or "schools" and referred to by students as their "alma mater"?

It all starts in *kindergarten*, a German concept meaning "children's garden," where the atmosphere for learning should be as pleasant for a child as being in a garden. *School* follows the same philosophy and is from a Greek word for leisure. When university students refer to their *alma maters*, they are speaking Latin for "nursing mother," in this case one which nourishes the mind.

Why do we say "A is for effort" if *effort* starts with *e*?

When someone is given an "A for effort," it is usually a backhanded compliment meaning "even though what you did sucked, we know you gave it your best!" In elementary schools, "A for effort" is used so as not to discourage failing students or their parents. The reason *A* is used instead of *E* is found in the common A–F school grading system where there is no E: A = excellent; B = good; C = fair or average; D = poor, but just barely passing; and F = failure.

fraud
and trickery

Why, if you're insincere, do we say you're "talking through your hat"?

Saying something without conviction might be called a lie, or you could be accused of "talking through your hat." Around 1850, an Englishman refused to kneel before sitting in a church pew, a serious breach of religious etiquette. Instead, he whispered a prayer while covering his mouth with his hat before sitting down. This shocked the other worshippers, and although many copied him, "talking through your hat" took on the meaning of false and irreverent.

Where did the word *gimmick* come from?

Gimmick or *gimac* — either way it's spelled, a *gimmick* is a gadget or idea that gives you an advantage. The second spelling is an anagram of *magic*; the word comes from the language of professional magicians and means a small, secret device, like a mirror or sliding panel, that makes an illusion possible. Carnival barkers picked up *gimac* in the 1920s as a reference to a hidden control over their wheels of chance that ensured the wheel would stop when the barkers wanted it to stop. Today, a gimmick is most often used in advertising or selling, but it's still part of an illusion.

Why is mischief called "hanky-panky"?

Sleight of hand using handkerchiefs or "hankies" was introduced by magicians during the mid-1800s. The idea was to draw the audience's eye line to a moving hanky in one hand while the other accomplished the trick. It was from this that the hanky became associated with all things shifty or clandestine. The addition of the word *panky* was simply for colourful rhyming in the same manner as were the words presented by magicians themselves when they said "hocus pocus."

What is a "goldbricker"?

A person who shirks their responsibility through trickery and fraud is called a goldbricker. The word is First-World-War armed forces slang for fellow soldiers who avoided their duties through lies or feigned illness. It comes from those who practiced the con game of selling false "gold" bricks around the turn of the last century.

Why is someone sneaky called "slick"?

The use of the word *slick* to describe a clever or deceptive person began in 1599, but it wasn't until 1959 that this cleverness became associated with a swindler. The word's origins explain its use. The Old Norse word *slikr* meant "smooth" like mud and its use in German as *schleiken* was "to creep or crawl" through mud or slime. A "city slicker" is someone streetwise (or slimy) looking for a country newcomer to exploit.

Why is something false or deceiving called "phony"?

Something fraudulent or counterfeit is called phony whether it's an individual or an item. The word *phony* arose from a confidence game the Irish called a "fawney rig" wherein a player or victim would end up with a gilt brass ring having been pawned off as gold. In the Irish language, the word *fawney* was slang for *fainne* meaning "ring." The alteration of *fawney* to *phony* took place around 1900 and ever since, *phony* has meant bogus.

What is the origin of the slur "Indian Giver"?

It should be of no surprise that European settlers had little respect for the traditions of the Native Americans. The common greed of commerce wasn't a part of Indian culture and so the newcomers took advantage of the natives at every turn. The expression "heads I win, tails you lose" would be the approach to bartering with the naïve Native Peoples who were more used to trusting that a deal would be to the benefit of both parties. Once the First Nations caught on to being cheated, they would return demanding a fair trade, insisting on an honest deal. The embittered European, who thought he'd successfully made a profit by cheating the native, called the person insisting on fairness an "Indian Giver." Rather than a slur, the expression is a compliment!

Why is cheating on corporate accounting ledgers called "cooking the books"?

If someone is using creative accounting, she is usually breaking the law, and so she needs someone with sophisticated bookkeeping skills comparable to those of a skilled chef who can prepare a dish so artfully that no one can tell how it was done. If authorities discover that the books have been cooked and criminal charges are laid, it is said that the accountant and the employer have "cooked their own goose."

How did "skulduggery" come to mean deceitful behaviour?

"Skulduggery" suggests crafty, sneaky, or obscene behaviour because it is from the early Scottish word *sculdudrie*, meaning "adulterous fornication." The planned seduction of a married or committed person, which is conceived in secrecy and committed as a deception is skulduggery. (Sometimes spelled *skullduggery*.)

Why do we say that someone tricked has been "hoodwinked"?

To have been hoodwinked means to have been put at a disadvantage. The term derives from early children's games like Pin the Tail on the Donkey and Blind Man's Bluff, where someone was either blindfolded or hooded and required to complete a task without being able to see. Muggers also employed the hood to blind and rob innocent victims on the street. Wink was really a half-wink, a reference to the blind point where the eye is covered by the lid.

friend or foe?

How did *dude* become a greeting between friends?

The word *dude* originated as a Victorian slang word for a man who was effeminate. It's a variation of *dud* or *duds*, from the Arabic word for *cloak* (*dudde*), and was a reference to fancy or foppish clothes. When vain, fashion-conscious city slickers wanted a taste of the West, they went to a Dude Ranch. *Dude* was kept alive by California surfers and took on its current fellowship meaning from a generation weaned on the Teenage Mutant Ninja Turtles.

Why do men call a good friend their "buddy"?

Buddy is a masculine term for a close companion who can be counted on in a crisis. In wartime, males become buddies during combat or while watching each other's back in a foxhole. The word originated with seventeenth-century Welsh and English coalminers who referred to a workmate with whom they shared the responsibilities of survival as a "butty," which became "buddy" in North America.

Why are close partners said to be "in cahoots" with each other?

Cahoots suggests a conspiracy, and is derived from the French Canadian fur trappers' word *cahute*, meaning cabin. It entered American English about 1820 and because trappers spent long cold days and nights together sharing ideas and dreams, isolated in a cahute, the word took on the meaning of working tightly together.

Why, when embarking on a difficult project, does a group say they must "all hang together"?

The meaning of "all hanging together" is that our only hope is to combine our resources because we are already doomed as individuals. It's a quote from John Hancock, who was the first to step forward and sign the American Declaration of Independence. He said to those gathered, "We must all hang together; else we shall all hang separately," and the hanging he was referring to was death on the gallows for treason.

What is the origin of the expression "hail-fellow-well-met"?

"Hail-fellow-well-met" is an archaic reference to someone who is always cheerful but who is perhaps overdoing his or her enthusiasm. The expression began pleasantly enough as the medieval Scottish greeting *hail*, which is how the Scots pronounced *heal*. "Hail fellow" meant "health to you, friend." In the sixteenth century, the expression became associated with the words *buddy* or *mate*. "Well met!" followed, meaning, "It's good to meet you!" The two expressions became combined in a fuller phrase, "Hail-fellow-well-met," in the late sixteenth century and is used today to suggest that a person's exuberance is perhaps exaggerated.

Why do we say that someone looking for trouble has a "chip on his shoulder"?

In early England, one man would challenge another to a duel by slapping his face with a glove. The challenge was a serious matter of honour, and if the slapped man did not accept it, he would be branded a coward. Having a chip on your shoulder was kind of an early Wild West equivalent of the glove slap, though generally less mortal in nature. Boys and men would place a woodchip on their shoulder, challenging anyone who dared knock it off to a fistfight. So, if a man had a "chip on his shoulder," he was clearly in an aggressive mood and spoiling for a fight.

Why do we say that someone with a hidden agenda has "an axe to grind"?

As a boy, Benjamin Franklin was sharpening tools in his father's yard when a stranger carrying an axe came by and praised the boy on how good he was with the grindstone. He then asked Franklin if he would show him how it would work on his own axe. Once his axe was sharpened, the stranger simply laughed and walked away, giving young Franklin a valuable lesson about people with "an axe to grind."

Why, when looking for a showdown, do we say "I've got a bone to pick"?

Wild pack animals will eat from a carcass only after the alpha male has finished. Having a bone to pick establishes superiority and comes from an ancient Sicilian wedding ritual. At dinner's end, the bride's father would give the groom a bone and instruct him to pick it clean. This ritual signalled the groom's authority over his new wife, establishing that in all future decisions, he would have the final word.

question and feature list

WAR AND THE MILITARY

ANIMALS

A HORSE IS A HORSE …

THE HUMAN CONDITION

HE SAID, SHE SAID: CELEBRITY SPLIT-UPS

THEATRE AND THE ARTS

LITERARY LANGUAGE

SAILING ON THE HIGH SEAS

HOLIDAYS AND CELEBRATIONS

CHRISTMAS

RELIGION AND SUPERSTITION

POLITICS

SCIENCE AND TECHNOLOGY

FASHION AND CLOTHING

GENERAL SPORTS

MURDER MOST FOUL

ORDER IN THE COURT

FOOD AND DINING

OH CANADA!